International Aviation Law Library

Volume 1

Series Editor

Ludwig Weber, Quebec, Canada

The International Aviation Law Library is a series of high quality research books by authors from all over the world. They deal primarily with international aviation law issues of practical importance for governments, airlines, aircraft manufacturers, or other related stakeholders, particularly those that are relevant for regulatory and/or commercial aviation activities. The series also deals with those international legal issues that directly relate to national regulatory problems in civil aviation, including safety, security, economic regulation, and environmental matters.

The series welcomes monographs and edited volumes.

Maria Piera Rizzo • Federico Franchina
Editors

Drones in the Digital European Sky

Theoretical Foundations and Aviation Law Perspectives

Springer

Editors
Maria Piera Rizzo
Department of Law
University of Messina
Messina, Italy

Federico Franchina
Department of Law
University of Messina
Messina, Italy

ISSN 3004-9539 ISSN 3004-9547 (electronic)
International Aviation Law Library
ISBN 978-3-032-16690-6 ISBN 978-3-032-16691-3 (eBook)
https://doi.org/10.1007/978-3-032-16691-3

This work was supported by Ministero dell'Istruzione, dell'Università e della Ricerca (PRIN_2022F4FLSF_001).

This Springer imprint is published by the registered company Springer Nature Switzerland AG
The registered company address is: Gewerbestrasse 11, 6330 Cham, Switzerland

Acknowledgment

This volume collects research papers related to the PRIN (Research Project of Relevant National Interest) 2022 “ATM, Drones and D.A.N.T.E. (Digitalization, Artificial Intelligence and New Technologies for Environment)”, funded by the European Union—Next Generation EU, Mission 4, Component 2, CUP J53D23009300006—identification code PRIN_2022F4FLSF_001.

This study is the result of the contribution from the following research units: University of Messina, Principal investigator, Prof. Maria Piera Rizzo; University of Macerata, Vice Principal Investigator, Prof. Stefano Pollastrelli; University of Modena and Reggio Emilia, Associate Investigator, Prof. Simone Vernizzi; University of Naples “Parthenope”, Associate Investigator, Prof. Francesca Salerno.

Contents

Contributors

Federico Franchina Department of Law, University of Messina, Messina, Italy

Cinzia Ingratoci Department of Law, University of Messina, Messina, Italy

Silvio Magnosi Department of Sciences and Technologies, Parthenope University of Naples, Naples, Italy

Adele Marino Department of Legal and Political Sciences, University of Messina, Messina, Italy

Michela Pandolfino University of Messina, Messina, Italy

Giuseppina Panebianco Department of Law, University of Messina, Messina, Italy

Francesca Pellegrino Department of Law, University of Messina, Messina, Italy

Stefano Pollastrelli Department of Law, University of Macerata, Macerata, Italy

Maria Piera Rizzo Department of Law, University of Messina, Messina, Italy

Francesca Salerno Department of Law, Parthenope University of Naples, Napoli, Italy

Chiara Vagaggini Department of Management and Law, "Tor Vergata" University of Rome, Rome, Italy

Emilia Vermiglio University of Messina, Messina, Italy

Simone Vernizzi Department of Law, University of Modena and Reggio Emilia, Modena, Italy

List of Abbreviations

AI	Artificial Intelligence
AAM	Advanced Air Mobility
AA	Autonomous Aircraft
ACP	Aeronautical Communications Panel
ACV	Air-Cushion Vehicle
AIC	Aeronautical Information Circular
AIS	Aeronautical Information Services
AMC/GM	Acceptable Means of Compliance/Guidance Material
ANC	Air Navigation Commission
ANS	Air Navigation Services
ATM	Air Traffic Management
ATS	Air Traffic Services
C-ITS	Cooperative Intelligent Transport Systems
CORUS	Concept of Operations for European U-space
CNS	Communication, Navigation and Surveillance
EASA	European Union Aviation Safety Agency
EMAAS	Electric Mobility as a Service
ENAC	National Authority Civil Aviation
ENAV	Italian Air Navigation Service Provider
FAA	Federal Aviation Administration
FF2020	Flying Forward (European project)
GEV	Ground Effect Vehicle
IAM	Innovative Air Mobility
IAS	Innovative Aerial Services
ICAN	International Commission for Air Navigation
ICC	Italian Criminal Code
IMC	Italian Military Code
IPMCC	Italian Peacetime Military Criminal Code
ITU	International Telecommunication Union
JARUS	Joint Authorities for Rulemaking on Unmanned Systems
MAAS	Mobility as a Service

MET	Meteorological Services
NHTSA	National Highway Traffic Safety Administration
PANS	Procedures for Air Navigation Services
RPA	Remotely Piloted Aircraft
RPAS	Remotely Piloted Aircraft Systems
RPASP	Remotely Piloted Aircraft System Panel
SARPs	Standards and Recommended Practices
SES	Single European Sky
SESAR	Single European Sky ATM Research
SORA	Specific Operations Risk Assessment
UA	Unmanned Aircraft
UAM	Urban Air Mobility
UAS	Unmanned Aircraft System
UASSG	Unmanned Aircraft System Study Group
UAV	Unmanned Aerial Vehicle
U-SPACE	Unmanned space
VCA	Vertical Capability Aircraft
VEMS	Vertical Emergency Medical Services
VTOL / eVTOL	(Electric) Vertical Take-Off and Landing
WRC	World Radiocommunication Conference
xTM	Extensible Traffic Management

Introduction

Maria Piera Rizzo and Federico Franchina

This introduction, grounded in this comprehensive research volume, explores the theoretical foundations and evolving legal landscapes governing the transformation of air transport in the light of new technologies and digitalisation. The volume, a product of the PRIN 2022 research project "ATM, Drones and D.A.N.T.E. (Digitalisation, Artificial Intelligence, New Technologies for the Environment)" funded by the European Union under the Next Generation EU initiative, serves as a critical scholarly resource for understanding the "drone system" as a complex interplay of technology, law, and economics.

The integration of Unmanned Aircraft Systems (UAS) into civil aviation marks a paradigm shift comparable to the move from maritime to aerial navigation seen in the early twentieth century.

The terminology surrounding this technology is itself a subject of legal and academic development. While "drone" has entered popular language—originating from the German *drohne* (male bee), referring to the insect's buzzing sound and its expendability compared to the queen—regulatory authorities prefer more precise terminology.

European Union (EU) regulators use "Unmanned Aircraft" (UA) as the overarching term for the vehicle, and "Unmanned Aircraft System" (UAS) to refer to the aircraft, ground control station, and the command-and-control link.

The economic necessity for a comprehensive regulatory framework is unequivocal. According to estimates from the European Commission, the European market for drone services is projected to be worth €14.5 billion by 2030, with a compound annual growth rate (CAGR) of 12.3%. This growth trajectory spans various sectors, including logistics, agriculture, and the emerging domain of Urban Air Mobility (UAM), which aims to facilitate the transportation of passengers and goods using

M. P. Rizzo (✉) · F. Franchina
Department of Law, University of Messina, Messina, Italy
e-mail: mariapiera.rizzo@unime.it; federico.franchina@unime.it

M. P. Rizzo, F. Franchina (eds.), *Drones in the Digital European Sky*,
International Aviation Law Library 1,
https://doi.org/10.1007/978-3-032-16691-3_1

electric Vertical Take-Off and Landing (eVTOL) aircraft. Nonetheless, achieving this potential necessitates overcoming substantial legal challenges, particularly concerning safety, liability, and the integration of unmanned traffic with conventional manned aviation within the Single European Sky.

To regulate drones, it is essential to first establish their ontological status within aviation law. The primary inquiry concerns whether a drone qualifies as an "aircraft." This definition has evolved over a century through various international treaties. The *Convention Portant Réglementation de la Navigation Aérienne* (Paris, 1919) initially did not provide a specific definition, but subsequently adopted a broad scope in its annexes, encompassing any airborne vehicle.

The seminal document continues to be the 1944 Chicago Convention. According to Article 8, the classification of drones was arguably established *from the outset*: "pilotless aircraft" are explicitly acknowledged as aircraft and are subject to regulation accordingly, although they require special authorization to operate over the territory of a contracting state. This article establishes a legal continuity between the manned aircraft of the 1940s and the autonomous systems of the twenty-first century.

Nonetheless, the technical definition outlined in ICAO Annex 7 (*Aircraft Nationality and Registration Marks*) has necessitated continual re-evaluation to accommodate technological advancements. Originally characterised as "any machine that can derive support in the atmosphere from the reactions of the air," this definition encountered an interpretative dilemma in the 1960s with the emergence of hovercraft. The hovercraft, which employs an air cushion generated against the Earth's surface, challenged the demarcation between aviation and maritime law. In 1967, the ICAO Council amended the definition to exclude machines deriving support from "the reactions of the air against the earth's surface," thereby legally distinguishing hovercraft from the category of aircraft.

Current legal scholarship states that the drone is "a new type of aircraft," a classification that justifies the extensive revision of ICAO Annexes and EU legislation.

The current definition of aircraft is subject to scrutiny due to emerging technologies that transcend existing regulatory boundaries. Suborbital vehicles intended for point-to-point transportation on Earth pose a challenge to the conventional definition of "aircraft", as they may utilise rocket propulsion systems (endoreactors) rather than air-breathing engines (hexoreactors) during substantial phases of their flight. Endoreactors do not rely on "reactions of the air," which could potentially exempt these vehicles from the provisions of ICAO Annex 7.1.

Within the European framework, the drone is classified as an aeronautical product. Regulation (EU) 2019/945 establishes specific design and construction criteria for Unmanned Aircraft Systems (UAS), distinguishing between those that are subject to harmonised standards, requiring CE marking for the 'Open' category, and those necessitating comprehensive certification for the 'Certified' category. The classification of the drone as a "product" has significant legal implications concerning civil liability. A defect in design, manufacturing, or instructional documentation that renders the drone "unsafe" may give rise to product liability claims against the manufacturer, independent of the operator's liability for negligent operation.

The regulatory framework for UAS is built on a hierarchy of norms, ensuring consistency from the global to the local level.

The Chicago Convention provides the foundation, as ICAO has systematically amended its Annexes (1, 2, 6, 7, 8, 10, 11, 13, and 19) to incorporate RPAS. Notably, Annex 1 (*Personnel Licensing*) now includes definitions for Remote Pilot and Remote Pilot-in-Command, and Annex 6 (*Operation of Aircraft*) has added Part IV specifically for RPAS.

The EU has determined authority over all UAS regardless of weight, marking a notable shift from the previous system (Regulation 216/2008), which categorised drones under 150 kg as under national jurisdiction. The current "Basic Regulation" (Regulation (EU) 2018/1139) authorises the European Union Aviation Safety Agency (EASA) to regulate the entire scope of unmanned aircraft.

A fundamental aspect of the EU regulatory approach is the shift from weight-based classification to a risk-based system. This approach, implemented through Implementing Regulation (EU) 2019/947, classifies operations based on the inherent risk of the flight rather than the vehicle's mass.

From a practical standpoint, managing UAS operations involves a complex legal interplay between the UAS Operator, the Remote Pilot, and other crew members. This framework reflects, yet differs from, traditional aviation.

Under Regulation (EU) 2019/947, the UAS Operator is the central figure, comparable to an "accountable manager" in an airline. The operator assumes organisational responsibility for safety, compliance, and the legal status of the operation. They must establish procedures, appoint remote pilots, and ensure the drone is registered. The regulation allows the operator to be a legal or natural person, making the framework adaptable for all operators, ranging from hobbyists to major logistics companies.

Conversely, the Remote Pilot is the individual accountable for the safe execution of the flight. Although functionally equivalent to the traditional Pilot-in-Command (PIC), the physical separation from the aircraft introduces novel legal considerations regarding the "univocity of command." In complex operations, control may be transferred between pilots situated in different locations. EU Regulation 2019/947 employs the term "remote pilot" rather than "remote pilot-in-command," although the responsibilities remain substantially identical. Nevertheless, future advancements in automation may necessitate a legal distinction between a "pilot-not-in-command" (responsible for manoeuvres) and a "mission commander" (possessing legal authority).

However, the frontier of drone operations primarily resides within Urban Air Mobility (UAM), a subdivision of Innovative Air Mobility (IAM). This encompasses the utilisation of Vertical Take-off and Landing (VTOL) aircraft—commonly electric (eVTOL)—to facilitate the transportation of passengers and cargo in densely populated urban settings, necessitating entirely new physical infrastructure such as vertiports.

The regulation of vertiports resides at the nexus of aviation law and urban planning. In this context, EASA delineates distinct categories: *Vertihubs* (large transport centres with maintenance facilities), *Vertibases* (medium-sized terminals), and

Vertipads/Vertistops (basic landing sites). For Urban Air Mobility (UAM) to operate effectively, vertiports must be incorporated into urban planning frameworks, particularly Sustainable Urban Mobility Plans (SUMPs). The acceptance of UAM by local communities hinges on the mitigation of noise and visual pollution, which necessitates a collaborative effort between aviation authorities and municipal authorities.

From a broader perspective, the most critical challenge facing the future of aviation is the integration of unmanned traffic into existing airspace occupied by manned aircraft. The risk of collision necessitates the implementation of a sophisticated management system that surpasses traditional Air Traffic Control (ATC).

This integration takes place within the framework of the Single European Sky (SES) reform. The recently enacted Regulation (EU) 2024/2803, known as Implementation of the Single European Sky (SES II+), signifies a comprehensive overhaul, repealing the preceding framework (Regulations 549/2004, 550/2004, 551/2004). The aim of this regulation is to modernize air traffic management (ATM) to enhance performance, capacity, and environmental sustainability. It emphasises the independence of National Supervisory Authorities (NSAs) and introduces more rigorous performance review mechanisms for Air Navigation Service Providers (ANSPs).

To specifically address unmanned aerial vehicles, the European Union implemented the "U-Space" package in 2021 (Regulations 2021/664, 665, and 666). The U-Space framework comprises a collection of digital services and procedures engineered to facilitate safe, efficient, and secure access to the airspace for a substantial number of drones. It functions through the designation of U-Space Airspace, a geographically defined zone where unmanned aircraft system (UAS) operations are permitted solely with the support of obligatory digital services.

Within U-Space airspace, providers are required to deliver a minimum of four essential services: (i) Network Identification Service, which supplies real-time identification and positioning information of the drone and operator; (ii) Geo-awareness Service, which delivers data regarding airspace configuration and restrictions (such as no-fly zones); (iii) UAS Flight Authorization Service, which ensures that each flight is strategically de-conflicted from others prior to take-off; and (iv) Traffic Information Service, which informs operators of other air traffic, both manned and unmanned, within the vicinity.

These services represent a transition from human-centric control to automated, digital service delivery. Common Information Services (CIS) function as the authoritative data source within a U-Space volume, typically supplied by an entity appointed by the Member State. The legal classification of these services is intricate: whilst CIS is likely recognised as a Service of General Economic Interest (SGEI) subject to state designation, the remaining U-Space services are intended to be offered within a competitive market.[1]

As unmanned aerial vehicles advance towards greater autonomy through the integration of Artificial Intelligence (AI) and Machine Learning for purposes such as navigation and collision avoidance, conventional liability frameworks are experiencing significant disruption.

When a drone is operated by a self-learning algorithm, the connection between the human operator or programmer and the drone's actions diminishes. In instances where an AI makes an "unpredictable" decision resulting in damage (the "black box" phenomenon), establishing negligence or fault becomes increasingly challenging.

Legal scholarship indicates that the opacity of artificial intelligence necessitates the adoption of strict liability frameworks. This approach is consistent with the regulation of "dangerous activities" (e.g., Art. 2050 of the Italian Civil Code), whereby the operator is held liable for damages irrespective of fault, merely due to the creation of risk.

For damage caused to third parties on the surface, the 1952 Rome Convention provides a strict liability regime based on the concept of the "operator" (the entity with control).

The Convention is solely applicable to international flights and has been ratified by merely 51 states, including 10 European Union member states such as Italy and Spain. It does not encompass domestic drone operations, which comprise most flights.

The compensation limits established by the Rome Convention were originally intended for manned aviation and may be either excessively high or insufficiently low for drones, depending on the specific context.

Since the European Union is not a signatory to the Rome Convention, liability concerning surface damage during domestic flights is frequently regulated by national tort law, resulting in fragmentation. The establishment of a harmonized liability regime for drones within the EU is recognised as a necessary future initiative.

The criminal implications of drone use vary significantly by context.

The employment of armed drones for targeted killings prompts significant questions concerning the chain of command and the legality of the orders issued. Establishing individual criminal responsibility for "collateral damage" requires intricate evaluations of international humanitarian law and the possible liability of decision-makers and remote pilots.

In civil operations, criminal liability generally arises from negligence, such as a pilot losing control due to recklessness, or from intentional misuse, including privacy violations and interference with airport operations. The current technological capabilities of semi-automatic drones permit the application of traditional criminal law categories. Nonetheless, the advent of fully autonomous systems in the future could pose significant challenges to the principle of personal criminal responsibility, as the "behavioural choices' of such autonomous systems may be unforeseeable to human programmers or operators.

Conversely, drones serve as highly effective platforms for data collection during flight. Their capability to capture high-resolution imagery, thermal data, and geolocation information necessitates the application of the General Data Protection Regulation (GDPR).

The safeguarding of personal data within the UAS sector is both a legal right and a matter of public concern. Member States have the authority to designate UAS geographical zones or to prohibit operations to safeguard privacy. Manufacturers are obliged to embed privacy protection measures such as data minimization and encryption into the drone's architecture. Operators engaged in high-risk operations, such as those classified under the 'Specific' category, are frequently mandated to perform a Data Protection Impact Assessment (DPIA) to identify and mitigate potential privacy risks prior to conducting flights.

Finally, the digitisation of air navigation services is propelled by the SESAR (Single European Sky ATM Research) program. Currently evolving into the SESAR 3 Joint Undertaking under Regulation (EU) 2085/2021, this initiative seeks to establish a "Digital European Sky." It encompasses the virtualization of infrastructure, enabling service provision independent of physical location, and the comprehensive integration of data to optimize flight trajectories. The objective is to develop a scalable, automated system capable of accommodating mixed traffic, including both manned and unmanned aircraft efficiently.

In conjunction with digitalisation, the proliferation of drones and Urban Air Mobility (UAM) must be aligned with the objectives of the European Green Deal.

Electric propulsion (eVTOL) provides a route to decarbonised urban transport for short-distance missions.

Nevertheless, the expected increase in drone traffic brings new environmental challenges, especially noise pollution and visual intrusion in cities. The regulatory framework, including the SES II+ reform, clearly states that air traffic management should support the sustainable growth of the air transport system by optimising routes to reduce environmental impact.

The incorporation of unmanned aerial vehicles into the European airspace constitutes a dynamic process characterised by the tension between rapid technological advancements and the imperative for cautious legal regulation. This analysis, derived from the' Drones in the Digital European Sky" study, underscores that although the European Union has established a robust, risk-based regulatory framework through Regulations 2018/1139, 2019/945, and 2019/947, significant efforts are still required.

The key findings and future directions include: (a) the definition of "crew" remains inconsistent with ICAO standards, potentially leading to international disputes; (b) the effective implementation of Urban Air Mobility depends on the physical development of vertiports and their integration into municipal planning instruments such as Sustainable Urban Mobility Plans (SUMPs), a process that is still in its early stages; (c) the adoption of Regulation (EU) 2024/2803 (SES II+) establishes the necessary legal framework to modernize air traffic management; however, the practical implementation of U-Space services continues to present substantial technical and bureaucratic challenges; (d) the increasing prominence of artificial intelligence and autonomous flight necessitates a re-evaluation of liability frameworks, with a shift towards strict liability and product liability regimes to ensure compensation for victims in light of the opacity of algorithms.

The "drone system" represents more than an emerging sector within aviation; it serves as a case study for the broader digitalisation and automation of transportation. Navigating this digital landscape necessitates ongoing dialogue between aviation law, technological innovation, and societal values to uphold safety, privacy, and sustainability.

UAS and Aircraft

The Aircraft

Simone Vernizzi

Contents

Abstract The purpose of this chapter is firstly to provide a definition of the aircraft, through an evaluation that takes into account the indications deriving from the analysis of the most relevant provisions of the 1944 Chicago Convention and the ICAO International Standards and Recommended Practices, of those emerging from the recent European derivative law instruments on aeronautical safety, as well as from some significant definitions existing in the legal system of some ICAO member countries.

The definition in ICAO Annex 7 *Aircraft Nationality and Registration Marks* is examined by considering the various debates it has fuelled since its introduction, mostly in relation to the new frontiers opened up by technological progress.

With particular reference to suborbital vehicles, and to the imminent employment of such vehicles for the transport of people and/or payloads in suborbital flight

S. Vernizzi (✉)
Department of Law, University of Modena and Reggio Emilia, Modena, Italy
e-mail: simone.vernizzi@unimore.it

M. P. Rizzo, F. Franchina (eds.), *Drones in the Digital European Sky*,
International Aviation Law Library 1,
https://doi.org/10.1007/978-3-032-16691-3_2

at super or ultrasonic speeds, attention is dedicated to their non-immediate inclusion in the definition of aircraft, with all the consequences that this entails in terms of applicable legal framework.

Lastly, the aircraft is examined as a product, emphasising the importance of certification processes provided for by International Standards and Recommended Practices contained in Annex 8 *Airworthiness of Aircraft* for the safety of air navigation.

1 The Problem with Definitions; Introduction

The first definition of aéronef/aircraft is contained in the *Convention Portant Réglementation de la Navigation Aérienne*, signed in Paris on 13 October 1919: since this was not the convention's main objective, the text initially contained no definition of aircraft. Later on, after special intervention by ICAN (International Commission for Air Navigation), the Convention provided a definition of the vehicle, which appeared, however, only in one of its annexes, where "*aéronefs*" are referred to as all those vehicles that "*pouvant se soutenir dans l'atmosphère grâce aux reactions de l'air*".

This definition received strong criticism, especially from French scholars of the time, who considered it to be excessively broad: in any case, only few states referred to it in their domestic legislation (e.g. Belgium, Spain, Portugal and Greece), since most states preferred instead to distance themselves from the definition in the Convention.

In the Civil Aeronautics Act 1938, US legislators included within the scope of aircraft "*any contrivance now known or hereafter invented, used or designed for navigation of or flight in the air*"; such a definition would also seem to include rockets and ballistic missiles.

In other domestic legislations functional data prevail over technical data: the definition should refer to those machines *intended* for air navigation purposes (Germany and Panama), for air traffic *intended for the transport* of goods or persons (Soviet Union) or in any case *capable* of transporting persons for air navigation purposes (Japan and Italy).

Finally, some others, more or less consciously, concluded that they do not need to provide any definition, with the clear conviction that it was not necessary to define a term of general meaning that can be applied to all aircraft subject to aviation law, thus preferring to entrust the listing of the different categories of aircrafts/aéronefs to a regulatory instrument.

1.1 The Chicago Convention (1944) and the Provisions Relating to Aircraft

The 1944 Chicago Convention contains several provisions that refer to aircraft.[1]

In Chapter 1 (*General principles and application of the Convention*), Article 3 distinguishes between *civil* and *state* aircraft, affirming that state aircraft are those "*used in military, customs and police services*". It states in particular that the provisions of the Convention do not apply to state aircrafts and, unlike civil aircrafts, they also require prior authorisation to fly over the territory of another Contracting State.

In Chapter II (*Flight over the territory of contracting states*), Article 8 addresses pilotless aircraft, reaffirming also for this category of vehicles the need for special prior authorisation to fly over the territory of another contracting state. With regards to this specific matter, please refer to Drones (Ch. X).

Chapter III (arts. 17–21) is instead dedicated to the nationality of aircraft; all aircraft shall have the nationality of the state in which they are registered (art. 17), thus calling the principle according to which an aircraft cannot be validly registered in more than one state and, however, its registration may be transferred from one state to another (art. 18); registration or transfer of registration of aircraft in a contracting state shall be made in accordance with the laws and regulations of that state (Art. 20); each aircraft used in international air navigation shall bear its nationality and registration marks, with the further undertaking by each contracting state to provide, at the request of another contracting state or the International Civil Aviation Organisation, information concerning the registration and ownership of any aircraft registered in that state, as well as to provide ICAO with detailed reports concerning the ownership and control of aircraft registered in that state and ordinarily used in international air navigation (Art. 21).

Further important provisions are contained in Chapter V (*Conditions to be fulfilled with respect to aircraft*). Under Art. 29, each aircraft engaged in international navigation shall, in addition, carry the following documents in conformity with the conditions prescribed in this Convention:

> (a) Its certificate of registration; (b) Its certificate of airworthiness; (c) The appropriate licenses for each member of the crew; (d) Its journey log book; (e) If it is equipped with radio apparatus, the aircraft radio station license; (f) If it carries passengers, a list of their names and places of embarkation and destination; (g) If it carries cargo, a manifest and detailed declarations of the cargo.

Particular attention is to be paid to the provision of Article 31, whereby each aircraft shall be provided with a certificate of airworthiness issued or rendered valid by the state in which it is registered: such a certificate—as well as that of competency and licences issued or rendered valid by the contracting state in which the aircraft is registered—shall be recognized as valid by the other contracting states, provided that the requirements under which such certificates or licences were issued or rendered valid are equal to or above the minimum standards which may be established from time to time pursuant to this Convention. See also *infra*, chapter "Civil Liability Deriving from Artificial Intelligence Used in Air Navigation".

---

[1] See Dempsey (2008), 51 et seq.

1.2 In Particular, the Definition of Aircraft in Annex 7: The Technical Aspect

Like the earlier Paris Convention, the 1944 Chicago Convention defines aircraft in its technical annexes, which may have consequences in terms of the hierarchy of legal sources within the legal framework of each contracting state: although the Convention binds each contracting state "*to collaborate in securing the highest practicable degree of uniformity in regulations, standards, procedures, and organisation in relation to aircraft (...)*", the regulatory instrument by which each contracting state introduces such international standards and recommended practices into its own legal system are left to the state itself.

Annex 7 (*Aircraft Nationality and Registration Marks*) initially defined aircraft as "*any machine that can derive support in the atmosphere from the reaction of the air*", thus referring exclusively to the technical element by which the vehicle receives support in the air.

This characteristic of the definition imposes specific evaluation whenever a technological innovation is introduced. In terms of interpretation, it has been agreed, for example, that vehicles that exploit the density of the air for the purposes of airworthiness, as well as those that overcome the resistance of the air that is an obstacle to navigation by means of the dynamic thrust determined by the pre-compression of the air in the traction system, should be considered aircraft. Therefore, turbojet-engine (hexoreactor) vehicles have also been considered compatible with the definition in Annex 7, despite the great difference between such vehicles and those, equipped with a propeller or turboprop engine, in respect of which the aforementioned definition had been initially modelled.

In the second half of the 1960s, however, the definition of aircraft was amended to put an end to the international debate concerning the nature of hovercraft and other vehicles that receive their support by statically generated air cushions.

As is well known, the hovercraft generates underneath itself an "air cushion", capable of lifting it above the earth's surface (water, land), and is guided by one or more propeller rotors; the difficulties of framing this technical system are mainly due to the peculiar mix of factors (technology, environments and risks) involved in its construction characteristics and usage, and make it a vehicle that "hovers" between different modes of transport.

Considering the different perspective of its usage, on the other hand, the hovercraft should rather be assimilated to ships, since it covers routes normally operated by the latter and travels mostly on the sea surface.

In November 1967, the ICAO Council decided to specify the definition in Annex 7 by adding the words '*other than the reactions of the air against the earth's surface*', aircraft definition thus resulting in "*any machine that can derive support in the atmosphere from the reaction of the air other than the reactions of the air against the earth's surface*". As a consequence, the hovercraft and hovercraft-assimilated vehicles were definitively no longer to be considered as aircraft. Subsequently, at an international level, hovercrafts were included among the High-Speed Craft(s) in the

HSC Code drawn up by the International Maritime Organisation, where they appear as ACV ("Air-Cushion Vehicle").[2]

In the late 1960s and early 1970s, international scholarship also debated at length on the qualification of vehicles equipped with rocket-propelled engines (endoreactors). In such vehicles, propulsion is the effect of the thrust generated by the expulsion of a fluid already stowed on board, with the consequence, therefore, that, technically, there is no real reaction with the air, as required by the definition in Annex 7; so much so that such vehicles are perfectly capable of operating in conditions of rarefied atmosphere or even in the total absence of air. Consequently, rocket vehicles could not be considered as aircraft, a conclusion that led to new requests for intervention on the definition contained in Annex 7, which, however, were unsuccessful. See *infra*, Sect. 2.

In the same paragraph (1. *Definitions*), Annex 7 also classifies aircrafts on the basis of their technical characteristics, distinguishing lighter-than-air aircraft from heavier-than-air aircraft and providing the definition of peculiar types of aircraft: in the current version applicable as of 2 November 2023, the Annex identifies the following types of aircraft:

> Aeroplane. A power-driven heavier-than-air aircraft, deriving its lift in flight chiefly from aerodynamic reactions on surfaces which remain fixed under given conditions of flight. (…) Airship. A power-driven lighter-than-air aircraft. Balloon. A non-power-driven lighter-than-air aircraft. (…) Glider. A non-power-driven heavier-than-air aircraft, deriving its lift in flight chiefly from aerodynamic reactions on surfaces which remain fixed under given conditions of flight. Gyroplane. A heavier-than-air aircraft supported in flight by the reactions of the air on one or more rotors which rotate freely on substantially vertical axes. (…) Helicopter. A heavier-than-air aircraft supported in flight chiefly by the reactions of the air on one or more power-driven rotors on substantially vertical axes. (…) Ornithopter. A heavier-than-air aircraft supported in flight chiefly by the reactions of the air on planes to which a flapping motion is imparted. Remotely piloted aircraft (RPA). An unmanned aircraft which is piloted from a remote pilot station. Rotorcraft. A power-driven heavier-than-air aircraft supported in flight by the reactions of the air on one or more rotors (Annex 7, 1. Definitions).

The Annex also includes a synoptic table.

1.3 *The Aircraft and International Air Law Conventions: Potential Interferences of Functional Aspects*

At the international level, the legislation relevant to air navigation refers not only to that of a technical nature deriving from the ICAO annexes: numerous conventions regulate various aspects of international private law and, even when not concerned directly with aircraft, refer to the air carrier, the operator or the owner of the aircraft, while however not providing in any case a definition of aircraft, nor in any case explicitly referring to another legal source.

The situation described occurs for instance in conventions relating to air carrier liability, such as, first and foremost, the Warsaw Convention of 1929. In this respect,

[2] See Du Pontavice (1970), 136 et seq.

it is undoubtedly worth recalling that in the year immediately following the opening for signature of the convention, CITEJA (*Comité International Technique d'Experts Juridiques Aériens*)—which had promoted the adoption of the Convention—had proposed to amend the text by adding the definition of aircraft, without success. Neither the subsequent (complementary) Guadalajara Convention of 1961 nor the current Montreal Convention of 1999 contain any definition of aircraft.

The same may be said for the 1952 Rome Convention on the Operator's Liability for Damage to Third Parties on the Surface, in which the aircraft is in no way defined, or for the 1948 Geneva Convention on the International Recognition of Rights in Aircraft and its predecessor, the 1933 Rome Convention on the Preservation of Aircraft.

However, this lacuna is also to be found outside the field of private law, such as in the field of security and the suppression of crimes against the safety of navigation and other acts of unlawful interference in air transport.

Each of the conventions referred to mentions aircraft but none of them aims to define it: to overcome the silence of international legislation, it is then necessary to refer to the *lex fori* identified by the connecting factors that may be contained in any of those legal instruments or in other legislation applicable to the case.

Depending on the legal framework applicable on the basis of the criteria referred to, the definition of aircraft might include functional specifications (e.g. if the definition of aircraft contained in the applicable law refers to the aircraft as a vehicle '*intended for air transport purposes*', or similar expressions, as is the case in Italian law).

1.4 The Aircraft and EU Legislation

Until the late 1990s, even European Community-derived aviation legislation did not provide, even indirectly, any definition of aircraft.

With the beginning of the new millennium, Commission Regulation (EC) No 2042/2003—with which the legislator intended, among other objectives, to adopt common technical rules and administrative procedures for the continued airworthiness of aeronautical products, parts and appliances, as well as to ensure uniformity in the application of the same—in Art. 2 (definitions), para. 1(a), defines aircraft as '*any machine that can derive support in the atmosphere from the reactions of the air other than reactions of the air against the earth's surface*', thus repeating without any distinctions the definition contained in the ICAO Annexes.

The regulation was amended and supplemented on several occasions in later years and was finally repealed by Commission Reg. (EU) No. 1321/2014. However, the definition of aircraft contained in the new regulatory instrument remained unamended.

This definition applies, as expressly stated, for the purposes of the so-called 'basic' regulation—at that time, Reg. (EC) No. 216/2008, later replaced by the current Reg. (EU) No. 1139/2018—and, therefore, referring to aviation safety.

The same definition was then further contained in Commission Reg. (EU) No. 139/2014, and, especially, in Reg. (EU) No. 376/2014 of the European Parliament and of the Council, which partly amends the previous Reg. (EU) No. 996/2010 on safety investigations, which originally did not contain any definition of aircraft.

In light of the above, it cannot be doubted that such a definition of aircraft is, to all extents and purposes, an integral part of European safety legislation and, due to the horizontal effectiveness of the regulation and its direct applicability within the legal system of each the Member State, it is part of the existing legal framework of each individual Member State.

However, as referred to in respect of international (private) law conventions, even European legislation dedicated to, for example, the protection of passengers' rights (e.g. Regulation (EC) No. 261/2004) and, more generally, air carrier's liability (e.g. Regulation (EC) 2027/1997), do not provide any definition of aircraft, thus imposing once again to refer to the *lex fori* applicable to the specific case.

1.5 Some Conclusions: Technical and Functional Aspects of the Definition of Aircraft

In the light of the foregoing, it would appear, in the final analysis, that two distinct bodies of legislation are present and clearly identifiable within aeronautical legislation: one, which deals with safety and safety-related issues, in which the aircraft is defined on the basis of technical data; the other, of a more exquisitely private nature, relating to the situations of aircraft operators, air carriers and the protection of the rights of air transport passengers, which in many cases may fill out the definition of aircraft with details of a functional nature.

Consequently, technical data alone would no longer be useful to fully define aircraft: increasingly, the purposes for which a given (air) navigation activity is performed, and/or the environment (risks) within which it is carried out, would contribute to defining the vehicle, or rather to determining the system with which to regulate its operations.

These conclusions are of significant importance in relation to the issue of the legal classification of suborbital vehicles.

2 Suborbital Vehicles

The expression "suborbital vehicles" is used to identify specific devices that combine aerospace-type propulsion means (for all or most of the ascent phase) and aerodynamic gliding capabilities (during the descent phase), experiencing a few moments of micro-gravity, whose projected use involves the transport (of passengers and payloads) from one place to another on the earth's surface (point-to-point transport).

Already in the mid-1960s, such devices had aroused the keen interest of international scholarship. Forgotten then for decades, with the new millennium the influx of private capital has reawakened interest in this type of super(or even hyper)sonic transport vehicles.

As previously mentioned, the use of endoreactors puts them in conflict with the definition of aircraft, given that such engines are capable of operating even in the absence of air (and, therefore, without there being an effective reaction of air on the machine): in this regard, the international community has so far proved reluctant to amend the dictate of ICAO Annex 7, either because such vehicles were considered "space objects", or because they were judged to be state aircrafts for the purposes of the (non-)applicability of freedom of overflight.

Reasons connected to their possible different usage (not space missions, but rather the transport of people and payloads from one point to another on the earth's surface) and the progressive privatisation of experimentation activities have, however, once again re-opened the international academic debate, to identify the regulations applicable to them, even irrespective of their actual classification.

Traditionally, the interpretative solutions proposed by scholars are divided between those that give precedence to the type of activity actually carried out (the so-called "functionalist" doctrine), and those that, instead give greater prominence to the environment within which (and possibly to the means of propulsion by which) the activity is exercised, applying to the vehicle one regulatory regime or another, depending on the location (airspace or outer space) within which it operates (the so-called "spatialist" doctrine).

For the supporters of the former, the passenger/payload transport activity performed by suborbital vehicles would be nothing more than air transport activity, making it irrelevant that the vehicle uses, at least in part, means of propulsion that go beyond the notion of aircraft, or that it travels certain stretches in which the environment, due to the extreme rarefaction of the air, is more similar to that of space: "the nature of the activity rather than the location of the activity should be the determinant".[3]

By contrast, the advocates of the spatialist theory consider that the regime proper to the environment in which the navigation activity takes place, should be applied to suborbital vehicles, with the consequent fragmentation of the applicable regulations: the aircraft would thus be, in the course of the same voyage, aircraft, then space object (spacecraft) and then aircraft again, depending on the phase of flight.

The traditional criticism levelled at the spatialist theory, apart of course from the complexities relating to the choice of a composite system, is that it requires the establishment, at the level of uniform law, of a demarcation between airspace (atmospheric, so-called inner space) and outer space (outer space), an issue on which, however, the international community has never been able to agree, and the Karman line itself has only been effectively adopted for this purpose, at the level of positive law, by Australia.[4]

---

[3] See Di Paolo (2014), p. 623 et seq., in part., 628. Dasgupta (2013), p. 237 et seq., in part., 245. See also Fawcett (1968).

[4] See Gangale (2017), 151 et seq.

The need to reach a satisfactorily clear and unequivocal interpretative solution is felt with significant urgency with reference to the operator's liability regarding: (i) the people transported; (ii) third parties damaged on the surface, as well as (iii) aspects of the safety of traditional air navigation, due to the numerous possible interferences with the latter.

With reference to the specific subject of liability for the death or personal injury of the persons on board, the qualification of a suborbital vehicle as an aircraft or as a space object gives rise to significant divergences in regulatory terms. In fact, in the former case, provided the carriage meets the requirement of internationality (as in the case for point-to-point carriage between different States), the regime envisaged by the Montreal Convention 1999 would then probably apply. Otherwise, the injured person would be subject to the provisions of the 1972 Liability Convention, which, however, do not seem to provide adequate protection for the specific matter, unless the damage derives from a collision with another space object[5].

According to the EASA, "*suborbital aeroplanes deriving support from the atmosphere for the largest part of their flight, are considered as aircraft*".[6] One thinks, in this perspective, of all those suborbital vehicles that use aerodynamic flight modes for a large part of their flight: they could therefore be defined as aircraft and would not consequently cease to be such when they temporarily cease to receive support from a "reaction of the air".

The EASA would seem to believe that such vehicles should be subject to (albeit partial) *ad hoc* regulation, although the starting point must in any case be found in (the application of) the existing aeronautical certification system.

Another debated aspect concerns liability for damage (to persons and property) suffered by third parties as a result of the suborbital vehicle crashing, or of one or more of its parts becoming detached from the vehicle.

As is well known, the classification of suborbital vehicle as space objects would entail the application of the rules of the already mentioned 1972 Liability Convention, which—introduced in a context in which launch operations were conducted (exclusively) by states—in such cases imputes the entire liability (without limitation) to the launching state, without any reference to the (suborbital vehicle) operator.

However, the approach of this convention suffers from the fact that space activities were at the time conducted exclusively by states, while, at present, the role of private individuals is far from being marginal and is, indeed, positively encouraged. Consequently, the provisions of the Liability Convention 1972 prove to be incomplete with respect to the regulation of the cases under consideration and require individual states, within the framework of their domestic legislation, to define the

[5] *Convention on International Liability for Damage Caused by Space Objects*, London – Moscow – Washington, 29 March 1972 (Liability Convention 1972): in particular, according to article III, "*In the event of damage being caused elsewhere than on the surface of the earth to a space object of one launching State or to persons or property on board such a space object by a space object of another launching State, the latter shall be liable only if the damage is due to its fault or the fault of persons for whom it is responsible*".

[6] See Marciacq et al. (2010), pp. 187–212.

responsibilities of private companies wishing to conduct suborbital and space activities.

Otherwise, by qualifying suborbital vehicle as aircraft, the rules of the Rome Convention 1952 [and, possibly, of the two superseding conventions,[7] if and when they will come into force], which makes the "operator" liable for the case of damage to third parties on the surface, could be applied.

In any case, establishing appropriate regulatory instruments aimed primarily at avoiding possible threats to aviation safety has now become urgent. In fact, in the take-off (or launch) phase and, above all, in the descent phase, suborbital vehicles cross traditional airspace, resulting in the need to coordinate the civil (and military) management and control of airspace and traffic flows on the one hand, and suborbital aviation on the other.

Additionally, it is worth noting that the 1975 Registration Convention requires the registration of space objects only when they are launched into Earth's orbit or beyond, whereas suborbital vehicle would operate at lower (i.e., "suborbital") altitudes, consequently highlighting a significant shortcoming of the current uniform space law.

Some consensus is forming within international scholarship as to whether the status provided for aircraft should be applied to suborbital vehicles.

These considerations therefore lead to the identification of the ICAO as the most appropriate body for the regulation of suborbital activities, especially given its organizational structure and expertise in relation to international civil aviation[8].

The EASA believes that, also for suborbital activities, it is necessary to certify the operations, flight crew and passenger licensing and continued airworthiness in the manner provided by the technical regulations for aircraft, thus supporting its belief that suborbital vehicles should be considered as "aircraft with certain special features".

In this perspective, the ICAO, in Doc. No. 9750, also emphasized its interest in suborbital vehicles, considering that suborbital activities assume practical relevance as sustainable forms of transportation. In addition, the ICAO's Thirteen Air Navigation Conference, as part of the work conducted within Committee A, addressed issues related to "Operations above Flight Level 600" (5.1) and "Other emerging issues impacting the global air navigation system including unmanned aircraft systems (drones), and supersonic and commercial space operations" (5.5).

Far from taking a position on the debated qualifying profile of suborbital vehicles, the ICAO is currently promoting those actions designed to safeguard the safe conduct of operations within the airspace used by traditional civil aviation, while encouraging the growing development of activities (CST and SST) conducted at higher altitudes and inviting states to share their experiences in this area in order to prepare the ground for future regulation.

---

[7] *Convention on Compensation for Damage Caused by Aircraft to Third Parties* and *Convention on Compensation for Damage to Third Parties, Resulting from Acts of Unlawful Interference Involving Aircraft*, both signed on 2 May, 2009.

[8] See Fitzgerald (2014), p. 3 et seq., in part., 23 et seq.

3 Ground Effect Vehicles (GEV)

Ground Effect Vehicles (GEVs), also known as Wing In Ground effect (WIG) Craft, flarecraft, and sea skimmers, are often thought to be the connecting link between hydrofoils and seaplanes and are therefore of certain interest for definitional and disciplinary purposes.

The most significant examples of such vehicles are ekranoplanes (= "sea skimmers"), large military vehicles employed to cover considerable distances over the large sheets of water of the Soviet Union, and capable of reaching considerable speeds.

A common feature of such vehicles is that they dynamically generate a particular kind of air cushion: this is the so-called "ground effect," which improves the performance of the vehicle, causing it to emerge and separate completely from the water, even by several metres.

Initially, the ekranoplane was conceived to combine the carrying capacity of a ship and the speed of an aircraft: although referred to as an aerodine, its qualification among aircraft nevertheless seemed somewhat dubious, in view of the fact, above all, that its "flight" was by no means free, since it turned out to be ultimately constrained within the confines of the body of water over which the vehicle operated, being unable to overcome large obstacles (much less mountainous terrain).

At present, the so-called GEVs constitute a rather heterogeneous category: these vehicles, whose dimensions have been greatly reduced compared to those of the Soviet ekranoplanes, are in fact configured as hybrid, i.e., normally aircraft (but often also boats) that nevertheless take advantage of the ground effect when they are flying at low altitude (or, as the case may be, sailing at high speed); there are also amphibious models, capable of moving easily on land as well.

Their qualification therefore appears uncertain, and ultimately depends on the nature (ship, aircraft) peculiar to the individual type based on its specific structural and operational characteristics:[9] it has also been proposed that they should be considered as *sui generis* vehicles, which, in any case, would not exempt them from the application of the rules peculiar to operation in a given environment.

---

[9] The International Maritime Organization (IMO) has outlined the rules based on the International Code of Safety for High-Speed Craft (HSC Code), which was developed for high-speed vessels such as hydrofoils, hovercrafts, catamarans and the like. The Russian Rules for the Classification and Construction of Small ekranoplanes (Type A) is the document on which the design of most of these GEVs (short for Ground Effect Vehicles) is based. In 2005, the IMO classified certain GEVs under the category of ships. The International Maritime Organisation recognises three classes of such vehicles, denoted A, B and C. Type A cannot operate outside 'ground effect', while type B can overcome obstacles by converting kinetic energy (speed) into potential energy (height) but cannot maintain flight without the support of 'ground effect'. As for Type C, they are certified as aircraft, as they can operate safely and efficiently even without ground effect.

4 Flying Cars

The possibility of putting on the market a vehicle capable of combining the functions of an ordinary passenger car and a small aircraft seemed to materialize during the 2010s, with solutions that were also quite different from each other. The U.S.-based Terrafugia (which became Chinese-owned as of 2017) has long experimented with the Transition prototype, a roadable aircraft that obtained a special Light-Sport Aircraft (LSA) airworthiness certificate from the FAA in 2021, and was on its way to road use approval, expected in 2022. However, the process was halted due to the company's decision to lay off the majority of its employees, and plans to close its U.S. operations and re-establish in China. Another prototype publicized by the same company is the TF-X, a VTOL flying car equipped with two rotor engines. Subject of intense experimentation is also the AeroMobil 4.0, a vehicle conceptually similar to the Terrafugia Transition. In terms of qualification, it seems difficult to doubt that such vehicles, in flight mode, fall within the definition of aircraft in the international technical regulations, and the aforementioned FAA's obtaining of an airworthiness certificate would confirm this. In addition, in road mode, they are certainly motor vehicles, albeit of a particular kind. Rather, the issues raised by flying cars concern the potential implications related to the dual nature of such vehicles, and, in particular, the difficult coexistence, in a single vehicle, of the dual purpose, alternative and not cumulative, of road and air transport. In addition to the need to obtain a dual certification (both as a passenger car and as an aircraft), the driver will need to obtain a dual licence for use of the vehicle, as well as dual registration and dual insurance. These circumstances undoubtedly add to the administrative burden of flying cars and may convince of the advisability of providing for special regulations, which take into account their eccentricity with respect to the traditional concept of aircraft (and motor car).

5 The Aircraft as a Product

The aircraft and/or its parts are to all extents and purposes (aviation) products, since they are the result of industrial production.

Indeed, after aviation ceased to be conceived as a pioneering experience, the war period fostered the birth and growth of the aviation industry. With the end of World War II and the advancement of civil aviation internationally, aviation increasingly became an integral part of and a key strategic factor in the growth and development of each country's economic and social life. The experience gained in the military field had thus been transferred and reconverted to the civilian field, and the manufacturing companies undertook industrial mass production of each type of aircraft and its components, so much so that today, and subject in any case to the customization activities required by the customer/client, the non-serial production of individual aircraft is to be considered the true exception.

In this perspective, the ICAO Annexes place the aircraft and its parts within type-certification and type-conformity certification procedures, incorporating the demands of the concrete experience of the aviation industry and the needs of large-scale production.

5.1 *ICAO Annex 8 (Airworthiness of Aircraft)*

The international technical regulations contained within the ICAO Annexes were intended to coordinate the needs of the aviation industry with those inherent in the need to ensure and guarantee compliance with common aviation safety standards.

Annex 8 (*Airworthiness of Aircraft*), which is devoted to the airworthiness of aircraft, deals with the certification and type-approval procedures for the aircraft and its parts, thereby aimed at ensuring safe operation.

This objective is pursued by conducting initial controls and inspections, as well as periodic and unannounced inspections, intended to verify the existence and maintenance of the prescribed requirements and conditions necessary to ensure the initial presence and continued fitness of the aircraft, engine propeller and its parts for safe operational use, in accordance with the concept of "Continuing Airworthiness," which consists of

> the set of processes by which an aircraft, engine, propeller or part complies with the applicable airworthiness requirements and remains in a condition for safe operation throughout its operating life (Annex 8, Part I, Definitions).

The system outlined in the Annex is based on a twofold certification: the first consists of the issuance of the Type Certificate, a document

> issued by a Contracting State to define the design of an aircraft type and to certify that this design meets the appropriate airworthiness requirements of that State (Annex 8, Part I, Definitions)

and refers to the design of the aircraft (the "type"), which must meet the airworthiness requirements prescribed for that class of aircraft ("Type Certification"—Chapter 1.); the other, concerning each individual aircraft specimen produced, certifies that the individual vehicle is actually capable of performing the air navigation activity for which it was built, and for which it is or will be used, in a safe condition (Chapter 3), and coincides with that "Certificate of Airworthiness," required by Article 31 of the 1944 Chicago Convention.

The first certificate thus concerns the design, and is issued, as a rule, in response to a request from a party (Manufacturer) to proceed with mass production of that model.

The second, on the other hand, concerns each individual aircraft, which, once it has been found to conform to the type certified in the Type Certificate, also demonstrates, as a result of tests and inspections, that it can undertake the air navigation activities for which it is intended under safe conditions (Airworthiness). This second certificate must also be maintained in a constant state of validity, to meet the principles of Continuing Airworthiness referred to above.

Between the issuance of the first and second certificates lies the (serial) production of the aircraft (Production, Chapter 2), an activity for which the annex in question provides that specific responsibility lies with the state of construction, which is called upon to ensure that the aircraft and its parts are airworthy and manufactured in accordance with the certified design.

Therefore, the dual consideration of the aircraft emerges: as a "product," since the Type Certificate is aimed at the subsequent serial production of aircraft in accordance with the certified type; further, and with respect to the individual specimen, as a means suitable for the safe performance of airworthy activities: indeed, this is attested through the issuance of the Certificate of Airworthiness.

5.2 *Airworthiness and EU Legislation*

In the European context, the notion of "product" referring to the aircraft, engine, and propeller already appeared in EEC Reg. No. 3922/91 on the harmonization of technical regulations and administrative procedures in the field of civil aviation safety. However, with the EASA's founding regulation, the approach set forth in ICAO Annex 8 received significant regulatory attention from the EU.

Reg. (EC) No. 1592/2002, in fact, in Chapter II, relating to substantive requirements, deals, with reference to aircrafts as indicated under Art. 4 (*Basic Principles and Applicability*), with Airworthiness (in part, Art. 5), an issue referred to in the very first recitals of the measure regarding the concept and notion of aeronautical safety, to which the legislator also adds environmental protection, in line with the provisions of international technical regulations.

Airworthiness is then considered as a tool and/or set of procedures aimed at ensuring (i) that an aeronautical product complies with common safety and environmental protection rules; and, at the same time, (ii) that any aircraft complying with the certification basis is also a suitable means of safely conducting flight operations.

The system set up within the regulation addresses the subject of airworthiness: in general, in relation to the type, and with reference to the individual aircraft.

With regard to the first aspect, for EU legislators, the product must comply with the type certification basis, which consists of the applicable airworthiness code and the other specifications provided in Articles 14 and 15. With reference to the second aspect, the individual aircraft, as a product, has its own type certificate, but becomes airworthy when it has been proven that it conforms to the design approved in its type certificate (conformity of the product to type) and that "*relevant documentation, inspections and tests demonstrate that the aircraft is in a condition to safely conduct flight operations*" (fitness of the means for their proper usage), through the issuance of a certificate of airworthiness.

As can be seen, therefore, with this regulation EU legislators intended to reproduce and specify the contents and principles referred to in international technical regulations, while also providing for the specific competencies of EASA and the relationship between the Agency and the Civil Aviation Authorities of individual member states in relation to certification procedures.

The so-called "Basic Regulation" also consists of special detailed implementing measures, contained within second-level regulations adopted by the European Commission and constituting the so-called "Implementation Rules."

The subsequent Reg. (EC) no. 216/2008 is set in the perspective of a progressive expansion of the Agency's competences and powers; while repealing the previous basic regulation, however, with reference to aeronautical products it does not deviate from the approach contained in the previous measure, of which it clarifies certain aspects without, however, altering its general architecture.

With the new basic regulation, EU Reg. no. 1139/2018, which repeals the previous Reg. (EC) no. 216/2008, we see a further contraction of the competences of the individual national authorities in favour of the EASA and the European Commission: the regulation aims to adapt the European regulatory framework on aviation safety to the challenges of the next fifteen years, seeking to foster competitiveness through the adoption of measures "*proportionate to the nature and risk of each particular activity*" to which they refer and innovation in the field of the aviation industry, with the aim of simplifying and rationalizing the regulatory system, without however affecting the high levels of safety achieved.

With regard to airworthiness and environmental protection, the regulation outlines a system that does not innovate with regard to the previous legislation and yet organizes the subject in a more rational manner with respect to the essential airworthiness requirements, the concept of compliance, and the issuance of the certificate of airworthiness for individual aircraft.

5.3 The Aircraft and Its Parts as Unsafe or Defective Products: Aspects of Liability

Considering the aircraft as a product opens up important issues in the field of civil liability: for example, we should think of the cases in which an accident (or an incident) depends wholly or even only in part on a technical failure due to a manufacturing defect or to the incorrect maintenance of the aircraft or of one of its parts.

The liabilities that may eventually arise may obviously be contractual in nature, as is the case, for example, in the relationship between manufacturer and purchaser, or in that between the aircraft operator (or carrier) and maintainer.

Far more interesting, however, are the responsibilities to which the manufacturer, parts supplier, and maintainer may be exposed outside and independently of a relationship of a contractual nature (whether of sale, air enlistment, or service contract), in relation to damage suffered by third parties, such as, in particular, the air transport user (i.e., his successors in title), the captain, the pilot, as well as the third party on the surface damaged in his person and/or property as a result of a design, production, or documentation defect relating to an aircraft or any of its parts.

There may be awarded, in such cases, damages resulting from non-contractual liability. While the injured party may take advantage of a longer statute of limitations and the absence of limits to indemnity (present, on the other hand, both in contractual actions against the air carrier and in non-contractual actions against the operator for surface damage), the claimant is subject to a substantial burden of proof.

However, the consideration of the aircraft and its parts as "products" allows at least partial relief of this burden in favour of the injured party, due to the system provided by the EU-derived product liability legislation.

Indeed, the definition of "safe product" (and that of "dangerous product," which can be derived in reverse), and the producer's obligation to place only safe products on the market, seem to take on sufficiently precise connotations when assessed in the light of European Community-derived safety legislation.

In particular, consider, from this point of view, the airworthiness codes as well as the other technical specifications provided by the basic regulation, its annexes and other measures complementary to it for the purpose of identifying the basis of type certification. The manufacturer's failure to comply with these provisions at the design stage or at the production stage, or even, in any case, the non-compliance with them of any parts subsequently installed during maintenance, determines the unsafety of the product and, therefore, its dangerousness, with all the consequences that follow for the safety of navigation, the safety of users and third parties, and operator liability.

On the other hand, mere compliance with airworthiness codes would not seem to certify the safety of the product(s) definitively at trial stage: in fact, there would be no preclusion for the injured party to otherwise prove the defectiveness of the aircraft or any of its part(s).

The burden of the injured party or its successors in title may be further facilitated, moreover, by the findings contained in the investigation reports drawn up by the authorities in charge by individual states under international technical regulations (in part, ICAO Annex 13), if, of course, there are events that fall under the notion of an accident or (serious) incident.

References

Dasgupta U (2013) Legal issues on sub-orbital space tourism: international and national law perspectives. Ann Air Space Law XXXVIII:237 ff

Dempsey PS (2008) Public international air law. Montreal

Di Paolo AJ (2014) The definition and delimitation of outer space: the present need to determinate where "Space Activities" begin. Ann Air Space Law XXXIX:623 ff

Du Pontavice E. (1970), Le statut de l'aéroglisseur. Rev. gén. de l'air, 136 ff

Fawcett J (1968) International law and the uses of outer space. Clarendon, Oxford

Fitzgerald PP (2014) Inner space: ICAO's new frontier. J Air Law Commer, 3 ff

Gangale T (2017) The Non-Karman line: an Urban legend of the space age. J Space Law, 151 ff

Marciacq JB, Morier Y, Tomasello F, Erdelyi Z, Gerhard M (2010) Accommodating sub-orbital flights into the EASA regulatory system. In: Pelton JN, Jakhu RS (eds) Space safety regulations and standards, 187 ff

Drones

Simone Vernizzi

Contents

Abstract After a discussion of terminology, the chapter aims to provide an analysis of drones by and within the 1944 Chicago Convention with their undoubted qualification as aircraft: the notion of pilotless aircraft (Article 8) is also examined to understand whether the limitations established in that provision refer exclusively to aircraft flying a predetermined route or more generally to all aircraft without a pilot on board.

The growing interest in unmanned aircraft shown by the ICAO since the early 2000s, with the aim of achieving the objective represented by the progressive use of such vehicles in non-segregated airspace, is thus evidence of an enlightened approach, as is the adoption of the Manual *on Remotely Piloted Aircraft Systems* (RPAS), in 2015, and, most of all, the gradual amendment of the relevant ICAO Annexes.

The EU Institutions began to consider the importance of integrating traditional and unmanned aviation only after 2010 and with a rather cautious attitude. They became convinced of the need to implement a unified regulatory approach only afterwords, with Reg. 2018/1139 and with the following legislative measures relating to the design and manufacture of UAS, the rules for their operation in the Single European Sky and those dedicated to the regulation of U-Space.

S. Vernizzi (✉)
Department of Law, University of Modena and Reggio Emilia, Modena, Italy
e-mail: simone.vernizzi@unimore.it

M. P. Rizzo, F. Franchina (eds.), *Drones in the Digital European Sky*,
International Aviation Law Library 1,
https://doi.org/10.1007/978-3-032-16691-3_3

1 Introduction

The etymological origin of the term 'drone' would seem to be in the German word 'drohne', i.e. 'drone', the male of the bee. For some, the reason should be sought in the typical buzzing noise of remotely piloted aircraft, similar to that of a swarm of drones, especially during the mating season; for others, the reference to drones is due to the fact that they are more expendable members of the hive than the females–if only because they do not produce honey—just as an unmanned aircraft is more expendable than a traditional aircraft with a pilot and possibly crew on board.

A recent international encyclopaedic work reports, moreover, that at present there is an appreciable consensus within the ICAO and in Europe on the use of the English term '*drone*' to designate an aircraft without a crew on board, as an alternative to the more specific '*Unmanned Aircraft*': the former is mainly used in the popular press and sometimes in academia, while the latter is currently '*the umbrella concept in regulatory materials*'.[1]

On a technical-legal level, therefore, the expression 'Unmanned Aircraft' (abbreviated to 'UA') is the definitive term used to designate any type of unmanned aircraft, at the same time replacing and encompassing within it that congeries of terminological expressions, often not interchangeable, used since the early post-war period, such as: Drones, Model Aircraft, Remotely Operated Aircraft (ROA), Remotely Operated Vehicle (ROV), Remotely Piloted Aircraft (RPA), Remotely Piloted Aircraft System (RPAS), Remotely Piloted Vehicle (RPV), Unmanned Aircraft System (UAS), Unmanned Aerial Vehicle (UAV) and, most recently, Unmanned Aircraft (UA).[2]

On the other hand, the expression 'Unmanned Aircraft' ('UA') refers only to the vehicle, and in this way is well suited to encompass both aircraft operating autonomously on the basis of a pre-programmed route ("*Autonomous Aircraft*"—"AA": "*an unmanned aircraft that does not allow pilot intervention in the management of the flight*"[3]), and those piloted from a remote station ("*Remotely Piloted Aircraft*"—"RPA": "*an aircraft where the flying pilot is not on board the aircraft*"[4]). Meanwhile, to designate the vehicle, the ground control station and the other components that allow the remote pilot to operate the vehicle, international technical language currently adopts the expression "*Remotely Piloted Aircraft System*" ("RPAS"),[5] which would appear to be preferred to the previous "*Unmanned Aircraft System*" ("UAS"),[6] which is still current, as will be explained below, in European legislation.

---

[1] See Scott and Huttunen (2023), p. 506.

[2] See Dupont (2015), 359 et seq.; see also Scott (2016), 7 et seq.

[3] See ICAO Cir 328-AN/190 Unmanned Aircraft Systems (UAS), lett. (ix).

[4] See ICAO Cir 328-AN/190 Unmanned Aircraft Systems (UAS), lett. (x).

[5] See Cir 328-AN/190, in part., (x). See also ICAO Doc 10019-AN/507 Manual on Remotely Piloted Aircraft Systems (RPAS), First. Ed., 2015.

[6] See ICAO Cir 328-AN/190 Unmanned Aircraft Systems (UAS), cit., (x).

2 Drones and the Chicago Convention 1944: "Pilotless Aircraft"

In the international context, the qualification of drones seems to have been clear from the outset: 'pilotless aircraft' are in fact undoubtedly considered 'aircraft', and are regulated as such, except for the special authorisation required for overflight and for the further aspects pertaining to traditional civil aviation safety regulated by Article 8 of the 1944 Chicago Convention, whereby:

> No aircraft capable of being flown without a pilot shall be flown without a pilot over the territory of a contracting State without special authorization by that State and in accordance with the terms of such authorization.

Previously, Article 15 of the Paris Convention of 1919, as amended by the Protocol of 15 June 1929, regulated the matter according to the same principle.

International academic scholarship has, however, questioned the scope of the expression 'aircraft capable of being flown without a pilot', and, in particular, whether this also includes remotely piloted aircraft, or only those operating according to a pre-programmed route.[7]

This question received an official answer in the context of the Eleventh ICAO Air Navigation Conference, held in Montreal in September-October 2003, where the Unmanned Aerial Vehicle (UAV) was defined as a 'pilotless aircraft' for the purposes of Article 8 of the aforementioned convention text: this is the case both when the aircraft in question are 'flown either remotely and fully controlled', and when the aircraft is 'programmed and fully autonomous'.[8]

The acronym UA ('Unmanned Aircraft') is instead subsequently used in Cir no. 328/2011 Unmanned Aircraft Systems (UAS), in which the characteristic of this category of aircraft is the fact that it is operated without a pilot on board, thus being able to include both RPAs and AAs within it.[9]

3 RPA(S), UASSG and RPASP

Since the second half of the first decade of the 2000s, ICAO has intensified its interest in UAS, with the aim of providing an international regulatory framework through Standards and Recommended Practices (SARPs), with supporting Procedures for Air Navigation Services (PANS) and guidance material, to underpin routine operation of RPAS throughout the world in a safe, harmonised and seamless manner, comparable to that of manned operations and in order to pursue the ultimate goal of

---

[7] See Abeyratne (2016), 289 et seq.

[8] See ICAO AN-Conf/11-WP/4, Eleventh Air Navigation Conference, Montreal, 22 September to 3 October 2003, in part., Appendix B Explanation of Terms, A-43.

[9] See ICAO Cir 328-AN/190 Unmanned Aircraft Systems (UAS), in part., 3, Ch. 2 ICAO Regulatory Framework, par. 2.1.

'supporting a safe, secure and efficient integration of UAS into non-segregated airspaces and aerodromes'.

To this end, during the Second Meeting of the 175th Session (19 April 2007) of the Air Navigation Commission (ANC), the Unmanned Aircraft System Study Group (UASSG) was set up, with the mandate of assisting the ICAO Secretariat in the coordinated development of International Standards and Recommended Practices (SARPs) and Guidance material relative to unmanned aircraft systems.

According to the UASSG working programme, the UASSG shall:

> a) serve as the focal point and coordinator of all ICAO UAS related work, with the aim of ensuring global interoperability and harmonization; b) develop a UAS regulatory concept and associated guidance material to support and guide the regulatory process; c) review ICAO SARPs, propose amendments and coordinate the development of UAS SARPs with other ICAO bodies; d) contribute to the development of technical specifications by other bodies (e.g., terms, concepts), as requested; and e) coordinate with the ICAO Aeronautical Communications Panel (ACP), as needed, to support development of a common position on bandwidth and frequency spectrum requirements for command and control of UAS for the International Telecommunication Union (ITU)/World Radiocommunication Conference (WRC) negotiations.

On the other hand, as early as 2009, the UASSG restricted its scope of activity exclusively to RPAs and unmanned free balloons, in the belief that only such vehicles, and not autonomous aircraft, could effectively be integrated with traditional manned aircraft in non-segregated airspace and airport environments.

This circumstance clearly emerges from the analysis of Annex 7—Aircraft Nationality and Registration Marks—6th Ed. 2012, where the definitions include RPA, while there is no mention of Autonomous Aircraft. Then, significantly, in Article 2, '*Classification of Aircraft*', paragraph 2.2, RPAs are coherently reinstated in the broader category of Unmanned Aircraft, which however, according to the following 2.3, includes RPAs and unmanned free balloons, while, once again, it does not mention AAs.

More specifically, in 2011, the UASSG developed the aforementioned Circ. no. 328/2011—Unmanned Aircraft Systems (UAS), which lists the issues that will be addressed in the Annexes, to ensure the compliance of RPAS with the provisions of the Chicago Convention. The following year saw the adoption of the first package of SARPs concerning RPAS in relation to Annex 2—*Rules of the Air*, and the aforementioned Annex 7—*Aircraft Nationality and Registration Marks*. Finally, the UASSG contributed to the development of ICAO Doc. 10019 AN/507 Manual on Remotely Piloted Aircraft Systems (RPAS), discussed below.

Subsequently, at the Second Meeting of the 196th Session of the ANC (6 May 2014), the establishment of the Remotely Piloted Aircraft System Panel (RPASP) was approved, and called upon to continue and advance the work begun by the UASSG, identifying the following objectives to guide its action:

> a) serve as the focal point and coordinator of all ICAO RPAS-related work, with the aim of ensuring global interoperability and harmonization; b) develop an RPAS regulatory concept and associated guidance material to support and guide the regulatory process; c) review ICAO SARPs, propose amendments and coordinate the development of RPAS SARPs with other ICAO expert groups; d) assess impacts of proposed provisions on existing manned

aviation; and e) coordinate, as needed, to support development of a common position on bandwidth and frequency spectrum requirements for command and control of RPAS for the International Telecommunication Union (ITU)/World Radio Communication Conference (WRC) negotiations.

4 ICAO Manual on Remotely Piloted Aircraft Systems (RPAS) and the Subsequent ICAO Perspectives

The result of more than 3 years of collaboration by numerous expert groups (including the UASSG), the ICAO Doc. 10019 AN/507 *Manual on Remotely Piloted Aircraft Systems* (RPAS), on a strictly classificatory level, brings no innovations with respect to the previous approach: firstly, Ch. I, *ICAO Regulatory Framework and Scope of the Manual*, expressly reiterates that all unmanned aircraft (whether fully autonomous, remotely piloted or a combination of the two) are subject to the provisions of Art. 8 of Conv. Chicago 1944 (1.1.1), justifying this conclusion in Sect. 1.2 *History of the Legal Framework*, at paras. 1.2.4 et seq. where it is observed that:

> To understand the implications of Article 8 and its incorporation from the Paris Convention of 1919 (Article 15) into the Chicago Convention of 1944, the intent of the drafters must be considered. Remotely controlled and uncontrolled (autonomous) aircraft were already in existence at the time of the First World War, operated by both civil and military entities. "Aircraft flown without a pilot" therefore refers to the situation where there is no pilot on board the aircraft. 1.2.5 The Eleventh Air Navigation Conference (ANConf/11), Montréal, 22 September to 3 October 2003) endorsed the global air traffic management (ATM) operational concept which contains the following text: "[a]n unmanned aerial vehicle is a pilotless aircraft, in the sense of Article 8 of the Convention on International Civil Aviation, which is flown without a pilot in-command on-board and is either remotely and fully controlled from another place (ground, another aircraft, space) or programmed and fully autonomous." 1.2.6 This understanding of unmanned aerial vehicles (UAVs) was endorsed by the 35th Session of the ICAO Assembly in 2004. 1.2.7 As a consequence, any unmanned aircraft is a "pilotless" aircraft, consistent with the intent of the drafters of Article 8. Emphasis was placed on the significance of the provision that aircraft flown without a pilot on board "should be so controlled as to obviate danger to civil aircraft", indicating that the drafters recognized that "pilotless aircraft" must have a measure of control applied to them in relation to a so-called "due regard" obligation, similar to that of State aircraft.

Also in Ch. 1, Figure 1-1. illustrates that the category of Unmanned Aircraft is made up of three subsets (Remotely piloted aircraft, Autonomous aircraft and Model aircraft), of which the main one, i.e. Remotely piloted aircraft, nevertheless partly overlaps, in terms of operations and activities, both with the subset of Model aircraft (in particular, 'Remotely piloted aircraft used for recreational purposes' and "Model aircraft used for other than recreational purposes"), and with that of Autonomous aircraft ('RPA conducting autonomous flight/segments' and "Autonomous aircraft conducting remotely piloted flight segments"). This will certainly have future consequences.

Moreover, in paragraph 2.2.1, the ICAO Manual provides a clear systematic reconstruction that covers aircraft, unmanned aircraft, and remotely piloted aircraft, thus reaffirming the undoubted inclusion of the latter in the group of aircraft for the purposes of international technical regulations:

> an aircraft is defined as any machine that can derive support in the atmosphere from the reactions of the air other than the reactions of the air against the earth's surface. An aircraft which is intended to be operated with no pilot on board is classified as unmanned. An unmanned aircraft which is piloted from a remote pilot station is an RPA.

This paragraph finally concludes with a statement that unveils the disruptive potential of RPAs, reporting that all aircraft classified in the subsequent Table 2-1 (the well-known Table 1 Classification of aircraft contained in Annex 7) '*could be remotely piloted*', so that, in the not too distant future, the classification of aircraft according to their different technical characteristics should apply as much to manned aircraft as to Remotely Piloted Aircraft(s).

More recently, in the ICAO Unmanned Aviation Bulletin 01/2020, under the title '*Key Terms for Unmanned Aviation*', we find a circular diagram where Unmanned Aircraft is divided into four sectors: RPA, Small UA ('Drone'), Unmanned Free Balloons and Model Aircraft. In more detail, according to the document, the RPA sector contains within it the sub-sector RPA [INTL. IFR], relating to those RPA '*integrated into the airspace for international, instrument flight rules (IFR) operations, which will require full regulatory certification*'; Small UA are those UA '*generally weighing less than 25 kg*', and, it adds, '*this subset of smaller UA is commonly referred to as drones*'; the expression 'Unmanned Free Balloon(s)' '*describes non-power driven, unmanned, lighter-than-air aircraft in free flight*', and, finally, 'Model Aircraft' means a '*small size unmanned aircraft, generally representing a scaled down version of full size aircraft and used for recreational purposes in the sport and pastime of aeromodelling*'.

Once again, Autonomous Aircraft are not mentioned at all; however, this circumstance must be read in terms of confirmation of the approach initially adopted by the UASSG, which considered AA to be excluded from the objective of integrating manned and unmanned aviation.

5 Drones and EU Legislation

Unlike ICAO, the interest of the European institutions in the regulation of remotely piloted aircraft emerges more recently: it was not until 2013 that the European Commission published the '*Roadmap for the Integration of Civil Remotely-Piloted Aircraft Systems into the European Aviation System*' and, in December of the same year, the European Council welcomed '*the development of remotely piloted aircraft systems (RPAS) in the period 2020-2025*'.[10]

Subsequently, in the important Communication from the Commission to the European Parliament and the Council, *A New Era for Aviation Opening the Aviation Market to the Civil Use of Remotely Piloted Aircraft Systems in a Safe and Sustainable Manner*, dated 8 April 2014 [COM. (2014), 207 final], the European

[10] See Conclusions of the European Council (19–20 December 2013) EUCO 217/13, par. 11, 5.

Commission pushed for a gradual integration of RPAS in the common European airspace as from 2016, in the belief that the possibility of operating in a non-segregated airspace is the only suitable condition to allow the development of these new means, of their relevant and numerous application potentialities and to fully enjoy the benefits of those new services that such vehicles are able to make available, with particular consideration of low-altitude operations, which are particularly relevant in relation to the performance of commercial services within inhabited centres.

In this context, it is stated that '*from a formal point of view, RPAS are aircraft*'. However, the fact that they are aircraft 'from a formal point of view' highlights the difficulties of immediately identifying them with manned aviation vehicles. The approach adopted by the EU in terms of qualification seems to be more cautious: unlike the international legislator, it does not intend to directly identify drones with aircraft, preferring, at least initially, to opt for a formal assimilation.

A similar approach can be seen in the subsequent 2015 Riga Declaration, a document adopted at the end of a conference attended by, among others, representatives of the European Commission, the heads of the civil aviation authorities of each Member State, data protection authorities and leading representatives of the aviation industry and service providers, which ended with a declaration endorsed by the Commissioner for Transport and the Department for Mobility and Transport (DG-MOVE). The Declaration refers to the principles and guidelines of the future European policy on UAS, and proposes to ensure the necessary support for the aviation industry for the safe and sustainable development of innovative drone services, while adequately addressing the concerns of EU citizens. It also emphasises the importance of abandoning national particularisms in favour of the creation of a common legislation on UAS, which is considered the only way of guaranteeing the integration of drones in the common airspace and the faster achievement of the sector's growth objectives, while safeguarding the fundamental aspects linked to maintaining the high levels of aviation safety achieved in Europe. The European Aviation Safety Agency (EASA) has therefore been identified as the most suitable body to take the lead in developing safety standards for unmanned aircraft through its regulatory process. In terms of qualification, the 2015 Riga Declaration states that '*drones need to be treated as a new type of aircraft*', and it therefore seems evident that the use of the verbal expression '*need to be treated*' is intended to express an awareness of the fact that drones are not, or at least are not immediately perceived as, aircraft, a circumstance further underlined by the fact that they are in any case '*new types*' of aircraft.

This timid initial approach has progressively changed since the second half of the 2010s, especially due to the need to accelerate the development of unmanned aviation and its integration with traditional aviation in a safety context, pursued through the option for a common EU safety regulatory approach and the inclusion of unmanned aircraft in the overall EU aviation safety framework; the central role of EASA in this context certainly contributes to bringing the approach of European legislation closer to that of ICAO regulations.

A sure expression of this change of perspective can be found in the regulatory measures of that period. First of all, in the context of reg. 2018/1139 (the so-called new 'Basic Regulation'): inspired by the indications expressed by EASA in the document '*Concept of Operations for Drones: A risk-based approach to regulation of unmanned aircraft*', dated 29 May 2015, and in the subsequent Opinion no. 01/2018, '*Introduction of a regulatory framework for the operation of unmanned aircraft systems in the "open" and "specific" categories*'. The new Basic Regulation introduces the essential requirements to ensure that unmanned aerial vehicles for civil use can be operated in the airspace of the Single European Sky.

The previous regulation (Reg. no. 2008/216) adopted assigned competences based on the total weight of the remotely piloted aircraft system, and attributed competence to the European Union only in relation to unmanned aircraft with an operational take-off mass of more than 150 kg. For those with a mass less than or equal to 150 kg, the civil aviation authorities of each Member State held jurisdiction. The new measure, meanwhile, covers all unmanned aircraft,

> since unmanned aircraft also operate within the airspace alongside manned aircraft, this Regulation should cover unmanned aircraft, regardless of their operating mass.

The regulation therefore adopts a new approach and introduces requirements based on the level of risk of the operations, according to principles inspired by the criteria of proportionality (as the risk increases, the requirements become more stringent) and progression (the requirements are constructed in such a way as to favour the growth of the sector with progression).[11]

In Art. 3 (*Definitions*) the Basic Regulation defines 'Unmanned aircraft' as

> any aircraft operating or designed to operate autonomously or to be piloted remotely without a pilot on board,

and the increased alignment with the approach accepted by the international ICAO technical regulations is also reiterated in Sect. VII, dedicated to "Unmanned aircraft", where the European Commission is given extensive powers. In fact, on the basis of the provisions of Articles 57 (implementing acts) and 58 (delegated powers), it is called upon, in particular, to adopt: (i) implementing acts aimed at establishing detailed provisions on specific rules and procedures concerning the operation of unmanned aircraft, personnel and remote pilots, as well as the organisations involved in such operations [cf, Article 57(1)(a)), as well as (ii) delegated acts laying down detailed rules concerning specific conditions for the design, production and maintenance of unmanned aircraft, engines and their parts (see, Article 58(1)(a)), with binding effect on manufacturers and users of unmanned aircraft in the EU.

In line with the above, the Commission is also assisted in the exercise of these powers by EASA (see Art. 76 "Agency measures"), which does so upon request and by means of opinions issued in execution and within the scope of its mandate.

Significantly, therefore, unmanned aircraft are now also considered to be aircraft under European law.

---

[11] See Masutti and Tomasello (2018), 65 et seq.

Accordingly, Regulation 2019/945, on the design and manufacture of unmanned aircraft and their commercialisation, and Regulation 2019/947, on rules and procedures for the operation of unmanned aircraft in the Single European Sky, both subsequently amended and supplemented, adopt the same approach as in the Basic Regulation and include the definition of Unmanned Aircraft System (UAS).

The EU regulatory landscape relating to drones is completed by the measures constituting the so-called U-Space framework. The U-Space regulatory framework, which aims to create and harmonise the conditions necessary for manned and unmanned aircraft to operate safely in airspace, prevent collisions between aircraft and mitigate air and ground risks. These are the provisions introduced by reg. 2021/664 of 22 April 2021, on a regulatory framework for U-space; reg. 2021/665 of 22 April 2021, amending reg. 2017/373 as regards requirements for providers of air traffic management and air navigation services and other air traffic management network functions in U-space designated controlled airspace; and by reg. 2021/666 of 22 April 2021, amending reg. 923/2012 as regards requirements for manned aviation operating in U-space.

6 Conclusions: Drones in the existing legal context

In light of the remarks made in the previous sections, it is now possible to outline the concept of "drone" under the current regulatory landscape.

The drone:

- is an Unmanned aircraft in non-legal or otherwise journalistic parlance;
- however, it is also an Unmanned aircraft with a weight of less than 25 kilograms (Small UA), according to ICAO;
- is an 'Aircraft', and international technical regulations apply to it;
- is a 'Pilotless' aircraft, within the meaning of Article 8 of the Chicago Convention (1944);
- is a 'new type of aircraft', and this circumstance therefore justifies the activities of revising the ICAO Annexes and the evolving EU legislation;
- within the theory of property and assets, is a movable asset, sometimes also registered, due to technical/physical characteristics and possibly to its usage (see, in part, Art. 14, Reg. (EU) No. 2019/947);
- moreover, the unmanned aircraft, the engine, the propellers and its parts, as well as the relevant remote-control devices are aeronautical products to all intents and purposes, as, moreover, expressly provided for by reg. 2019/945, which establishes precise conformity requirements for UAS belonging to the 'open' category (parts 1 to 6 of the Annex). They are also subject to the safety and health protection requirements of EC dir. 2006/42 with regard to risks other than those relating to flight safety. UAS belonging to the 'specific' and 'certified' categories are, instead, subject to the provisions of art. 40 of reg. 2019/945, which establishes the conditions under which the design, production and maintenance of UAS must be certified, and in this case the product must comply with the requirements set out in EU Commission regs. 748/2012, 640/2015 and 1321/2014.

As an aircraft, moreover, in the event of a drone or its parts falling, it could be subject to the provisions of the Rome Convention (1952); the transport of persons and payloads that will be performed by such means in the near future must evidently be qualified as air transport, with the consequent applicability of the provisions of the Montreal Convention (1999) regarding air carrier liability for delays, loss or damage to goods and baggage, death and personal injury to passengers, as well as, possibly, those of Reg. (EC) No. 261/2004, for cases of denied boarding, flight cancellation or delay.

In this perspective, in the recent Communication "*A Drone Strategy 2.0 for a Smart and Sustainable Unmanned Aircraft Eco-System in Europe*" of 29 November 2022 [COM (2022), 652 final], the Commission expressed great interest in the development of innovative air mobility (IAM), which

> consists of vehicles ranging from small drones used for cargo delivery operations to eVTOL aircraft, i.e. electrically powered aircraft capable of vertical take-off and landing for the transport of both goods and people. Indeed, multiple eVTOL developers are targeting passenger operations, built on economic efficiencies of electric power, nodal networks, and scalability to achieve competitive pricing and provide sustainable alternatives to existing travel services.

Initially, these vertical take-off vehicles will be equipped with an on-board pilot. However, in the near future, the Commission hopes that these services will be operated first through remotely piloted eVTOLs and eventually also through fully autonomous platforms, thus helping to clarify that, unlike the ICAO—whose focus is, as mentioned above, at present exclusively on Remotely Piloted Aicraft, of which it envisages the proliferation of new and different types - the action of the European institutions is by no means limited to these means, but extends also to Autonomous Aircraft.

References

Abeyratne R (2016) Remotely piloted aircraft systems: some unexplored issues. Air Space Law, 289 ff

Dupont PM (2015) Les drones ou la révolution aéronautique du 21eme siècle. Rev. fr. dr. Aérien et Spatial, 359 ff

Masutti A, Tomasello F (2018) International regulation of non-military drones. Cheltenham, UK – Northampton, USA

Scott BI (ed) (2016) The law of unmanned aircraft systems: an introduction to the current and future regulation under national. Regional and International Law, Kluwer Law International, Alphen aan den Rijn

Scott BI, Huttunen MT (2023) Unmanned aerial systems. In: Masutti A, De Leon PM (eds) Elgar Concise Encyclopedia of Aviation Law, Cheltenham, pp 506–509

The Regulatory Framework of UAS

The International Regulatory Framework on Drones

Francesca Pellegrino

Contents

Abstract The international framework on drones aims to standardize and regulate the use of unmanned aerial vehicles, including international instruments, standards, guidelines and other relevant documents, in order to ensure the safe and responsible operation of these vehicles.

This chapter examines the current international regulatory framework on drones regulation, focusing on the ICAO Annexes, containing international standards and recommended practices (SARPs), and other Documents (Procedures for Air Navigation Service - PANS, Circulars, etc.). Additionally, the ICAO is actively involved in developing the framework for UAM (Urban Air Mobility), a new safe, secure and more sustainable air transportation system for passengers and goods in urban environments.

F. Pellegrino (✉)
Department of Law, University of Messina, Messina, Italy
e-mail: fpellegrino@unime.it

M. P. Rizzo, F. Franchina (eds.), *Drones in the Digital European Sky*,
International Aviation Law Library 1,
https://doi.org/10.1007/978-3-032-16691-3_4

1 Introduction: The Chicago Convention

The international framework on drones[1] aims to standardize and regulate the use of unmanned aerial vehicles. It includes international instruments, standards, guidelines and other relevant documents, in order to ensure the safe and responsible operation of these vehicles.

At an international level, the Convention on International Civil Aviation (also known as the Chicago Convention),[2] signed on 7 December 1944, is the starting point for drawing up the international regulatory framework governing drones.

This fundamental treaty laid down several key principles governing the use of international airspace.

In particular, Article 8[3] of this Convention forbids a pilotless aircraft from operating without special authorization by a contracting state. In fact, the expression 'aircraft capable of being flown without a pilot', contained in Article 8 of the Chicago Convention, refers to aircraft without a pilot on board.

In addition, this article requires states to take all necessary safety measures to prevent accidents resulting from pilotless aircraft.

This article is based on Article 1[4] of the same international instrument according to which every "State has complete and exclusive sovereignty over the airspace above its territory".

According to the principle that every state has complete and exclusive sovereignty over the airspace above its territory, foreign aircraft need prior permission to enter a state's airspace (except in specific circumstances).[5]

The Chicago Convention also established the International Civil Aviation Organization (ICAO),[6] a UN specialized agency with the aim to promote safe and orderly development of international civil aviation, through a global framework of standards and practices.

---

[1] Franchi (2018), p. 1788 ff.

[2] See Abeyratne (2013); Havel and Sanchez (2014), p. 28 ff.; Sipos (2024), p. 25 ff.

[3] See Abeyratne (2013), sub Article 8; La Torre (2022), p. 469 ff.: Sipos (2024), p. 61 ff.

[4] See Abeyratne (2013), sub Article 1.

[5] This applies to unmanned flights. For non-scheduled conventional flights, Article 5 of the Chicago Convention grants aircraft of contracting states the right to make flights into or in transit non-stop across its territory and to make stops for non-traffic purposes, without the necessity of obtaining prior permission, and subject the right of the State flown over to require landing.

[6] For the history and evolution of ICAO, see Mackenzie (1953), pp. 107 ff., 276 ff.

2 The ICAO Legal Framework

The ICAO Council issues international standards and recommended practices (SARPs),[7] contained in nineteen technical Annexes, cover various aspects of safety, security, and flight operation efficiency.

In addition, the ICAO Council issues other legal documents such as the PANS (Procedures for Air Navigation Service),[8] also known as DOCs, that contain the SARPs implementing rules. The difference between them is that SARPs are mandatory standards, while PANS provide detailed guidance and procedures.

The ICAO also issues Circulars that provide additional information and guidance on specific topics.

Finally, ICAO Manuals are a collection of documents that provide guidance and standards concerning a wide range of topics, including aviation safety and security, air navigation services etc.

Given the above, it is worth mentioning that in 2015 the ICAO published a Manual on Remotely Piloted Aircraft Systems (Doc 10019, AN/507)[9] to provide guidance on technical and operational issues applicable to the integration of RPA in non-segregated airspace and aerodromes in order to guide the development of future SARPs.

This Manual contains Guidelines on drone operations, certification, licensing and air traffic management, useful for developing coherent and integrated national policies at a global level.

It must be also stated that international rules concerning drones are contained in several amendments to ICAO annexes.[10]

Specifically, in Annex 1—"Personnel Licensing"[11] a global framework for the regulation of RPAS licensing has been introduced. In particular, Amendment 175[12] introduces provisions for remote pilots, licensing, competency-based training, and medical standards. In fact, this Annex now includes new standards and recommended practices aimed to ensure that remote pilots possess the necessary knowledge, skills, and medical fitness to operate drones safely. Pilots must demonstrate their ability to perform specific tasks and functions related to drone operations.

In Annex 2—"Rules of the Air",[13] high level provisions regarding certification, licensing, operating rules and special authorizations of aircraft, including unmanned

[7] See Milde (2008), p. 165; Van Antwerpen (2008), Ch. 2; Salih (2021), p. 115 ff.; Sipos (2024), p. 206 ff.

[8] See Milde (2008), p. 164 f.; Van Antwerpen (2008), p. 27 ff.; Salih (2021), p. 121 ff.; Schubert (2024), p. 206.

[9] 1st Edition, 2015.

[10] For a commentary of all ICAO Annexes, see *ex multis* Weber (2023), Ch. III, par. III.

[11] 14th Edition, July 2022.

[12] This Amendmentt, adopted in 2018, focuses on personnel licensing for remote pilots of RPAS.

[13] 10th Edition, July 2005.

vehicles, have been introduced. This Annex has been adapted to address the integration of UAS into non-segregated airspace.

Annex 6—"Operation of Aircraft",[14] at its new Part IV, entitled "Remotely Piloted Aircraft Systems" (RPAS),[15] contains standards and recommended practices for the international operation of all types of unmanned vehicles, including requirements for operator certificates, remote pilot licensing, and airworthiness.

Annex 7—"Aircraft Nationality and Registration Marks"[16] defines RPA as unmanned aircraft, and ensures that nationality and registration marks can be applied regardless of size or type of aircraft.

Annex 8—"Airworthiness of Aircraft"[17] has been expanded to cover RPAS and C2 (Command and Control) Link, that refers to the communications link between a UAV (Unmanned Aerial Vehicle) and its ground station.

Volume VI of Annex 10—"Aeronautical Telecommunications"[18] establishes communication systems and procedures for RPAS, including provisions for the above mentioned Command and Control (C2) Link.

Although ICAO Annex 11 on "Air Traffic Services"[19] does not specifically deal with unmanned aircraft systems in detail, it contains provisions about their integration into existing air traffic management (ATM) systems.

Integrating UAS into the existing ATM system poses challenges, such as the need for new procedures, technologies, and regulatory frameworks.

In Annex 13 on "Aircraft Accident and Incident Investigation",[20] unmanned aircraft have been included in the definition of "accident",[21] contained in Chapter 1. It states that an accident is an "occurrence associated with the operation of an aircraft which […] in the case of an unmanned aircraft, takes place between the time the aircraft is ready to move with the purpose of flight until such time as it comes to rest at the end of the flight and the primary propulsion system is shut down".

The provisions of Annex 19 on "Safety Management",[22] including the SMS (Safety Management System) framework, are extended to RPAS operators engaged in international operations and their approved maintenance organizations.

RPAS operators are required to implement an SMS, which involves a systematic approach to managing safety risks.

[14] 11th Edition, July 2018.

[15] Panzeri (2016), p. 39 ff.

[16] 6th Edition, July 2012.

[17] 13th Edition, July 2022.

[18] 1st Edition, July 2021.

[19] 15th Edition, July 2018.

[20] 13th Edition, July 2024.

[21] Pellegrino (2007), p. 110 ff.

[22] 2nd Edition, July 2016.

Circular 328-AN/190 ("Unmanned Aircraft Systems (UAS)"[23] of 2011 provides an overview of issues that need to be addressed in the Annexes in order to ensure compliance of RPAS with the provisions of the Chicago Convention.

In particular, according to para. 2.5 of this Circular, "whether the aircraft is manned or unmanned does not affect its status as an aircraft". The subsequent para. 2.6 adds: "To the maximum extent possible, all terms in common use in ICAO documents will remain unchanged by the introduction of UAS" and the function of the pilot "remains unchanged despite the person or persons being located other than on board the aircraft".

Therefore, in principle, the ICAO considers drones to be aircraft and includes them in its regulatory framework accordingly. Existing references to aircraft contained in current regulations are also applicable to drones.

The decision to not separate the regulatory frameworks for manned and unmanned aircraft is justified by the fact that there is not a complete lack of regulations to govern pilotless vehicles. However, some gaps remain to be filled, due to the absence of harmonization.

In order to support UAS regulatory harmonization, in December 2020 ICAO developed the UAS Model Regulations as a living instrument that evolves in parallel with the evolution of the industry. They provide guidance on drone operations, including parts on general provisions and operating rules, such as Part 101 and Part 102. The first one (Part 101) defines the "open category" for Unmanned Aircraft Systems (UAS) weighing 25 kg or less, operating under standard conditions without requiring additional operational approval or authorization. Instead, Part 102 covers UAS weighing more than 25 kg and is designed to ensure a safe and effective culture for unmanned aircraft operators, providing the necessary safety requirements for certification and operation.

In addition, ICAO has established the "Remotely Piloted Aircraft Systems Panel" (RPASP),[24] an entity that coordinates and develops SARPs, Procedures and Guidance material for remotely piloted aircraft systems, in order to facilitate a safe, secure and efficient integration of drones into non-segregated airspace and aerodromes.[25]

This Panel is actively involved in amending the Annexes to the Chicago Convention, taking into account the real problems arising from the widespread use of unmanned aerial vehicles (UAVs).

In order to safely manage unmanned aircraft operations at low altitudes, a collaborative ecosystem, named Unmanned Aircraft System Traffic Management (UTM),[26] has been built within a framework of regulatory requirements, technical capabilities, and interoperable services.

[23] Approved by the Secretary General and published on 1st January 2011.

[24] See ICAO Doc. 10019, Manual on Remotely Piloted Aircraft Systems (RPAS), 2015.

[25] See Scott (2022), Ch. 3.

[26] Barnhart et al. (2021), p. 439 ff.

In this respect, ICAO issued the document "Unmanned Aircraft Systems Traffic Management (UTM) – A common Framework with Core Principles for Global Harmonization".[27]

In this document, UTM has been defined as "a specific aspect of air traffic management which manages UAS operations safely, economically and efficiently through the provision of facilities and a seamless set of services in collaboration with all parties and involving airborne and ground-based functions".

In fact, separate from but complementary to Air Traffic Management (ATM) services, UTM enables many functions such as authorization, flight planning, surveillance and conflict management to mitigate risks associated with unmanned vehicles flights and ensure safe, efficient operations, especially beyond visual line of sight (BVLOS) operations.

In 2023 the ICAO released Edition 4 of its "Unmanned Aircraft System Traffic Management (UTM) – A Common Framework with Core Principles for Global Harmonization" in order to facilitate harmonization between UTM and ATM.

This document follows a stepped approach towards integration of drones into the ATM system.

The UTM Common Framework provides the foundations for consistent rules and regulations, facilitating consensus on standards and best practices. It also supports the development of common guidance material. It is intended to provide a framework with core capabilities of a typical UTM system.

3 Urban Air Mobility: The ICAO approach

As far the future use of drones,[28] the challenge today is UAM (Urban Air Mobility),[29] a new safe, secure and more sustainable air transportation system for passengers and goods in urban environments. Transportation is performed by electric aircraft taking off and landing vertically (e-VTOL, electric vertical take-off and landing), remotely piloted or with a pilot on board.

Commercial operations that involve these vehicles are expected to become a reality within at least three years, thanks to new technologies, such as electric propulsion and enhanced battery capacity.

This system aims to solve urban traffic congestion, improve urban logistics, provide new transport opportunities and deliver societal benefits to municipalities and their citizens.

The ICAO is actively involved in developing the framework for UAM.

---

[27] IV Edition, 2023.

[28] Kasprzyk and Konert (2023), Ch. 4; Comenale Pinto et al. (2024), p. 251 ff.

[29] Pruneddu (2024), p. 173 ff.; Pruneddu and Lamon (2023), p. 495 ff.

In this context, the Working Paper entitled "Legal and Societal Stakes for the Emerging Air Mobility in Metropolitan Areas", adopted in 2022,[30] deserves to be mentioned. In this document, a clear legal/governance framework in the emerging domain of urban innovation is required to modernize the governance management of airspace operations above cities, by involving local authorities and ground mobility stakeholders. This makes it possible to adopt a citizen-centric approach to the responsible integration of UAM operations/services with sustainable urban mobility plans of cities and regions.

This is the current international regulatory framework for drones, composed of several key organizations, treaties, soft law documents and national policies. It is still evolving. Several indicators predict this trend, including an increasingly marked shift towards risk-based regulation, the integration of remotely piloted vehicles into airspace management systems, and the growing importance of cybersecurity and data protection.

References

Abeyratne R (2013) Convention on international civil aviation: a commentary. Springer, Berlin

Barnhart RK, Marshall DM, Shappee E (eds) (2021) Introduction to unmanned aircraft systems, 3rd edn. CRC Press, Taylor & Francis

Comenale Pinto MM, Pruneddu G, Lamon M (2024) Swarm drones in multiple and cooperative configuration. Le sfide del volo autonomo. Il Diritto marittimo 2:251–277

Franchi B (2018) L'evoluzione della normativa internazionale e UE relativa agli "unmanned aircraft", detti anche "droni": profili ricognitori. Responsabilità civile e previdenza 6:1788–1810

Havel BF, Sanchez GS (2014) The principles and practice of international aviation law. Cambridge University Press, New York

Kasprzyk P, Konert A (2023) Drones – future of aviation law?: Interference of public law in private law. Peter Lang, Berlin

La Torre U (2022) Spunti sulla nozione di aeromobile. Rivista del Diritto della Navigazione 2:469 ff

Mackenzie D (1953) ICAO. A history of the international civil aviation organization. University of Toronto Press, Toronto, Buffalo, London

Milde M (2008) international air law and ICAO, 4th edn. Eleven International Publishing, Utrecht

Panzeri S (2016) I sistemi aerei a pilotaggio remoto (SAPR): profili giuridici. Rivista di Diritto dell'Economia, dei Trasporti e dell'Ambiente:39–60

Pellegrino F (2007) Sicurezza e prevenzione degli incidenti aeronautici: nella normativa internazionale, comunitaria e interna. Milano, Giuffrè

Pruneddu G (2024) La "Urban Air Mobility" (UAM) e le nuove frontiere della mobilità. Rivista del Diritto della Navigazione 1:173–187

Pruneddu G, Lamon M (2023) I nuovi orizzonti dei servizi di trasporto aereo: la mobilità aerea avanzata. Il Diritto marittimo 3:495–518

Salih C (2021) International aviation law for aerodrome planning. Springer, Berlin

Schubert F (2024) The law of air navigation services. Elgar Publishing, Cheltenham

Scott B (ed) (2022) The law of unmanned aircraft systems, 2nd edn. Kluwer, Alphen aan den Rijn

[30] During the 41st Session of the ICAO Assembly that took placein Montreal, from 27 September to 7 October 2022.

Sipos A (2024) International aviation law: regulations in three dimensions. Springer, Berlin
Van Antwerpen N. (2008), Cross-border provision of air navigation services with specific reference to Europe. Safeguarding transparent lines of responsibility and liability. Kluwer, Alphen aan den Rijn
Weber L (2023) International civil aviation organization, 5th edn. Kluwer, Alphen aan den Rijn

The Basic EU Regulation on UAS

Adele Marino

Contents

Abstract The chapter will examine the key points of European legislation on unmanned aircraft systems.

After a brief historical excursus on the steps that have laid the foundations of the European drone policy, the EU regulations will be analyzed.

With the basic regulation of 2018/1139 it was established that all drones are subject to the rules on civil aviation safety.

To promote investments in the sector, the EU adopted the delegated regulation (EU) 2019/945, amended several times, which establishes the technical characteristics and the capacity that drones must possess to be authorized to fly safely. The regulation also identifies the conditions that third-country operators must respect to operate in the airspace of the single European sky.

The implementing regulation (EU) 2019/947 on rules and procedures for the operation of unmanned aircraft identifies three categories of operations: "open", "specific" and "certified". The regulation establishes the requirements and procedures to be followed based on the severity of the risk that their use could cause.

A. Marino (✉)
Department of Legal and Political Sciences, University of Messina, Messina, Italy
e-mail: admarino@unime.it

M. P. Rizzo, F. Franchina (eds.), *Drones in the Digital European Sky*,
International Aviation Law Library 1,
https://doi.org/10.1007/978-3-032-16691-3_5

With a view to implementing the development of the drone industry, in 2020 the EU also adopted regulations on U-space in order to guarantee maximum safety for operations carried out by unmanned aircraft in airspace.

1 Evolution of the Reference Regulatory Framework

Remotely piloted aircraft, commonly known as drones, now have a complete international, European and national regulation that has allowed ever-increasing development. Drones are used in various sectors: agriculture, commerce, land monitoring, border control and transport.

At a European level, the process of harmonizing legislation began in small steps, to ensure a gradual integration of the new vehicles into the civil aviation system.[1]

The European Union, aware of the importance of exploiting remotely piloted aircraft for civil purposes, launched a series of consultations between 2009 and 2012 on the future of remotely piloted aircraft system services (RPAS) in Europe. The consultations highlighted the importance of integrating these innovative means into the aeronautical system and to this end the Commission established the European RPAS Steering Group (ERSG)[2] in July 2012. This is a group of stakeholders that was brought together the main organisations and experts interested in integrating RPAS into the European aeronautical system. In June 2013, the group presented a Road Map to guide the various organisations in developing RPAS applications, ensuring high levels of safety, security and privacy for citizens and other airspace users.

At the end of 2013, at the European Council,[3] the Member States reaffirmed their commitment to "the development of Remotely Piloted Aircraft Systems (RPAS) in the 2020-2025 timeframe: preparations for a program of a next-generation European Medium Altitude Long Endurance RPAS; the establishment of an RPAS user community among the participating Member States owning and operating these RPAS; close synergies with the European Commission on regulation (for an initial RPAS integration into the European Aviation System by 2016)".

A few months later, the Commission adopted Communication COM(2014) 207 final of 8 April 2014[4] in which it aimed to introduce RPAS into the European market "with a combination of new and existing regulatory action at the European level dealing with all relevant issues, including the insertion of safety, security, privacy and data protection requirements within existing EU rules in these areas".

---

[1] See Vernizzi (2025), p. 153; see also Gaspari (2020), p. 139.

[2] Roadmap for the integration of civil Remotely-Piloted Aircraft Systems into the European Aviation System, Final report from the European RPAS Steering Group, June 2013.

[3] Conclusions of the European Council on 19-20 December 2013, EUCO 217/13.

[4] Communication from the Commission to the European Parliament and the Council, 8 April 2014 "A new era for aviation. Opening the aviation market to the civil use of remotely piloted aircraft systems in a safe and sustainable manner".

One year later, in December 2015, in the communication COM (2015) 598 final "an aviation strategy for Europe",[5] the Commission decided to entrust the European Aviation Safety Agency with the task of preparing more detailed rules enabling the use of drones and the development of industry standards, and included the rules on drones in the new basic aviation regulation.

To this end, Regulation 1139/2018[6] was issued, establishing common rules in the civil aviation sector, the so-called Basic Regulation. The regulation, which introduced innovations with respect to the repealed Regulation 216/2008, presented a new approach that took into account, in its preparation, the risk of operations based on the criteria of "proportionality (as the risk increases, the requirements become more stringent) and progression (the requirements are constructed in such a way as to favour the growth of the sector with progression)"[7].

Regulation 1139/2018, which was amended several times,[8] recognises EASA's competence in defining common rules for operations conducted with drones, including requirements for design, construction and use, as well as rules on pilot training and certification (Chapter V of the Regulation).

Pursuant to Article 55, the design, production, maintenance and operation of unmanned aircraft must meet the requirements set out in Annex IX "Essential requirements for unmanned aircraft". The Regulation also recognises the power of the Commission to adopt delegated acts (Article 57) and implementing acts (Article 58) for the safety and operation of drones.

The Commission, assisted by EASA, in compliance with Regulation 1139/2018, therefore adopted:

- Regulation (EU) 2019/945[9] (and subsequent amendments) on unmanned aircraft systems and on third-country operators of unmanned aircraft systems.

---

[5] Communication from the Commission to the European Parliament, The Council, The European Economic and Social Committee and the Committee of the Regions, 7.12.2015, "An Aviation Strategy for Europe".

[6] Regulation (EU) 2018/1139 of the European Parliament and of the Council of 4 July 2018 on common rules in the field of civil aviation and establishing a European Union Aviation Safety Agency, and amending Regulations (EC) No 2111/2005, (EC) No 1008/2008, (EU) No 996/2010, (EU) No 376/2014 and Directives 2014/30/EU and 2014/53/EU of the European Parliament and of the Council, and repealing Regulations (EC) No 552/2004 and (EC) No 216/2008 of the European Parliament and of the Council and Council Regulation (EEC) No 3922/91.

[7] Morandi et al. (2022a), p. 1087.

[8] Commission Delegated Regulation (EU) 2024/1107 of 13 March 2024 supplementing Regulation (EU) 2018/1139 of the European Parliament and of the Council by laying down detailed rules for the continuing airworthiness of certified unmanned aircraft systems and their components, and on the approval of organisations and personnel involved in these tasks.

[9] Commission Delegated Regulation (EU) 2019/945 of 12 March 2019 on unmanned aircraft systems and on third-country operators of unmanned aircraft systems; emended by Delegated Regulation (EU) 2020/1058 of 27 April 2020 and by Regulation (EU) 2024/1108 of 13 March 2024.

- Regulation (EU) 2019/947[10] (and subsequent amendments) on the rules and procedures for the operation of unmanned aircraft.

The policies launched by the EU in the 2015 aviation strategy have achieved their objectives and have enabled the definition of a set of common rules for flights with remotely piloted aircraft.

In 2022, this prompted the Commission to adopt[11] a new strategy 2.0 for a smart and sustainable ecosystem of unmanned aircraft in Europe, to be implemented by 2030 with actions "that will facilitate the transition from demonstrations to large-scale commercial operations". According to the Commission, to be able to achieve these further steps, "sufficient support from all stakeholders, in particular the European institutions, Member States and their authorities at all levels of government, stakeholders and businesses is needed, and, if the involvement of citizens is ensured".

The Union, in fact, highlights that the drone services market includes "innovative air services or the set of operations and/or services made possible by new air technologies. Such operations and/or services include both the transport of passengers and/or goods and air operations (for example surveillance, inspections, mapping, telecommunication networks)". Urban air mobility (UAM) represents the future evolution in the use of drones and includes those operations carried out with types of aircraft, new technologies, with vertical take-off and landing capabilities that are used in congested urban areas, using air and ground infrastructure integrated into a multimodal system.

2 UAS Design and Manufacturing Requirements: Reg. 2019/945

Delegated Regulation 2019/945,[12] with subsequent amendments, establishes the design and manufacturing requirements for unmanned aircraft systems, providing obligations for manufacturers, importers and distributors. The Union seeks to ensure

[10] Regulation (EU) 2019/947 of 24 May 2019 on the rules and procedures for the operation of unmanned aircraft, Commission Implementing Regulation (EU) 2024/1110 of 10 April 2024 amending Regulation (EU) No 748/2012 regarding the initial airworthiness of unmanned aircraft systems subject to certification and Implementing Regulation (EU) 2019/947 as regards the rules and procedures for the operation of unmanned aircraft.

[11] Communication from the Commission to the European Parliament, The Council, The European Economic And Social Committee and the Committee of the Regions "A Drone Strategy 2.0 for a Smart and Sustainable Unmanned Aircraft Eco-System" 29 November 2022 (COM 2022.652). See Masutti and Tomasello (2018); Franchina (2020); Lamon (2020); Morandi et al. (2022b).

[12] Commission Delegated Regulation (EU) 2019/945 of 12 March 2019 on unmanned aircraft systems and on third-country operators of unmanned aircraft systems, amended by Commission Delegated Regulation (EU) 2020/1058 of 27 April 2020 amending Delegated Regulation (EU) 2019/945 as regards the introduction of two new unmanned aircraft systems classes and by

that products placed on the market are safe and compliant with predetermined standards to protect consumers. The aircraft are classified into 7 classes from C0 to C6, based on their mass, technical specifications, automatic functions and performance. To be placed on the market, the aircraft must have the "CE" marking, in addition to the indication of sound power level and possibly label of the class to which they belong, if it falls within the cases provided for, to ensure high levels of safety. The annexes to the regulation detail the procedures for controlling the production phases and for verifying the specific requirements, based on the classes of the vehicles and their additional remote identification components. In fact, from 2024 all drones operating in the specific category and/or with class markings operating in the open category must be equipped with direct remote identification, which "means a system that ensures the local broadcast of information about a UA in operation, including the marking of the UA, so that this information can be obtained without physical access to the UA"(art. 3, 31 Reg. 945/2019).

This system, which sends a series of information in real time (see part 6 of annex reg. 945/2019), is essential to guarantee the safety and traceability of drones, especially if they fly in densely populated areas or in environments where traditional aircraft also operate.

The design, production, maintenance and operation activities of UAS must comply with the essential requirements set out in Annex IX of Regulation (EU) 2018/1139.

Based on the class marking obtained—C0, C1, C2, C3, C4, C5, or C6–, it is possible to carry out different types of operations according to the technical characteristics of the UAS, the distance from people on the ground and the flight performance.[13]

3 Operating Rules and Procedures: Reg. 2019/947

Commission Implementing Regulation (EU) 2019/947 of 24 May 2019, "on rules and procedures for the operation of unmanned aircraft", identifies three types of operations according to different levels of risk: Open, Specific and Certified.

It has been observed that "The relevant rules and procedures vary depending on the category, as the rules are operation-centric, and risk and performance-based. The various risk mitigation measures are mandated depending on the impact on safety. In other words, the greater the risk, the greater the risk mitigation measures will be required".[14]

Commission Delegated Regulation (EU) 2024/1108 of 13 March 2024 amending Regulation (EU) No 748/2012 as regards the initial airworthiness of unmanned aircraft systems subject to certification and Delegated Regulation (EU) 2019/945 as regards unmanned aircraft systems and third-country operators of unmanned aircraft systems.

[13] Avagliano (2025), p. 177.

[14] Truxal and Scott (2024).

3.1 Open Category

The "open" category provides for low-risk operations and therefore does not require authorization from the competent authority or a preliminary declaration by the operator (art. 3 letter a). According to art. 4, operations may be carried out with unmanned aircraft with a maximum take-off mass (MTOM) of less than 25 kg, within 120 m from the closest point to the earth's surface and within the visibility distance.

In the "open" category, operations are divided into three further subcategories based on operational limitations, and technical requirements for UAS and for pilots.

Annex to the regulation, Part A, identifies the following subcategories: A1, A2 and A3. Subcategory A1 concerns the less risky operations carried out with unmanned aircraft, falling within class C0 or C1 with a maximum take-off mass of less than 250 g. The remote pilot must ensure that the unmanned aircraft is kept at a safe distance and that it does not fly over crowds of people. In order to operate with class C1 aircraft, the pilot must have completed an online training course, while this is not required for class C0.

Subcategory A2 involves operations with unmanned aircraft marked C2, with a maximum take-off mass of less than 4 kg and a maximum height of 120 m, the vehicle must not fly over uninvolved persons and operations must be carried out so that the UAS are at a safe horizontal distance of at least 30 m from such persons. The regulation specifies that the remote pilot can reduce the horizontal safety distance to a minimum of 5 m from uninvolved persons during the operation of an unmanned aircraft in which the low-speed mode function is active and after an assessment of the situation with respect to: (a) meteorological conditions, (b) performance of the unmanned aircraft, (c) separation of the area flown over. In order to operate in this subcategory, the pilot must have completed a theoretical course and independent practical training.

Subcategory A3 may be operated by an aircraft with a mass of less than 25 kg, belonging to class C2, C3 or C4 and involves the performance of operations that may develop at a safe horizontal distance of at least 150 m from residential, commercial, industrial or recreational areas, by a pilot who can reasonably foresee not putting at risk any uninvolved person within the limits of the area in which to fly the unmanned aircraft during the entire period of the UAS operation.

The remote pilot must also complete an online training course and pass the related theoretical knowledge exam (referred to in paragraph 4, letter b), point UAS. OPEN.202° Implementing Regulation (EU) 2019/947.

3.2 Specific Category

The "specific" category includes those operations characterized by a medium risk, for which, pursuant to art. 3 letter b), a declaration by the operator is mandatory, preceded by a risk assessment (art. 11—operational risk assessment), and consequent operational authorization issued by the competent authority of the Member State in which the UAS is registered (art. 12).

If the operation is conducted in a state other than the one of registration, the operational authorization is issued by the National Civil Aviation Authority of the state of registration, while the authority of the state in which the operation is carried out must provide "confirmation".

The requirement for operational authorization ceases if the operation falls within one of the standard scenarios or when the pilot has a light UAS operator certificate.

In the former case, the standard scenarios are UAS operations that follow pre-defined procedures and have previously undergone risk assessment (art. 2.6). These scenarios allow operators to benefit from a simplified authorization procedure (art. 12, par. 5), reducing administrative complexity. In fact, the competent authority, having verified that the declaration required by art. 5.5 is positive and compliant with point UAS.SPEC.020, paragraph 2, of the Annex, provides the UAS operator with confirmation of receipt and completeness of the declaration, without undue delay, so that the operation can begin.

In the latter case, the operator can avoid prior checks by the authority if they hold the so-called Light Unmanned Certificate (LUC). The LUC allows drone operators to self-assess the risks of their operations and to independently carry out operations in accordance with the privileges granted by the certificate, without having to submit each individual operation to ENAC. This certificate of unlimited duration requires that the operator demonstrate a high level of competence and reliability in safety management (part C annex reg. 947/2019).

"The purpose of such a mechanism is to streamline the authorisation process for the requesting organisation and to reduce the burden on competent authorities, while ensuring the accepted levels of safety are met".[15]

3.3 Certified Category

Operations in the "certified" category, art. 3 letter c) are those with a high risk that require higher safety standards. These are operations that involve flying over crowds of people, transporting people and dangerous goods that may pose a high risk to third parties in the event of accidents (art. 6). These also include those operations that, based on risk assessment pursuant to art. 11 of reg. 947/2019, according to the competent authority, present excessive risk, which requires certification of the UAS and the operator. To carry out these operations, certification of the remotely piloted aircraft, including airworthiness, certification of the operator issued by the competent authority, and possession of a remote pilot licence are required.

[15] Truxal and Scott (2024), p. 51.

This category, although expressly provided for both by Delegated Regulation (EU) 2019/945 and by Implementing Regulation (EU) 2019/947, is not yet regulated in detail.

Those aircraft capable of transporting people, such as air taxis, must possess adequate certifications; moreover, the UAS operator must obtain air operator authorization issued by the competent authority, and the remote pilot must be in possession of a specific licence. EASA is working in particular on the certification of VTOLs, vertical take-off and landing aircraft, with a pilot on board, and has specified that operations with such vehicles are classified as "certified" when they are used for the transport of people flying over urban areas.[16]

On the EASA website, the Agency clarifies that also in this case it will proceed in steps, divided into three phases.

Type 1: Operations with certified cargo drones conducted under instrument flight rules (IFR).

Type 2: Operations with drones in urban or rural environments using predefined routes in airspaces where U-space services are provided.

Type 3: operations as in type 2 but conducted with an aircraft with a pilot on board.

3.4 *Remote Pilot Requirements*

Regulation 947/2019 also provides requirements and qualifications for the remote pilot. Specifically, this "means a natural person responsible for safely conducting the flight of a UA by operating its flight controls, either manually or, when the UA flies automatically, by monitoring its course and remaining able to intervene and change its course at any time" (art. 2.27 reg. 945/2019).

Pursuant to art. 9 of reg. 947/2019, they must be at least 16 years old to carry out open and specific category operations, with the exception of the cases regulated by art. 9.2 (open operations in subcategory A1, with class C0 UAS, as per the Annex, part I, operations with UAS built by private individuals or without class marking with MTOM less than 250 g., or if they operate under the direct supervision of a remote pilot who has the minimum age and skills referred to in art. 8).

Under the regulation, member states may lower the minimum age of pilots, after a risk assessment, by up to a maximum of four years in the open category and two years in the specific category, taking into account (art. 9.3).

The necessary skills for pilots for the open and specific categories are set out in Annex A (art. 8).

[16] Commission Implementing Regulation (EU) 2024/1111 of 10 April 2024 amending Regulation (EU) No 1178/2011, Implementing Regulation (EU) No 923/2012, Regulation (EU) No 965/2012 and Implementing Regulation (EU) 2017/373, as regards the establishment of requirements for the operation of manned aircraft with a vertical take-off and landing capability.

4 U-Space

The European regulation on drones is further integrated by the U-Space regulation aimed at allowing safe operations between manned and unmanned aircraft to prevent collisions in flight and to mitigate the risks of drone traffic on the ground.

Since 2016, the European Union, together with SESAR Joint Undertaking and EUROCONTROL, has started a process to prepare a single regulatory framework that allows drones to operate in the air navigation system in general. Four phases of implementation of U-space have been identified:

U1—U-Space foundation services provide e-registration, e-identification and geofencing.
U2—U-Space initial services support the management of drone operations and may include flight planning, flight approval, tracking, airspace dynamic information, and procedural interfaces with air traffic control.
U3—U-Space advanced services support more complex operations in dense areas and may include capacity management and assistance for conflict detection.
U4—U-Space full services support the full operational capability of U-Space, particularly services offering integrated interfaces with manned aviation.

To carry out this ambitious project, the commission adopted the U-Space Regulatory package on 22 April 2021, which entered into force on 26 January 2023, divided into three implementing regulations:

- Regulation (EU) 2021/664 on a regulatory framework for U-space.
- Regulation (EU) 2021/665 amending Implementing Regulation (EU) 2017/373 regarding requirements for providers of air traffic management/air navigation services and other air traffic management network functions in the U-space airspace designated in controlled airspace.
- Regulation (EU) 2021/666 amending Regulation (EU) no. 923/2012 regarding requirements for manned aviation operating in U-space airspace.

This legislative package represents "the corner stone of the new EU drone regulatory framework, facilitating the development of the drone industry and the drone services market" (COM (2022) 652 final of 29/11/2022, 2).

The regulations establish "a uniform and directly applicable discipline in the matter of U-space within the Member States. Some margins of intervention remain, however, for national legislators through the loopholes left open by the EU regulation".[17]

The rules and procedures for the safe conduct of UAS operations are mainly established in the framework regulation 2021/664.

Pursuant to Art. 3, states may establish a 'U-space airspace', i.e. UAS geographical zone where UAS operations are only allowed to take place with the support of U-space services.

---

[17] Rizzo (2025).

In this zone, states, following a careful assessment of operational and safety risks, may establish the capacity and performance requirements of UAS, the performance of U-space services and the applicable operating conditions and airspace restrictions. U-space airspace may also be created in a controlled airspace, but in this case States are required to ensure a dynamic reconfiguration of the airspace, to respect the segregation between manned and unmanned aircraft.

Within the U-space airspace, defined by the states, reg. 2021/664 will apply to UAS operators, U-space service providers and communication service providers, in all cases of operations carried out with UAS in the open and specific category.

UAS operations carried out with drones with a take-off mass of less than 250 g falling within the A1 subcategory, class C0 vehicles and operations within authorized aeroclubs or associations are excluded from application of the regulation.[18]

For the management of unmanned aircraft traffic, states must ensure a "common information service" in U-space providing static and dynamic data for U-space services, detailed in Article 5 (horizontal and vertical boundaries, relevant UAS geographical zones, possible restrictions, list of certified U-space service providers, etc.). A single common information service provider may be designated in all U-space airspaces or several providers may be designated.

UAS operations in U-space are subject to the following four mandatory services:

(1) Network identification service (Article 8): provides the operator's registration number, the aircraft serial number, the geographical position and the direction of flight, as well as any emergency status, in real time. The data are shared with other users;
(2) Geo-awareness service (Article 9): provides information on the applicable operating conditions and any airspace restrictions;
(3) UAS flight authorization service (Article 10): assigns UAS operators the authorization for each individual UAS flight, establishing its terms and conditions;
(4) Traffic information service (Article 11): notifies operators of the presence of other air traffic in the vicinity.

States may also provide other types of services:

(5) meteorological information (art. 12): provides meteorological information useful for operational decisions.
(6) Conformance monitoring service (art. 13): notifies any violations of the authorizations granted.

U-space services are provided by "U-space service providers", i.e. legal persons who have obtained certification, issued in accordance with Chapter V of the Regulation. Pursuant to Art. 7, the provider is responsible for providing the service to operators in the airspace in which it operates and must coordinate with air traffic service providers (ATS), with other U-Space Service Providers (USSP) and with the

[18] Huttunen (2019), p. 69; Barrado et al. (2020), p. 7.

Common Information Service Provider (CISP) for the exchange of information and the correct functioning of all operations.

The second measure of the U-Space package, reg. 2021/665 regulates coordination between ATS units, U-space service providers and UAS operators to ensure safe operations between manned and unmanned aircraft in U-space.

Finally, Regulation 2021/666 which maintains high levels of safety in U-space, provides that manned aircraft that are not provided with an air traffic control service must be electronically visible by signalling their presence within the U-space through surveillance technologies.

When the U-space harmonization process is completed there will be a single integrated airspace that will include manned aviation and operations in the upper airspace, innovative air mobility and small drones.

References

Avagliano R (2025) Riammissione sul mercato UAS, marcatura Ce e definizione C-Class. ATM, Drones and Digitalization, Artificial Intelligence And New Technologies For Environment. Rivista di Diritto dell'Economia, dei Trasporti e dell'Ambiente, Supplemento XXIII:177 ff

Barrado C, Boyero M, Brucculeri L, Ferrara G, Hately A, Hullah P, Martin-Marrero D, Pastor E, Rushton AP, Volkert A (2020) U- space concept of operations: a key enabler for opening airspace to emerging low-altitude operations, Aerospace, 7

Franchina F (2020) The new European Union regulation on unmanned aircraft system and the air navigation services. Dir Pol Trasp I:40 ff

Gaspari F (2020) La regolazione multilivello degli aeromobili a pilotaggio remoto e la disciplina 'speciale' dell'ENAC nel contesto della pandemia covid-19. Riv. dir. nav., 139 ff

Huttunen MT (2019) The U-space concept. Air Space Law:69–89

Lamon M (2020) Il ruolo dei mezzi aerei a pilotaggio remoto durante l'emergenza sanitaria del covid-19, in Rivista di Diritto dell'Economia, dei Trasporti e dell'Ambiente, 177 ff

Masutti A, Tomasello F (2018) International regulation of non-military drones. Edwar Elgar

Morandi F, Ancis L, Toneatto F, Severoni C, Vernizzi S (2022a) Il panorama normativo in materia di mezzi aerei a pilotaggio remoto e lo stato della sua implementazione in Italia. Parte I. Resp. civ. e prev., 1087

Morandi F, Ancis L, Toneatto F, Severoni C, Vernizzi S (2022b) Il panorama normativo in materia di mezzi aerei a pilotaggio remoto e lo stato della sua implementazione in Italia. Parte II. Resp. civ. e prev., 1452

Rizzo MP (2025) I Servizi U-Space: dalla certificazione del fornitore all'accesso alla fornitura. Profili qualificatori e disciplinari, ATM, Drones and Digitalization, Artificial Intelligence and New Technologies for Environment. Rivista di Diritto dell'Economia, dei Trasporti e dell'Ambiente, Supplemento XXIII, 257

Truxal S, Scott BI (2024) The regulation of unmanned aircraft systems in the European Union, Civil Regulation of Autonomous Unmanned Aircraft Systems in Europe. Elgar on line, 31–63, https://doi.org/10.4337/9781035312344.00008

Vernizzi S (2025) La nozione di drone alla luce del panorama normativo vigente e delle future prospettive di sviluppo, ATM, Drones and Digitalization, Artificial Intelligence and New Technologies for Environment. Rivista di Diritto dell'Economia, dei Trasporti e dell'Ambiente, Supplemento XXIII:153

Basic National Regulation on UAS: Italy and Other Countries

Michela Pandolfino

Contents

Abstract The national regulatory framework governing remotely piloted aircraft systems (RPAS) has evolved in following technological advancements and increasing safety requirements, thanks to its foundation established in Article 743, paragraph 2, of the Italian Navigation Code. This provision equates remotely piloted aerial vehicles to traditional aircraft, defined as any machine intended for the air transport of persons or goods, thereby fully incorporating these special aircraft within the Italian civil aviation legal system. On that basis, in 2013 the Italian Civil Aviation Authority (ENAC) adopted the first edition of the Regulation on Remotely Piloted Aircraft Systems, subsequently updated in 2015 and 2019, aimed at regulating the use of RPAS weighing less than 150 kg. This Regulation, now repealed, introduced an operational classification based on maximum take-off mass (MTOM), distinguishing between RPAS below or above 25 kg and imposing stricter obligations on operators of the latter, such as mandatory registration in the RPAS Registry. Aircraft with a maximum take-off mass equal to or exceeding 150 kg fell under the jurisdiction of the European Union Aviation Safety Agency (EASA).

However, the weight-based criterion has progressively been replaced by a risk-based approach, introduced at the European level by Regulation (EU) 2018/1139 and both implementing (No. 947) and delegated (No. 945) regulations of 2019. In 2021, this EU regulatory framework has been fully incorporated in the Italian legal system through the ENAC UAS-IT Regulation.

M. Pandolfino (✉)
University of Messina, Messina, Italy
e-mail: mipandolfino@unime.it

M. P. Rizzo, F. Franchina (eds.), *Drones in the Digital European Sky*,
International Aviation Law Library 1,
https://doi.org/10.1007/978-3-032-16691-3_6

The last chapter of the part examines the developments in legislation regarding unmanned aircraft systems (UAS) in France and Spain. Both legal systems have aligned with the European framework and, in particular, Regulation (EU) 2019/947, while adopting different legislative approaches. France has implemented a centralized and risk-averse model, emphasizing public safety through prohibitions of "open" operations in urban areas and imposing substantial technical and administrative requirements. Conversely, Spain has pursued a more pragmatic and operationally flexible framework, with the issuing of Royal Decree 517/2024, which introduced National Standard Scenarios (STS-ES) and Temporary Zones in order to facilitate legal certainty and procedural simplification.

1 The Italian Regulatory Framework

The Italian regulations regarding remotely piloted aircraft are contained in the Navigation Code and, in addition, in the regulations issued by ENAC (National Civil Aviation Authority), according to Article 743, para. 2, Navigation Code.

The first edition of the ENAC regulation on "*Remotely Piloted Aircraft*" (RPA) was adopted on 16 December 2013,[1] followed by the second in 2015 and the third in 2019.[2]

In addition, on 24 May 2019, Circular ATM 09[3] "*Remotely Piloted Aircraft. Criteria for use of airspace*" was adopted, aimed at defining rules and procedures for the use of segregated and non-segregated airspace by such aircraft.

The first definition of RPA was contained in Article 5 of the above-mentioned ENAC Regulation of 2013, which qualified it as a "*remotely piloted aerial vehicle without persons on board, not used for recreational or sporting purposes*"

This Regulation, in Article 1, para. 1, relied on Article 743 of the Italian Navigation Code, as amended in 2005-2006, that defined aircraft as "*any machine intended for the air transport of persons or goods. Remotely piloted aerial vehicles are also considered to be aircraft*".[4] Remote-piloted vehicles were thus considered aircraft.

Similarly, Article 246 of the Italian Code of Military Organization[5] defines RPA as "*an aircraft piloted by a crew operating from a remote command and control station*" expressly referring to operational aspects and not—unlike the Italian Navigation Code – to its function (air transport of persons or goods).

[1] Issue 1 of 16 Dec. 2013, adopted by Board Resolution No. 42/2013, which came into force on 30 April 2014. For an in-depth discussion.

[2] Scott (2022), pp. 65–67.

[3] ENAC Circular dated 24 May 2019 ATM-09, Air Traffic Management series, called "Remotely piloted aircraft airspace use criteria," which came into effect on 1 July 2019.

[4] Severoni (2016), p. 69.

[5] Legislative decree no. 66 of 15 March 2010.

Based on the provisions of the above-mentioned ENAC Regulation, all remotely piloted aircraft under Italian jurisdiction, *i.e.* those weighing no more than 150 kg and all those designed or modified for research, experimental or scientific purposes,[6] were classified according to their "maximum take-off mass" (MTOM), depending on whether they weighed less or more than 25 kg.

This distinction entailed relevant legal consequences: for example, this Regulation required RPAs with a MTOM of 25 kg or more operating in Italian airspace to be registered in the Registry of Remotely Piloted Aircraft.[7]

RPAs weighing more than 150 kg were, however, subject to European Regulation (EC) No. 216/2008[8] and thus regulated similarly to other traditional, pilot-operated aircraft.

In other words, the weight limit (150 kg) established shared responsibility between EASA (EU Aviation Safety Agency) and national aviation authorities.

The ENAC Regulation "*Remotely Piloted Aircraft*" remained in force until 2020, and then was replaced in 2021 by the current ENAC "UAS-IT" Regulation,[9] which was adopted after the issuing, at European level, of Regulation (EU) 2018/1139 of 4 July 2018,[10] followed by Implementing Regulation (EU) No. 2019/947[11] of 24 May 2019 and Delegated Regulation (EU) No. 2019/945[12] of 12 March 2019.

Regulation (EU) No. 1139/2018 defines unmanned aerial vehicles as *"any aircraft operating or designed to operate autonomously or to be piloted remotely without a pilot on board"* (Art. 3, No. 30), understanding in turn aircraft as "*any machine that can derive support in the atmosphere from the reactions of the air other than reactions of the air against the earth's surface"* (Art. 30, No. 28). The last definition derives in turn from technical annexes to the 1944 Chicago Convention on International Civil Aviation, adopted by ICAO. In fact, Article 8 of this Convention refers to unmanned aircraft, without defining them, in order to prohibit them from flying over a contracting state, unless special authorization from that country has been obtained.

6 Art. 2.2 of the ENAC "Remotely Piloted Aerial Means" Regulations of 2013.

7 Severoni (2016), p. 74.

8 Regulation (EC) No. 216/2008 of the European Parliament and of the Council of 20 February 2008, on common rules in the field of civil aviation and establishing a European Aviation Safety Agency, and repealing Council Directive 91/670/EEC, Regulation (EC) No. 1592/2002 and Directive 2004/36/EC (O.J.E. L 79, 19 March 2008, 1-49).

9 UAS-IT Regulations - Edition 1 of 4 January 2021. The Director General of the Civil Aviation Authority, the absence of the President of the Authority persisting, urgently adopted (provision DG 01/2021) the UAS-IT Regulations of 2021, pursuant to Article 4 of Legislative Decree No. 250 of 25 July 1997, "Establishment of the National Civil Aviation Authority" (E.N.A.C.).

10 Regulation (EU) 2018/1139 of the European Parliament and of the Council of 4 July 2018 on common rules in the field of civil aviation, establishing the European Union Aviation Safety Agency.

11 Commission Implementing Regulation (EU) 2019/947 of 24 May 2019 on rules and procedures for the operation of unmanned aircraft (OJEU L 152, 11 June 2019).

12 Commission Delegated Regulation (EU) 2019/945 of 12 March 2019 on unmanned aircraft systems and third-country operators of unmanned aircraft systems (OJEU L 152, 11 June 2019).

Instead, at the international level, the definition of RPA is contained, for example, in ICAO Annex 7[13] on aircraft nationality and registration marks, which defines it as "*an unmanned aircraft which is piloted from a remote pilot station*" (Article 1)

Specifically, Regulation (EU) 2019/947 amends the pre-existing European provisions, stating that "*unmanned aircraft, irrespective of their mass, can operate within the same Single European Sky airspace, alongside manned aircraft, whether airplanes or helicopters*" (Recital 1).

In fact, the EU regulatory framework of 2018-2019 does not give central importance to the weight of the aircraft, since even a small drone can cause serious damage, but prefers the operational risk criterion.

In other words, after putting aside the criterion based only on the weight of the aircraft, it became necessary to identify a more appropriate and flexible parameter which could be evaluated, on a case-by-case basis, in relation to the specific operational circumstances.

The risk-based criterion enables a proportionate analysis on to the characteristics and potential implications of the underlying operations.

In this regard, Regulation (EU) 2019/947 defines three categories of operations ("open", "specific" and "certified") and establishes applicable procedures and requirements, by applying the risk-based criterion, and the "principle of proportionality".[14] In other words, rules and procedures applicable to this industry must be proportionate to the risk involved in each operation.

In this context, risk assessment and the proportionality parameter become pivotal elements, especially following the integration of AI (Artificial Intelligence) systems into airspace. This phenomenon has recently been governed by Regulation (EU) 2024/1689,[15] the so-called "Regulation on Artificial Intelligence", aimed at establishing global standards for secure and reliable AI systems, while ensuring that fundamental rights of European citizens are respected.[16]

After this brief reference to the new European regulatory framework, it is necessary to examine the current Italian legislation on the use of RAPs.

In fact, following the entry into force of the European regulatory framework of 2018-19, the ENAC UAS-IT Regulation was issued with the aim to ensure high levels of safety for the different types of operations that can be carried out with SAPRs (Remotely Piloted Aircraft Systems), according to the risk-based criterion.

As previously said, the open category includes all low-risk drone operations and is characterized by flight altitude, distance and zones where flight is permissible. According to the national regulation, these operations do not require prior authorization or a declaration from the drone operator.

---

[13] Annex 7 to the Convention on International Civil Aviation, "Aircraft Nationality and Registration Marks", dated 18 February 2003.

[14] See Huttunen (2019), p. 2.

[15] Regulation (EU) 2024/1689 of the European Parliament and of the Council of 13 June 2024 laying down harmonized rules on artificial intelligence.

[16] See, in doctrine, on this matter: Andritsos et al. (2022), p. 5; Andritsos and Agouridas (2022), pp. 313–317.

According to the current ENAC UAS-IT Regulation, designed to work in harmony with the European legislation on UAS, additional rules, specific to the Italian context, apply, focusing on safety, operational categories, registration, pilot qualifications, and specific zones with restrictions.

It applies to all drone operators in Italy, both recreational and professional, particularly for operations falling in the "specific" and "certified" categories under EU law.

One of the key issues is the definition of geographical zones where drone flights are limited, or subject to specific conditions. These include areas near airports, military zones, urban centres and nature reserves. ENAC coordinates with other authorities to manage these zones, which are marked in official maps and NOTAMs.

Drone operators and certain categories of drones must be registered, in compliance with EU rules. In addition, all drones weighing 250 g or more, or equipped with a camera or other sensors capable of collecting personal data, must be subject to electronic identification systems (e.g., remote ID).[17]

The fact that the operation falls into the open category does not exempt the UAS operator from consulting, before the flight, the ENAC Circular ATM-09A of 2021,[18] which contains rules regulating the use of airspace and procedures for geographical zones. In particular, this Circular aims to align UAS operations with the EU Regulation 2019/947.

Therefore, it is also necessary to verify the operational area by using the maps available on the D-flight portal,[19] which show the "UAS geographical zones" referred to in Article 15 of Regulation (EU) 2019/947.

These zones, in which flight restrictions may be imposed, fall into three categories:

(a) zones established for "safety reasons" in order to protect airports, heliports, helipads;
(b) zones established for "security" reasons;
(c) zones established for environmental protection reasons.

In order to operate in these areas, it is necessary to first check whether additional restrictions apply. If it is not possible to fly within the open category's limitations, the "specific" category is the next step for drone operations.

---

[17] Palmierini et al. (2020), pp. 425–426.

[18] Circular ATM-09th, ed. 1, dated 24 March 2021, "UAS-IT: Implementation Criteria and Procedures for Geographical Zones", cited above, and the related Model for "Airspace Reserve for UAS Operations".

[19] D-flight S.p.A. is a company of the ENAV Group, the Italian public company that operates, in the form of a joint stock company, as the exclusive provider of services for civil air navigation in the airspace under Italian jurisdiction. D-flight is involved in the development and delivery of services for low altitude air traffic management of remotely piloted aircraft (APRs) and all other types of approaches falling under the category of unmanned aerial vehicles (UAVs). The company is owned by an industrial partner, selected through a public bidding process, consisting of Leonardo S.p.A. and Telespazio S.p.A.

The last category, involving medium risk, requires prior approval from the competent aviation authority or a declaration submitted to this authority by a UAS operator, in accordance with a standard scenario.

It is necessary to create an airspace reserve for UAS operations in the cases listed in Article 8.1 (a), (b) and (c) of ENAC Circular ATM-09-A, namely: (a) for operations taking place within the geographic zones located in the vicinity of airports (both civil and military); (b) when a risk assessment is carried out; (c) for operations carried out more than 120 metres above the earth's surface.

The "certified" category includes operations with the highest level of risk such as transporting people or dangerous goods. In this case, the design, construction and maintenance of drones must be certified by the relevant aviation authorities.[20]

In addition, UAS operations falling under the "certified" category are subject to the operational requirements of Commission Implementing Regulation (EU) No. 923/2012[21] and Commission Regulations (EU) Nos. 965/2012[22] and 1332/2011.[23]

Additionally, the UAS-IT Regulation establishes national rules also for model aircraft.

Aeromodelling is a recreational activity, considered as a non-specialized operation, that falls outside the scope of the above-mentioned legislation and represents an autonomous category.[24] In fact, for such drones lighter than 250 g and not equipped with sound/image recording systems, the operator has no obligation to register drones on the D-flight portal, laid down in Article 8 of the current ENAC Regulation.

Although aeromodelling is a recreational activity, it is not entirely exempt from aviation legislation, but is in any case subject to regulations concerning airspace and safety.[25]

A new draft of the UAS- IT Regulation, which will soon replace the version of January 2021, introduces some innovations for pilots and operators and integrates some provisions already in force but issued with circulars.

A significant new, contained in the draft, is the requirement to pre-post flight planning on the d-flight portal for all specific categories of operations, including those conducted under standard scenarios.

---

[20] Dei et al. (2023), p. 299 ff.

[21] Commission Implementing Regulation (EU) No. 923/2012 of 26 September 2012, laying down common air rules and operational provisions concerning air navigation services and procedures and amending Implementing Regulation (EU) No. 1035/2011 and Regulations (EC) No. 1265/2007, (EC) No. 1794/2006, (EC) No. 730/2006, (EC) No. 1033/2006, and (EU) No. 255/2010 (O.J.U. L 281, 13 Oct. 2012, 1-66).

[22] Commission Regulation (EU) No. 965/2012 of 5 October 2012, laying down technical requirements and administrative procedures related to air operations pursuant to Regulation (EC) No. 216/2008 of the European Parliament and of the Council (O.J.E. L 296, 25 Oct. 2012, 1-148).

[23] Commission Regulation (EU) No. 1332/2011 of 16 December 2011, laying down common airspace usage requirements and common operating procedures for airborne collision avoidance (O.U.E. L 336, 20 Dec. 2011, 20-22).

[24] Gasparri (2020), p. 152 ff.

[25] Trimarchi (2024), p. 197 ff.

2 The French Regulatory Framework

After having examined the regulation adopted in Italy following the entry into force of the EU regulatory framework of 2018–2019, it is interesting to stress that implementation of these regulations has not been uniform in all Member States.

Therefore, a comparative analysis deserves to be carried out by critically examining the French and Spanish legal systems, in order to identify similarities and divergences between them.

These two national legal systems have developed autonomous and differentiated regulatory solutions with particular attention to the authorization/registration systems and the management of UAS geographic zones where drone operations are managed in order to ensure safety, security, and privacy.

The first significant French legislation on drones was Law No. 2016-1428 of 24 October 2016,[26] which established a comprehensive legal framework aimed at regulating the use of remotely piloted aircraft, with particular attention to public safety, airspace protection and operator accountability.[27]

This Law intervenes at both the administrative and criminal levels, imposing specific obligations on operators, manufacturers and public authorities. It required electronic registration for unmanned aircraft, provided that their mass is equal to or greater than a certain weight established by law and, in any case, not exceeding 800 g. This obligation was an exception to the general principle according to which UAS weighing less than 25 kg are exempt from registration, provided that they comply with the technical specifications laid down in the same law.

In addition, this legislation provides for the possibility of exemptions for certain aircraft with special characteristics, defined by implementing decrees of the *Conseil d'État.*

This national regulatory framework was subsequently modified, repealing all national provisions that were redundant or in conflict with EU Regulation 2018/1139 and its 2019 delegated and implementing regulations.

First of all, it is necessary to mention the Decree of 3 December 2020,[28] relating to the use of airspace by drones, that implements and integrates the EU regulations, governing in detail the use of French airspace by unmanned aircraft and defining national standard scenarios. It also addresses operational requirements for flights in the vicinity of runways and landing areas.

This decree applies not only to civilian drones, but also to those used for security, emergency, public order or civil defense purposes, following a risk management approach: its focus is not the mere classification of drones, but the nature and type of flight operations with drones, as well as the responsibility of operators.[29]

[26] Journal officiel électronique authentifié n° 0249 du 25/10/2016.

[27] See Delebecque (2022), p. 1.

[28] Entered into force on 31 December 2020.

[29] Choné-Grimaldi and Glaser (2018), alerte 1.

In fact, the underlying principle of this decree is the protection of aviation safety: drones must operate in a manner that does not create any danger to other airspace users, particularly manned aircraft. For these reasons, maintaining visibility and adhering to distance restrictions from airports, sensitive infrastructure and densely populated areas are pivotal for safe drone operations.

In addition, the decree in question gives the remote pilot a central role and full legal responsibility, imposing stringent aviation safety obligations[30] in order to ensure that this activity does not create risks to other airspace users.[31]

Ordonnance No. 2022-456[32] of 30 March 2022 does not replace the 2020 Decree in its entirety, but rather supplements and updates it as part of a comprehensive reform of civil aviation regulations, including those relating to the drone sector.

This Ordinance is part of a broader regulatory reform aimed at harmonising national legislation with European Regulation (EU) 2018/1139, simplifying certain administrative procedures (such as the declaration procedures for certain air transport activities) and strengthening penalty and safety provisions.

It introduces exemptions from registration for those weighing less than 25 kg, while imposing an electronic registration requirement for those above a certain weight limit, with the introduction of training requirements for remote pilots. The provisions are also extended and adapted to French overseas communities.

It also introduces a new declaration regime for certain air transport activities, reducing the bureaucratic burden for operators, especially those operating light aircraft.

The Ordinance amended and supplemented the *Code des transports* in order to improve safety, stipulating that the operation of public air transport is subject to possession of a certificate issued by the competent authority. It introduces more severe criminal penalties than for operators who fly without the required certificates or in violation of safety and airworthiness regulations.

It is clear that the 2022 Ordinance does not automatically eliminate or repeal all the provisions of the 2020 Decree, which remain valid where it is not incompatible with the new provisions.

This Ordinance has a significant impact both on operators, who must adapt to new procedures and requirements, and on the competent authorities, called upon to implement these new rules, with the ultimate aim of ensuring a high level of safety in public air transport, harmonising national legislation with European legislation.[33]

---

[30] Brun (2018), p. 176.

[31] Debard and Guichard (2020), p. 543.

[32] Journal officiel électronique authentifié n° 0076 du 31/03/2022.

[33] Langer (2024) France, in Jacques Hartmann, Benjamin I. Scott, Steven Truxal, Andrea Bertolini, E. Anna Masutti, Civil regulation of autonomous unmaned aircraft systems in Europe.

3 The Spanish Regulatory Framework

Passing now to the Spanish legal system, in the absence of previously existing comprehensive legislation, the *Ley* 18/2014,[34] enacted on 15 October 2014, firstly introduced urgent measures for the growth, competitiveness, and efficiency of the drone sector and the use of these vehicles in certain areas and under certain conditions.[35] This law established a regulatory framework for the use of drones for professional or research tasks.[36] In particular, it introduced a provisional legal regime aimed at regulating the civil use of remotely piloted aircraft with an operating mass of less than 150 kg.

Operations were authorised exclusively in uncontrolled airspace and above non-urban areas. The use of UAS for scientific, technical, agricultural, emergency, surveillance and communication purposes was regulated by this legislation. Minimum technical requirements had been established, such as aircraft identification and possession of a pilot's licence.[37] For drones weighing less than 25 kg, there was no obligation to register and obtain a certificate of airworthiness.

The 2014 regulations represented the technical and legal basis for the subsequent evolution of national UAS regulations.

The obvious inadequacy of the above-mentioned transitional regulations in relation to rapid technological developments and the operational expansion of drones made it necessary to adopt more comprehensive and structured legislation, resulting from Royal Decree No. 1036/2017 of 15 December[38] and the subsequent Royal Decree No. 1180/2018 of 21 September.[39]

---

[34] Law 18/2014 of 15 October, on urgent measures for growth, competitiveness, and efficiency. Published in *Official State Gazette* ("BOE") No. 252, dated 17/10/2014.

[35] See Guerrero Lebrón et al. (2014), pp. 63–106; Franco García, M. A. (2014), "El régimen jurídico de las aeronaves civiles pilotadas por control remoto: análisis del Decreto Real-Ley 8/2014, de 4 de Julio" (*Il regime giuridico degli aeromobili civili pilotati a distanza: analisi del Decreto Reale-Ley 8/2014 del 4 luglio*), *Diario La Ley*, n. 8370, Sezione Dottrina, 4 settembre 2014, 4971/2014, p. 1.

[36] Converted into law on 17 October 2014.

[37] Ramírez Ciriza (2015), p. 46.

[38] Royal Decree 1036/2017, of 15 December, regulating the civil use of remotely piloted aircraft and amending Royal Decree 552/2014, of 27 June, establishing aviation regulations and common operating provisions for air navigation services and procedures, and Royal Decree 57/2002, of 18 January, approving the air traffic regulations. Published in "BOE" No. 316, of 29 December 2017 [Provision repealed].

[39] Royal Decree 1180/2018, of 21 September, which develops the Air Traffic Regulations and common operating provisions for air navigation services and procedures and amends Royal Decree 57/2002, of 18 January, which approves the Air Traffic Regulations; Royal Decree 862/2009, of 14 May, approving the technical standards for the design and operation of public airports and the Regulations for the certification and verification of airports and other public airports; Royal Decree 931/2010, of 23 July, regulating the certification procedure for civil air navigation service providers and their regulatory control; and the Air Traffic Operating Regulations, approved by Royal Decree 601/2016, of 2 December. Published in BOE No. 272, of 10/11/2018.

Royal Decree No. 1036/2017 applied to UAS used in specialised or experimental civil operations, whose operating mass did not exceed 150 kg, as well as, under certain conditions, to UAS with a higher mass, if they did not fall within the scope of Regulation (EC) No 216/2008.[40]

This Decree intended to ensure the safe use of civil UAS, filling previous regulatory gaps and providing a stable regulatory reference for both economic operators and competent authorities.

It represents a milestone in the evolution of the Spanish regulatory framework for remotely piloted aircraft (UAS), used for non-military purposes, introducing a comprehensive and systematic set of rules that supersedes the previous provisional regime contained in Law 18/2014.

It governed the responsible and internationally compliant use of remotely piloted aircraft, setting out requirements for operators and operational conditions, including certification requirements, drone identification and flight limitation.

The decree established a complex system of technical, operational and administrative requirements, modulated according to the principle of proportionality based on the mass of the aircraft, the type of operation (visual or non-visual) and the operating environment. Among other things, it required UAS to be equipped with a fireproof identification plate, containing essential information about the operator, the type of aircraft and contact details. UASs weighing less than 25 kg were exempt from the obligation to be registered in the Aircraft Register and from airworthiness certification, except in the case of particularly critical uses, while for heavier aircraft, the general civil aviation certification provisions applied.

For operational safety purposes, VLOS (Visual Line of Sight) operations could only be carried out in uncontrolled airspace, within a height of 120 metres and a distance of 500 metres from the pilot, while BVLOS (Beyond Visual Line of Sight) operations were subject to the use of detect and avoid systems or the use of specially authorised segregated airspace was imposed.[41] In addition, for operations carried out in urban areas, over gatherings of people or in the vicinity of critical infrastructure, prior coordination with the competent authorities (including the Ministry of the Interior) was required in order to safeguard public order and collective safety.

The real motivation behind this legislation lies in the need to reconcile technological development in the sector with the protection of public order, airspace safety and fundamental human rights, with particular reference to privacy, civil liability and the physical integrity of third parties.[42]

Decree No. 1180/2018 did not go into detail on drones, but established a general regulatory framework for air traffic, applied to unmanned vehicles that operate in

---

[40] Regulation (EC) No 216/2008 of The European Parliament And of The Council of 20 February 2008.laying down common rules in the field of civil aviation and establishing a European Aviation Safety Agency, and repealing Council Directive 91/670/EEC, Regulation (EC) No1592/2002 and Directive 2004/36/EC (OJ L 79, 19.3.2008, 1).

[41] See Vv.Aa. (2015), *Los drones y sus aplicaciones a la ingeniería civil* (*Drones and their applications to civil engineering*), Fenercom, Madrid.

[42] Pauner Chulvi (2016), pp. 83–116.

regulated airspace, particularly with regard to airspace management, separation, communications and navigation services.

Spain has recently made a regulatory update with the issuing of *Real Decreto* No. 517/2024,[43] currently in force, which represents a major reform[44] in the field of civil unmanned aircraft.

This new Decree, that repealed the previous Spanish legislation, marking the full integration of Spanish legislation with the European regulatory framework of 2018–2019, incorporated the principle of risk classification and the distinction between "open", "specific" and "certified" categories of drones operations, introduced by EU regulations.

It is aimed at simplifying and rationalising the legal system, clearly distinguishing between operations regulated by European law and those excluded (e.g. security, customs, firefighting).

In particular, it regulates civil operations excluded from European legislation, such as those carried out by customs, police, rescue, firefighting and border surveillance services, providing them with a coherent national legal framework.[45]

It applies to the entire Spanish territory and its airspace, and is aimed at covering all unmanned civil aircraft, personnel and organisations involved in their activities, as well as air traffic service providers (ATS), airport and heliport operators, aeronautical information service providers, U-Space and information service providers. For example, it also defines different minimum ages for pilots and operators, made training for the "open" category more accessible, and introduced professional figures qualified to provide training.

In this regard, it is important to note that the new Royal Decree No. 517/2024 expressly establishes the cases in which it does not apply, clearly outlining the subjective and objective limits of its regulatory effectiveness. In particular, the following cases are excluded from its scope of application:

- UAS used exclusively in completely enclosed indoor environments, or in any case in operational contexts where the probability of the vehicle escaping is very low, such that it does not interfere with external airspace;
- military aircraft and those used for military or similar purposes or in military or similar contexts, including activities and services related to defence and national security, as well as personnel and organisations involved in such operations, which remain subject to separate and autonomous military regulatory regimes.

[43] Royal Decree No. 517/2024, of 4 June, which develops the legal framework for the civil use of unmanned aircraft systems (UAS) and amends various regulatory standards concerning controls on imports of certain products with respect to applicable product safety standards; civil aerial demonstrations; firefighting and search and rescue, as well as airworthiness and licensing requirements for other aeronautical activities; civil aircraft registration; electromagnetic compatibility of electrical and electronic equipment; aviation regulations and common operating provisions for air navigation services and procedures; and reporting of civil aviation accidents. Entered into force on 25 June 2024. Published in Boletín Oficial del Estado (BOE) No. 136, dated 5 June 2024.

[44] Such as Royal Decree 1036/2017 and Chapter XI of Royal Decree 1180/2018.

[45] Alvear Trenor (2015), p. 134.

A second aspect deserving of further consideration concerns the legal definition of the "National Standard Scenario" (STS-ES), officially introduced in the new regulatory framework. The decree establishes that "National Standard Scenario" means the reference operational scenario developed by the European Aviation Safety Agency (EASA), in particular in relation to UAS operations falling within the "specific" category and not subject to EASA European regulations.

"Standard National Scenarios" allow VLOS and BVLOS operations to be carried out even in the absence of the CE marking required at European level, highlighting a significant technical derogation, albeit confined to operations not falling within the scope of EASA.

In conclusion, the analysis of the legal framework governing unmanned aircraft systems (UAS) in France and Spain reveals common features of the regulatory harmonisation process initiated at European level with Regulation (EU) 2019/947, but also differences in regulatory approaches and systematic legal choices.

Both national systems have incorporated the fundamental principles of EU legislation, such as the classification of operations according to the risk-based approach and the distinction between the "open", "specific" and "certified" categories, adapting their internal regulatory framework to the requirements of safety, responsibility and airspace integrity.[46]

France has maintained a highly centralised and restrictive regulatory framework, based on the precautionary principle, following an approach that strictly complies with European standards. In this context, access to the "open" category is severely restricted, particularly for operations carried out in urban environments, where the "specific" category and the preparation of detailed operational scenarios are required. The remote pilot is responsible for these operations and the entire system is based on strict supervision by the aviation and public safety authorities.

In contrast, Spain, with the recent *Real Decreto* 517/2024, has chosen a more flexible and simplified regulatory approach, drawing a clear line between operations subject to European regulations and excluded activities, such as those carried out by customs, law enforcement, civil protection and fire brigades.

While converging on the common goal of ensuring the safe and responsible use of UAS, France and Spain have therefore taken two divergent paths: the former oriented towards regulatory precaution and centralised control, the latter inclined towards greater operational accessibility and a differentiated use of legal instruments, adapted to national specificities.[47]

---

[46] Freixes San Juan (2011), pp. 37–50.

[47] See Gómez Sánchez (2014).

References

Alvear Trenor I. De (2015) “Algunos retos del Derecho en relación con la regulación de la operación civil y militar de drones y RPAS” (Some legal challenges related to the regulation of the civil and military operation of drones and RPAS). In: Retos del Derecho ante las nuevas amenazas, Dykinson

Andritsos K, AgouridaS V (2022) Urban air mobility: legal and societal stakes of an upcoming mobility network. In: Scott BI (ed) The law of unmanned aircraft systems. Kluwer Law International, The Hague

Andritsos K, Scott BI, Trimarchi A (2022) What is in a name: defining key terms in urban air mobility. J Intell Robot Syst

Brun (2018) Responsabilité civile extracontractuelle, 5ª ed., LexisNexis, Paris, n. 176

Choné-GrimaldI A-S, Glaser Ph (2018) Responsabilité civile du fait du robot doué d’intelligence artificielle: faut-il créer une personnalité robotique? Contrats Concurrence Consommation, n. 1, gennaio 2018, alerte 1

Debard T, Guichard S (2020) Lexique des termes juridiques 2020–2021, 28ª ed., Dalloz

Dei M, Koban O, Lyseiuk A, Vetral A, Kravchenko L (2023) Legal regulation of the use of drones; challenges to human rights and privacy. Riv dir Nav 299 ff

Delebecque (2022) “Navires autonomes et drones maritimes: Nouvelles avancées du droit maritime. Énergie – Environnement – Infrastructures, n. 2, febbraio 2022, comm. 1

Franco García MA (2014) El régimen jurídico de las aeronaves civiles pilotadas por control remoto: análisis del Decreto Real-Ley 8/2014, de 4 de Julio. Diario La Ley, n. 8370, Sezione Dottrina, 4 settembre 2014

Freixes San Juan T (2011) Constitucionalismo multinivel e integración europea” (Multilevel constitutionalism and European integration). In: Constitucionalismo Multinivel y relaciones entre Parlamentos: Parlamento europeo, Parlamentos nacionales, Parlamentos regionales con competencias legislativas. CEPC, Madrid

Gasparri F (2020) Multilevel regulation of remotely piloted aircraft and Enac’s special regulation in the context of the covid-19 pandemic. Riv dir nav 152 ff

Gómez Sánchez Y (2014) Constitucionalismo multinivel. Derechos fundamentales (Multilevel constitutionalism. Fundamental rights), 2ª ed., Sanz y Torres, Madrid

Guerrero Lebrón MJ, Cuerno Rejado C, Márquez Lobillo P (2014) Aeronaves no tripuladas: Estado de la legislación para realizar su integración en el espacio aéreo no segregado. Revista de Derecho del Transporte, n. 12

Huttunen M. (2019) Drone operations in the specific category: a unique approach to aviation safety. Aviat Space J

Langer L (2024) France, in Jacques Hartmann, Benjamin I. Scott, Steven Truxal, Andrea Bertolini, E. Anna Masutti, Civil regulation of autonomous unmaned aircraft systems in Europe

Palmierini E, Biasotti MA, Aiello F (eds) (2020) Diritto dei droni. Regole, questioni e prassi. Giuffrè, Milano

Pauner Chulvi C (2016) “El uso emergente de drones civiles en España. Estatuto jurídico e impacto en Derecho a la Protección de Datos” (L’uso emergente dei droni civili in Spagna. Statuto giuridico e impatto sul diritto alla protezione dei dati), Revista de Derecho Político

Ramírez Ciriza JM (2015) “Aspectos reglamentarios” (*Regulatory aspects*). In: VV.AA., Los drones y sus aplicaciones a la ingeniería civil, Fenercom, Madrid

Scott BI (2022) The law of unmanned aircraft systems, 2nd edn. Kluwer Law International, The Hague

Severoni C (2016) The current regulatory of remotely piloted aircraft. Dir Trasp 69

Trimarchi A (2024) Italy. In: Hartmann J, Scott BI, Truxal S, Bertolini A, Anna Masutti E (eds) Civil regulation of autonomous unmaned aircraft systems in Europe, 197 ff

UAS Operation between Legal Theory and Technological Evolution

Operator, Pilot-In-Command and UAS Crew

Federico Franchina

Contents

Abstract This chapter examines the legal framework governing the roles of the Unmanned Aircraft Systems (UAS) operator, pilot-in-command (PIC), and crew within the European Union, primarily through the lens of EU Regulation 2019/947. It highlights the regulation's risk-based and proportional approach, which legally distinguishes between the UAS operator's systemic, organisational responsibilities and the remote PIC's in-flight operational duties. The operator is established as the key entity for safety and compliance, akin to an accountable manager in traditional aviation, while the PIC retains ultimate authority for the safe conduct of the flight.

The analysis explores the historical and legal development of the PIC concept, tracing its origins and how it has adapted to the specific context of remotely piloted operations. A key aspect of the discussion is the legal uncertainty surrounding the "UAS crew," as the EU regulation intentionally lacks a formal definition, leaving it

F. Franchina (✉)
Department of Law, University of Messina, Messina, Italy
e-mail: federico.franchina@unime.it

M. P. Rizzo, F. Franchina (eds.), *Drones in the Digital European Sky*,
International Aviation Law Library 1,
https://doi.org/10.1007/978-3-032-16691-3_7

to the operator to specify roles and responsibilities for supporting personnel in their operations manual. This contrasts with emerging ICAO standards in Annex 6, Part IV, which offer clear definitions for crew members, which may lead to future interoperability challenges.

Furthermore, the chapter examines future challenges caused by increasing automation and Artificial Intelligence (AI). The distinction between 'automatic' and 'autonomous' operations in regulation indicates an upcoming paradigm shift. This development will fundamentally alter traditional human-centric models of command and liability, potentially changing the PIC's role from a direct controller to a "system supervisor" and redefining accountability frameworks. The chapter concludes that although the current EU framework offers a scalable foundation, the rise of autonomy will require a major re-evaluation of control, responsibility, and liability within the UAS industry.

1 Introduction

There is no doubt that technological advancements in the field of aviation, particularly in UAS, have introduced both benefits and challenges.[1]

Among the main potential benefits are demand-adaptive or 'scalable' capacity, user flexibility and autonomy that may finally enable truly successful business strategies, and compatibility with current-day operations so that the implementation rate can be driven from within the user community.

In this direction, the evolution of unmanned aircraft systems (UAS) and their widespread adoption by society have also prompted a swift response from lawmakers and aviation experts.

The European Union Aviation Safety Agency (EASA) has submitted several proposals to the European Commission that have resulted in the development of a legal framework capable of regulating UAS operations safely.

Conversely, lawmakers and stakeholders have emphasised the importance of UAS development (and the deployment of their support IT ecosystem) as a key driver for economic growth, which has led to the adoption of a series of regulations and technical standards from EASA to ensure safe operations.

From a straightforward legal perspective and considering recent history, lawmakers have approached UAS by adopting the existing framework of "traditional" aviation, with most terms and references leading to a largely symmetrical system of rules and regulations.

The rapid development and dissemination of this new aviation technology have raised certain legal issues that must be considered purely from a theoretical perspective.

[1] On this topic see Scott (2022); Masutti and Tomasello (2018); Mendes de Leon and Scott (2016); Fellner and Zawistowski (2021); Konert and Kasprzyk (2021); Bustos Moreno (2025).

2 The EU Regulations on Drone Operators

The EU Commission Implementing Regulation 2019/947 represents a significant milestone in the governance of Unmanned Aircraft Systems (UAS) within the European Union. As a key element of the Single European Sky initiative, the regulation aims to replace a fragmented collection of national laws with a harmonised, risk-based framework that applies across all Member States. Its central philosophy is one of proportionality, adjusting regulatory burdens to the specific risks associated with each operation, thereby encouraging innovation while safeguarding the safety of people, property on the ground, and other aircraft in the air.

According to Regulation 2019/947, the UAS operator is regarded as the key entity responsible for the overall safety, compliance, and legal status of any UAS operation. This role is seen as the main center of organisational responsibility, dedicated to establishing and sustaining the entire system within which safe flights can take place.

Article 2 of the regulation defines the 'UAS operator' as "any legal or natural person operating or intending to operate one or more UAS." The deliberate inclusion of both "legal" persons (e.g., corporations, government agencies, NGOs) and "natural" persons (e.g., individual hobbyists, sole traders) is a fundamental concept and an adaptation to the realities of the drone market. Unlike traditional commercial aviation, where the operator is almost solely a complex legal entity such as an airline, the UAS ecosystem is understood to consist of a wide range of users. The definition provided by the regulation is therefore designed to be scalable, applying the same principles (and rules) whether the operator is a multinational logistics company managing a fleet of delivery drones or a photographer operating a single device for commercial purposes.

A drone operator must be registered with the National Aviation Authority of their Member State, where a natural person resides or where a legal entity has its principal place of business. It is explicitly forbidden to be registered in more than one Member State at the same time. This means that the operator registration establishes a clear line of accountability to a specific person or entity other than the pilot.

A key objective of the regulation is to facilitate seamless cross-border operations, achieved by ensuring that the UAS operator registration number is valid throughout the entire EU.

UAS.OPEN.050 and UAS.SPEC.050 of the regulation's Annex outline the responsibilities assigned to the UAS operator. These sections establish a series of systemic and comprehensive rules that assign a central role to the operator in ensuring the safety of drone operations.

In this context, the operator must establish and maintain procedures tailored to the specific type of operation and its associated risks, including an operation manual for 'specific' category flights, which serves as the relevant safety document.

On the other hand, he must formally designate a remote pilot ensuring that he is entitled for the mission (certification, competence, etc.) and that all other personnel involved in the operation are adequately trained.

The regulation also states that the operator must ensure that the unique registration number is visibly displayed on every UAS in operation and that the aircraft is maintained in a condition suitable for safe flight.

From an operational perspective, the operator should conduct a risk assessment of the planned operation. Let us suppose that the activity fails to meet the strict criteria of the 'Open' category. In that case, the operator must apply for an operational authorisation from their National Aviation Authority to operate in the 'Specific' category.

Meanwhile, the operator must ensure that the UAS geo-awareness system is updated with information about any relevant UAS geographical zones (such as no-fly zones) for the planned location of operation.

The highlighted legal framework places the operator in a role akin to the "accountable manager" within a traditional airline's Safety Management System (SMS). The responsibilities assigned—developing procedures, ensuring personnel competence, conducting risk assessments, and securing insurance—are not tactical, in-flight duties but systemic, long-term, organisational tasks. This mirrors the function of an airline operator, which is held accountable for the overall safety framework, including maintenance programmes and crew training, rather than the piloting of a single aircraft. As a result, the 'UAS operator' is legally defined not just as a user or owner but as a figure with a critical role in the accountability of the entire system of operation, which must at least ensure safety and compliance on the large scale envisaged for the drone market and industry.

3 The UAS Pilot-in-Command. The Legal Basis of the Pilot-in-Command Concept

As has been stated, while the UAS operator bears organisational responsibility, the remote pilot is the designated person responsible for the actual flight.

Annex 1 (and also Annex 2 and 6) to the ICAO Convention defines pilot-in-command (PIC) as "The pilot designated by the operator, or in the case of general aviation, the owner, as being in command and charged with the safe conduct of a flight", and the exact definition recurs in almost all other regulations at different levels.[2]

But this definition of PIC, its legal meaning and its content are not as clear as they seem.[3]

It is important to note that this definition was developed after a detailed evolution prior to the adoption of ICAO Annex 1.

The starting point was the Paris Convention of 1919, which established the general principle that "in case the operating crew of an aircraft is composed of more than one member, one of them shall be in command".[4]

---

[2] See La Torre (1997).

[3] See also Dilk (1987); Goodman et al. (1997).

[4] Annex E, paragraph 39.

In 1930, CITEJA[5] began to discuss a draft Convention on the Status of the Aircraft Commander within a specific framework.[6]

First of all, for the specialised committee, it was important that every aircraft had a commander, a method for appointment, and a succession plan in case of injury or incapacity. The commander had to have the authority to command-and-control persons on board as well as to do what was necessary to expedite the voyage - procure supplies and repairs essential for the voyage; and if a crew member dropped out, hire a suitable man to complete the voyage. His command of the crew began at a certain point: when they embarked, and continued until the formalities of arrival were completed, or until he was relieved by another commander.

Compared to maritime navigation, CITEJA considered at that time that there should be public notice that the commander could not do certain things such as sell, pledge, or mortgage the aircraft, perform marriages, or act as a notary. Still, from a public law perspective, the commander, according to CITEJA, should be allowed to go to the consul of any nation whose nationals were interested in the aircraft, its managers, cargo, or passengers and record births and deaths on board.

From a practical perspective, the drafted convention did not specify any competency tests for commanders.

In terms of application, the drafted convention would have applied to international flights of aircraft registered in a state that ratified, adhered to, or was the owner of the aircraft, and that was a national of such a state. In contrast, it did not cover military, customs, or police aircraft.

Despite the efforts made, aviation stakeholders (IATA, above all) highlighted that an international legal instrument dealing with the "aircraft commander" was unnecessary, since many of the subjects included in the draft already seemed to be covered by the carrier's conditions of carriage, personnel regulations, and employment contracts.

At that time, during the discussion of the drafted convention, another interesting point emerged, specifically the dual role of the aircraft commander as a "public entity" and at the same time as a crew member.

Regarding this issue, it has been observed that the discipline and arrangements of the flight personnel under the working contract remained within the jurisdiction of national laws and, as such, were not subject to any international regulations.

According to art. 1 of the draft convention, the requirement to have a "commander" was limited to international flights, where it was important to facilitate air navigation in general and to enable the aircraft commander to understand the extent and purpose of his powers without referring to different national legislations. This made the adoption of some universally accepted regulations more urgent.

Although most national laws referred to the "aircraft commander", the term "pilot-in-command" was found only in the legislation of Australia, Cuba, the Dominican Republic, Panama, and the United States. In the case of the United States, it referred to 14 CFR § 1.1, which states:

---

[5] Comité International Technique d'Experts Juridiques Aériens (CITEJA).

[6] For an historical perspective see Giannini (1943–48); Iaccarino (1936); Maschino (1930).

Pilot in command means the person who:

(1) *Has final authority and responsibility for the operation and safety of the flight;*
(2) *Has been designated as pilot in command before or during the flight; and*
(3) *Holds the appropriate category, class, and type rating, if appropriate, for the conduct of the flight.*

Beyond the terminology and according to early legal scholarship, there was the idea to consider the aircraft commander as distinct from the technical personnel responsible for handling the aircraft, and superior to the latter.

It has been pointed out that "*Il arrivera que dans un cas difficile, dans une situation critique, le pilote sera obligé de manoeuvrer rapidement, et ses manoeuvres seront par les responsabilités qu'il aura. Dans ces cas, genées il importe qu'il y ait un commandant, il y a intéret à ce que celui qui est responsable de la manoeuvre ne soit pas celui qui l'exécute. Ceci est tout à fait important*".[7]

Initially, economic considerations suggested that the appointment of a commander should be optional to prevent placing an unnecessary burden on airline operators.

Conversely, during that period, advancements in air navigation and safety requirements necessitated the mandatory appointment of a commander, also considering an aircraft's size and the distance to be travelled.

Also, it has been considered whether it was suitable to create an aircraft commander as a distinct person, non-pilot, and therefore never directly engaged in the technical handling of the aircraft.

In this context, the I.F.A.L.P.A. previously proposed this suggestion and outlined its functions as follows: supervisory capacity and complete control over the other crew members, without actively participating in navigation or other duties performed by the operating crew.

The efforts by the legal community (CITJEA) was handed over to the ICAO Legal Committee, but the initial interest shown resulted in the project being abandoned.

Moving to the core of the topic, we can affirm that the definition found in the United States legislation (see above) is the closest to that of the ICAO Convention, which has been repeated in European Union legislation.[8]

Legal scholarship on the issue has concluded that the regulatory pilot-in-command concept originated in the military and served as the foundation for the responsibility assumed by military pilots. *The concept recognises that only the pilot in command of the aircraft in flight knows their limitations and responsibilities.*[9] Such duties include a pre-flight inspection of the plane, pre-flight planning, evaluation of the weather, and maintenance of flight currency requirements.

This interpretation is the outcome of the close connection between the position of aircraft commander and the air traffic control system, and the consideration that the pilot has taken care of his responsibilities during the entire flight (even before take-off and after landing).

---

[7] Vivent, Compte Rendu des Réunions de la 4ème Commission, Mai 1930, C.I.T.E.J.A. Doc.37, 11.

[8] See Havel and Sanchez (2014); Mendes de Leon (2017); Milde (2023); Shawcross and Beaumont (updated).

[9] McChesney Goodman et al. (1997), p. 663.

Furthermore, the ATC system is based on the premise that pilots will do precisely what Regulations require, and that they will not need a timely reminder as to what such rules require. In other words, it has been said that "*If controllers could not rely on such assumptions, aviation would generally come to a halt*".[10]

Based on these considerations, legal scholarship has extensively relied on the role and position of the qualified pilot-in-command as the person in charge of other crew members.

For example, the decision to turn back, divert to an alternative airport, or land or not land in adverse weather conditions, etc., must rest with one person—the most highly trained individual onboard, with up-to-date knowledge of the procedures and practices relevant to the situation. No employer, company officer or shareholder should be able to override his judgment.

These assumptions led to the conclusion that it is not just a matter of the safety of a single aeroplane but a concern for the overall safety of all aviation users and society as a whole.

The evolution and growth of air transport during the 1960s also led to the consideration that there may be circumstances where a non-pilot aircraft commander could become indispensable onboard. He would be called upon to control and supervise the flight, which becomes a crucial task when the aircraft is operated far from its usual station on international routes. The commander's functions would therefore be limited to general supervision of navigation and piloting, technical services, passengers, and cargo handling.

Apart from the above considerations, according to the traditional approach, the pilot-in-command is ultimately responsible for the safety of their aircraft because only they have access to the flight controls.

In other words, it seems that in aviation, contrary to what happens with sea-going vessels, where the master has: (a) exclusive control of manoeuvres and navigation; (b) acts as the operator's representative; and (c) exercises powers granted by law towards persons with an interest in the aircraft and cargo, only one person on board the aircraft is responsible for its management, and such powers cannot be exercised in conjunction with others, nor can they be relinquished. However, this does not mean that these powers must be exercised personally by the commander throughout the entire flight, as is mandated for the ship's captain (article 298 of the Italian Code of Navigation).

Consequently, the pilot-in-command appears to respond to the need to distinguish between the person responsible for the aircraft's piloting and those who provide "assistance" to the manoeuvres (e.g., air traffic controllers).

As we will observe, this situation differs somewhat in UAS, where in most of its uses and categories (according to EU classification), the pilot/commander personally carries out all the flight (and control) activities.

Regulation 2019/947 clearly defines the remote pilot's role (and not the remote-pilot-in-command but the tasks assigned to him allow us to assume that there is no difference in terms of legal meaning) skills, and in-flight responsibilities, designating them as the ultimate authority for ensuring safe operations.

---

[10] Dilk (1987), p. 800.

The 'remote pilot' is defined as the natural person responsible for safely conducting the flight of a UAS, either by manually operating its flight controls or, in the case of automatic flights, by monitoring its course and being able to intervene at any time. This role is legally distinct from the UAS operator, although in many cases, particularly for individuals and sole traders, the same person will fulfil both roles.

To achieve an appropriate safety level, Regulation 2019/947 establishes a specific competency framework based on the type of operational risk and designed, as previously mentioned, for scalability. It also allows for "consumers" to participate in low-risk activities while maintaining strict standards for more complex operations.

In the "open category" (subcategory A1/A3), a remote pilot must complete an online training course and then pass an online theoretical knowledge examination. In contrast, in the subcategory A2, the pilot must first possess A1/A3 proof of training and then pass a more comprehensive theoretical knowledge examination.

On the other hand, for operations in the "specific category", the remote pilot must obtain operational authorisation after completing training that covers a wider range of skills, including the ability to apply complex operational procedures and manage aeronautical communications.

In short, the framework established by Reg. 2019/947 creates a complex hierarchy of qualifications where the legal validity of a flight operation is not only related to the pilot's certificate but also to the specific class identification label (C0-C4) of the drone being used.

From an operational perspective, sections UAS.OPEN.060 and UAS.SPEC.060 of the Annex to Reg. 2019/947 establish tasks that the remote-pilot should undertake and address, covering all phases of the operation.

In these latter terms and before the flight, the remote-pilot must ensure that their competency certificate is valid for the intended flight and stay informed about UAS geographical zones for the area of operation. The section for the "open category" also requires that the pilot conduct a visual inspection of the operational environment to identify obstacles, the presence of uninvolved persons, and other potential hazards. Meanwhile, they must also check that the UAS is in a condition suitable for safe flight and that its remote identification system is active and updated where required.

During the flight, the pilot must always maintain control of the aircraft and follow the procedures established by the UAS operator, considering all operational limitations.

In other words, Reg. 2019/947, in setting a legal (and technical) standard for remote-pilot duties, replicates principles already established for manned aviation.

4 What Does the Future Hold for the UAS Pilot-in-Command?

With the introduction of UAS technologies, the main technical innovation is that the remote-pilot is no longer onboard the aircraft, as it is operated remotely.

The operational characteristics of Unmanned Aircraft Systems (UAS), as outlined in frameworks such as Regulation (EU) 2019/947, necessitate a fundamental legal re-evaluation of the traditional concept of the pilot-in-command.

This raises the question of whether the already established concept of PIC still applies to the remote PIC or if a new idea needs to be developed.

As we have observed, the operator is responsible for the operations and must take any suitable actions to guarantee the safety of the operations. The operator also assigns a remote pilot for each flight (this provision is currently only available for the "open" and "specific" categories).

A primary consideration is the distribution of operational control involved in remote piloting. While not having an onboard pilot does not eliminate the legal requirement to designate someone responsible for flight safety and third-party liability, the operational approach is substantially different. Scenarios might include multiple licensed pilots, supervisors, and operator representatives who are co-located or situated in different geographical locations, all potentially able to influence the flight. This spread of control challenges the traditional idea of a single, localised commander. The remote nature of the flight means several actors could have direct access to flight controls (i.e., various qualified persons—operator, PIC, etc.—could be in the same room), raising complex legal questions about how command is transferred and where the final authority lies at any given moment.

This new operational reality reduces the traditional content of the pilot-in-command concept. Many historic functions, such as exercising public powers or managing international flight protocols, become less relevant or are taken on by the operator, diminishing the commander's role. This reduction in traditional duties highlights the need to clearly distinguish between the technical aspect of flying—the physical act of piloting—and the broader legal authority of command. Making such a distinction would, in turn, require a fundamental re-assessment of the legal frameworks of liability and responsibility, redefining the core meaning of the "command" role in law.

Furthermore, the idea of command for UAS must be placed within the context of emerging air traffic management systems like U-Space. In some operational environments, a UAS crew might be given the authority to plan and carry out flights flexibly, giving the pilot full responsibility for traffic separation. Conversely, in other situations, the pilot works within the strict limits set by an Air Traffic Service (ATS) provider, which fundamentally defines the extent of their command authority.

Additional complexities, such as the composition of the UAS flight crew and the rising prevalence of advanced automation, add to these considerations. The legal framework must be adaptable enough to support in-flight command handovers between pilots and the piloting functions carried out by automated or artificial intelligence systems. How the distinction between technical conduct and legal command is defined will directly influence the roles, responsibilities, and structure of the UAS crew.

Ultimately, these factors suggest that applying traditional aviation rules to the UAS pilot-in-command may require a significant paradigm shift. The legal concept of a single commander, designed for manned aviation, appears incompatible with the distributed, disaggregated, and technologically mediated nature of modern UAS operations. Therefore, a new legal framework might be necessary to properly assign authority, responsibility, and liability in a way that reflects these new operational realities.

In this context, the current provisions within the European aviation framework, such as Annex V of Regulation (EU) 2018/1139 and ORO.FC.105 of Regulation (EU) 965/2012, may be inadequate to address the task. Therefore, it is advisable that the definition and responsibilities of the 'remote pilot-in-command' be explicitly codified within relevant regulations.

Also, the principle of "univocity of command," which states that a single human individual must hold ultimate authority and responsibility for the safe conduct of a flight throughout its entire duration, could be challenged, particularly during very long endurance missions that surpass standard flight duty limits.

Looking towards the future, it is conceivable that increasing levels of automation will trigger a shift in command responsibility. Depending on the aircraft's design and its Concept of Operations (CONOPS), accountability could be transferred from the remote pilot to other entities, such as the Air Traffic Management (ATM) system or even the Original Equipment Manufacturer (OEM). This potential evolution highlights a vital need for a standardised, uniform methodology for measuring and classifying different levels of automation. Such a framework would be crucial for correctly appointing the individual or entity that holds PIC responsibility, ensuring they are granted the necessary authority and situational awareness for a given operational context.

The picture emphasises the necessity for a clear separation between the technical activity of ensuring a safe flight and other tasks undertaken by different individuals.

This could lead to the emergence of the role of "pilot-not-in-command" as a qualified, licensed individual responsible solely for conducting the manoeuvres of the UAS. The commander, also skilled, would have the role of overseeing flight activities, ensuring the safety of the UAS, handing it over if necessary, and managing private and public responsibilities. The commander would also bear the third-party responsibility for "pilot-not-in-command" activities.

A potential scheme could be considered in maritime pilotage, where the pilot acts solely as technical support, leaving the master with legal responsibility.

The "pilot-not-in-command" and the "commander" could be the same person (and also be the operator), or it could be assumed that there is one "commander" for several "pilots-not-in-command".

Considering this from a theoretical perspective, the evolution of the 'pilot-in-command' concept appears to support the above solution, as even at the dawn of modern civil aviation, scholars questioned the wholesale application of the maritime concept of commander and the need to clearly distinguish between the "command" and the 'manoeuvres' components in flight activities.

This new figure could be integrated into the existing regulatory framework, enabling, in this view, the full realisation of the practical opportunities offered by UAS and supporting their safe integration into society.

5 UAS Crew: The Lost Definition

UAS operations—as depicted in the regulatory framework and as in practice—demonstrate clear signs of complexity, which are increasingly involving more than a single remote pilot.

Examining activities in the "specific" and "certified" categories requires a team of individuals fulfilling essential roles. However, the regulatory framework of 2019/947 introduces a notable legal ambiguity in this area because it does not define 'crew', a term that is pivotal to the organisation of manned aviation as part of essential flight operations. This sharply contrasts with traditional aviation regulations, where the roles, responsibilities, and qualifications of 'flight crew' (pilots, flight engineers) and 'cabin crew' are clearly outlined. The absence of this definition could create a legal grey area regarding the status and accountability of personnel supporting the remote pilot.

To be more precise, the Annex of Reg. 2019/947, in section UAS.SPEC.050(e) refers to "personnel in charge of duties essential to the UAS operation, other than the remote pilot itself." As we have seen, the regulation places responsibility for the competence of these individuals squarely on the UAS operator, who must ensure that the "personnel" completes on-the-job training developed by the operator, is informed about the UAS operator's operations manual and procedures relevant to their duties and obtains updated information about any relevant geographical zones.

This legal approach demonstrates significant flexibility in adopting a risk-based model that informs the entire regulatory framework.

It is indeed possible to handle UAS operations with a single person (i.e., the "open category subcategory A1" in VLOS mode), as well as with a complex BVLOS mission involving multiple observers, a payload operator, and a ground station manager.

From this perspective, it is evident that a prescriptive definition of 'flight crew' would be disproportionate and impractical for most operations, while, on the other hand, it leaves the responsibility to the operator to define the necessary team roles and competencies as part of their operational risk assessment and operations manual. The absence of a universal definition of 'crew' thus represents a key aspect of the regulation's principle of proportionality, transferring the burden of definition from the regulator to the operator.

The practical solution provided by EU Reg. 2019/947 has also highlighted the need to define other entities with specific supporting roles.

In these terms, the regulation describes the Unmanned Aircraft Observer as the person who assists the remote pilot by maintaining continuous, unaided visual contact with the unmanned aircraft. The primary role is to support the remote pilot in fulfilling the "see and avoid" principle by monitoring the aircraft's position relative to other aircraft, people, and obstacles, especially when the pilot may need to concentrate on the command unit. The remote pilot is explicitly required to maintain "clear and effective communication" with any observers involved in the operation.

Along with this subject, we could consider, as part of the UAS crew and based on interpretation of Reg. 2019/947, the airspace observer as a person who visually scans the airspace (rather than the drone itself) to detect potential hazards, such as other air traffic. This role is particularly critical for enabling BVLOS operations where the remote pilot cannot see the surrounding environment, while the payload operator is responsible for managing the instruments, sensors, or other equipment carried by the UAS that are not essential for flight control.

The flexibility caused by not having a strict definition of 'crew', on the one hand, results in positive outcomes for adaptation and scalability; on the other hand, it risks creating a "liability system' crisis that the UAS operator must proactively address.

In the event of an incident caused by a supporting team member's error—for example, an unmanned aircraft observer failing to spot a conflicting aircraft—the allocation of liability becomes complicated, as the operator, according to the examined regulation, is responsible for training and procedures for these personnel. The pilot is responsible for effective communication with them.

This shared task of oversight could lead to complex legal questions. Is the observer merely an 'assistant' acting under the pilot's complete authority and liability? Or does the observer hold a degree of independent responsibility for their designated task?

The regulation does not explicitly address this, as it appears that these aspects are delegated to operators who must define all the roles, responsibilities, communication protocols, and emergency procedures for supporting personnel within the operations manual and through contractual agreements. These documents, in short, may become key evidence in any subsequent investigation or litigation, filling the liability gap left open by the regulation.

6 Evaluation from the Perspective of ICAO Annex 6, Part IV

While Regulation (EU) 2019/947 offers a comprehensive framework for the European single market, it is important to assess it against emerging global standards established by the International Civil Aviation Organisation (ICAO). The adoption of Annex 6, Part IV—*International Operations – Remotely Piloted Aircraft Systems*—in March 2024 marks a significant milestone, creating the first international Standards and Recommended Practices (SARPs) specifically for RPAS. Scheduled to take effect in November 2026, this section of Annex 6 provides a benchmark for evaluating the EU's efforts towards global harmonisation.

ICAO Annex 6, Part IV, shares several aspects with the EU UAS regulation, as both frameworks are built on a risk-based, operation-centric foundation and an operator-centric responsibility model, moving away from a one-size-fits-all approach towards one that is proportional to the specific operation's risk.

The clear indication of this common approach is evident in the fact that the EU's three-tiered risk categorisation ('Open', 'Specific', and 'Certified') is conceptually reflected in the ICAO framework, which also acknowledges the necessity for varying levels of regulatory oversight depending on operational complexity and risk.

For UAS activities classified as international flights, the ICAO Annex specifies that operators must obtain an RPAS Operator Certificate (ROC). This document can be seen as similar to the Air Operator Certificate (AOC) in manned aviation, requiring a comprehensive Safety Management System (SMS) and effective state oversight. These provisions align with the EU's requirements for operators in the 'Specific' and 'Certified' categories, who are obliged to obtain operational authorisation (or a Light UAS Operator Certificate—LUC) based on thorough risk assessment and an operation manual that serves as the foundation of their safety system.

Despite the "cultural" alignment, a key difference appears in how personnel are defined and regulated. ICAO, through Annex 1 (*Personnel Licensing*), offers clear and specific definitions for the entire team, including the 'Remote pilot', 'Remote pilot-in-command', 'Remote co-pilot', and 'Remote flight crew member'. This creates a standardised international classification and an official structure for team-based operations, clarifying roles and responsibilities within a multi-person crew. It contrasts sharply with Regulation 2019/947, which, as previously discussed, does not provide a formal definition for 'crew'.

Since international, complex operations involving multi-person crews could become more common, this situation might cause friction with the global standard, leading to interoperability challenges and legal uncertainty in cross-border scenarios.

Regarding flight operations, while the EU has established a detailed, tiered system of competency certificates aimed at the mass market in the 'Open' category, reserving formal licensing for the highest-risk 'Certified' category, the scope of ICAO Annex 6, Part IV, requires a formal Remote Pilot Licence (RPL) for international IFR flights, based on the existing Commercial Pilot Licence (CPL) and focusing on competency-based training.

Considering these points, it appears that although both systems are essentially competency-based and proportionate to risk, the EU model is more accessible at the lower levels, enabling wider participation. Conversely, ICAO's RPL establishes a higher, more consistent standard for professional international operations.

The EU's approach can be regarded as a practical realisation that covers the entire range of the drone market. Meanwhile, the ICAO standard concentrates on the requirements for incorporating RPAS into the same airspace and traffic management systems as manned commercial aircraft.

From a purely legal theoretical perspective, the European Union's decision not to establish a formal definition for 'crew' represents a notable deviation from the ICAO model. This may necessitate future amendments to ensure seamless integration and legal clarity for operators seeking to compete within a globally harmonised aviation ecosystem.

7 UAS Operator, PIC, and Crew. The Autonomous Frontier: Evolving Roles and Liability in the Age of AI

The legal framework at the EU and international levels, based on a human-centric model involving an operator and a pilot, is already confronted by highly autonomous and AI-driven UAS. This significant technological shift challenges existing ideas of control and responsibility.

The regulation itself anticipates this future by making a key distinction between 'automatic' and 'autonomous' operations. An 'automatic' operation involves a drone following a pre-programmed route, but the remote pilot remains responsible and must be able to intervene to deal with unexpected events. In contrast, an 'autonomous' operation is one where the UAS can operate "without the remote pilot being able to intervene," using AI to manage unforeseen circumstances and safely complete the mission.

Recognising the immense complexity and risk, the regulation prohibits fully autonomous operations in the low-risk 'Open' category. However, it explicitly allows them in the 'Specific' and 'Certified' categories, provided the operator can demonstrate to the competent authority through rigorous risk assessment that the operation is safe. This provision serves as a legal gateway for the introduction of AI.

These aspects challenge traditional roles. If an AI makes real-time safety decisions—such as performing a collision avoidance manoeuvre or selecting an emergency landing site—who is the 'remote pilot'? The human's role may shift from directly controlling the aircraft to acting as a 'system supervisor' or 'mission commander,' overseeing the AI's performance remotely. This potential shift will affect the responsibility framework for the flight, with clear implications for the traditional concept of a pilot-in-command.

8 Conclusion

The legal framework concerning the UAS operator, pilot-in-command, and crew shows several adaptations from that governing manned aviation. The risk-based approach and the legal distinction between the systemic responsibilities of the UAS operator and the operational duties of the remote pilot ensure safety and accountability, while also providing the necessary scalability and flexibility to manage a diverse and rapidly expanding industry.

However, the rapid evolution of technology applied to UAS has also uncovered significant points of friction and future challenges. The effectiveness of regulation is tested by the legal ambiguity surrounding supporting 'crew' roles, which imposes a heavy burden on operators to define these functions through internal governance. Most notably, the entire human-centric framework is set for disruption with the advent of AI and autonomous systems, which will require a paradigm shift in how control, responsibility, and liability are understood and adjudicated.

Drafting a comprehensive operations manual that carefully defines the roles, responsibilities, and communication protocols for all personnel involved in an operation, including observers and other supporting members, plays a significant role in ensuring accountability. Simultaneously, establishing clear procedures, maintaining thorough training and maintenance records, and documenting all aspects of their activities strengthen the positions of those involved. For those exploring autonomous capabilities, it is essential to begin engaging with the principles of the EU AI Act (Reg. 2024/1689), embedding "trustworthiness by design" into systems from the outset, which will be vital in mitigating future legal and financial risks.

International and Intergovernmental Materials (ICAO, CITEJA, IFALPA)

- C.I.T.E.J.A. Rapport sur la situation juridique du commandant." Doc. 17. [1930s]
- International Civil Aviation Organisation (ICAO). Annex 1 to the Convention on International Civil Aviation: Personnel Licensing. Montreal: ICAO, current ed.
- International Civil Aviation Organisation (ICAO) Annex 2 to the Convention on International Civil Aviation: Rules of the Air. Montreal: ICAO, current ed.
- International Civil Aviation Organisation (ICAO) Annex 6 to the Convention on International Civil Aviation: Operation of Aircraft, Part IV – International Operations – Remotely Piloted Aircraft Systems (RPAS). Montreal: ICAO, adopted 2024; applicable November 2026.
- International Civil Aviation Organisation (ICAO) Circular 328 (AN/190): Unmanned Aircraft Systems (UAS). Montreal: ICAO, 2011.
- International Civil Aviation Organisation (ICAO) Manual on Remotely Piloted Aircraft Systems (RPAS) (Doc 10019). 1st ed. Montreal: ICAO, 2015 (with subsequent amendments).
- ICAO, Legal Committee. First Session (Brussels, 1947), Doc. 4635, LC/71. Montreal: ICAO, 1947.
- ICAO, Legal Committee. Second Session (Geneva, 1948), Doc. 6014, LC/111. Montreal: ICAO, 1948.
- ICAO, Legal Committee. Seventh Session (Mexico City, 1951), Doc. 7157, LC/130. Montreal: ICAO, 1951.
- International Federation of Air Line Pilots' Associations (IFALPA). Resolutions Adopted in April 1950. In ICAO Doc. 7157-LC/130, 326–27.
- IFALPA. Proceedings of the Eighth Annual Conference (Chicago, April 1953); and ICAO documents C-WP/1805; AN-WP/1219; AN-WP/1375; C-WP/1805; AN-WP/1392; C-WP/2103; C-WP/2202; C-WP/2202 Addendum; CC-WD/542.
- Vivent. "Compte rendu des réunions de la 4e Commission (mai 1930)." C.I.T.E.J.A. Doc. 37.

Standards, Guidance, and Technical Frameworks

- European Union Aviation Safety Agency (EASA). Easy Access Rules for Unmanned Aircraft Systems (consolidated AMC/GM for Regs (EU) 2019/947 and 2019/945). Cologne: EASA, current ed.
- Joint Authorities for Rulemaking on Unmanned Systems (JARUS). Guidelines on Specific Operations Risk Assessment (SORA), JAR-DOC-06. Latest public version.
- SESAR Joint Undertaking. U-space Blueprint. Brussels: SESAR JU, 2017.
- Concept of Operations (CORUS) for U-space. Brussels: SESAR JU, latest ed.

European Union Legislation (Official Journal)

- European Union. Commission Delegated Regulation (EU) 2019/945 of 12 March 2019 on unmanned aircraft systems and on third-country operators of unmanned aircraft systems. Official Journal of the European Union L 152 (11 June 2019): 1-40.
- European Union. Commission Implementing Regulation (EU) 2019/947 of 24 May 2019 on the rules and procedures for the operation of unmanned aircraft. Official Journal of the European Union L 152 (11 June 2019): 45-71.
- European Union. Commission Implementing Regulation (EU) 2021/664 of 22 April 2021 on a regulatory framework for the U-space. Official Journal of the European Union L 139 (23 April 2021): 161-94.
- European Union. Commission Implementing Regulation (EU) 2021/665 of 22 April 2021 amending Implementing Regulation (EU) No 923/2012 as regards requirements for manned aviation operating in U-space airspace. Official Journal of the European Union L 139 (23 April 2021): 195-201.
- European Union. Commission Implementing Regulation (EU) 2021/666 of 22 April 2021 amending Regulations (EU) 2017/373 and (EU) No 923/2012 as regards requirements for ATM/ANS and U-space service providers. Official Journal of the European Union L 139 (23 April 2021): 202-11.
- European Union. Commission Implementing Regulation (EU) No 923/2012 of 26 September 2012 laying down the common rules of the air and operational provisions regarding services and procedures in air navigation (SERA). Official Journal of the European Union L 281 (13 October 2012): 1-66.
- European Union. Commission Regulation (EU) No 965/2012 of 5 October 2012 laying down technical requirements and administrative procedures related to air operations. Official Journal of the European Union L 296 (25 October 2012): 1–148.
- European Union. Regulation (EU) 2018/1139 of the European Parliament and of the Council of 4 July 2018 on common rules in the field of civil aviation and

establishing a European Union Aviation Safety Agency. Official Journal of the European Union L 212 (22 August 2018): 1-122.
- European Union. Regulation (EC) No 785/2004 of the European Parliament and of the Council of 21 April 2004 on insurance requirements for air carriers and aircraft operators. Official Journal of the European Union L 138 (30 April 2004): 1-6.

National/Comparative Legal Materials

- Italy. Codice della Navigazione. 1942, as amended (see art. 298).
- United States. Code of Federal Regulations, Title 14—Aeronautics and Space: § 1.1 (Definitions); § 91.3 (Pilot in Command); Part 107—Small Unmanned Aircraft Systems.

Historical Treaties

- Convention Relating to the Regulation of Aerial Navigation (Paris), 13 October 1919.
- Comité International Technique d'Experts Juridiques Aériens (C.I.T.E.J.A.). Draft Convention on the Status of the Aircraft Commander. Unadopted draft texts, 1930s.

References

Books and Treatises

Havel BF, Sanchez GS (2014) The principles and practice of international aviation law. Cambridge University Press, Cambridge

La Torre U (1997) Comando e comandante nell'esecuzione della navigazione, Napoli

Masutti A, Tomasello F (2018) International regulation of non-military drones. Edward Elgar, Cheltenham

Mendes de Leon P (2017) Introduction to air law, 10th edn. Kluwer Law International, Alphen aan den Rijn

Milde M (2023) Milde's international air law and ICAO, 4th edn. Eleven International Publishing, The Hague, Revised by Attila Sipos

Scott BI (ed) (2022) The law of unmanned aircraft systems, 2nd edn. Kluwer Law International, Alphen aan den Rijn

Shawcross and Beaumont: Air Law, London: LexisNexis, loose-leaf (updated)

Chapters in Edited Volumes

Bustos Moreno Y (2025) The implementation of U-space: open challenges from the legal-private perspective. In: Governance and control of data and digital economy in the European single market. Springer, Cham, pp 489–515

Mendes de Leon P, Scott BI (2016) An analysis of unmanned aircraft systems under air law. In: Završnik A (ed) Drones and unmanned aerial systems: legal and social implications for security and surveillance. Springer, Cham, pp 49–72

Journal Articles

Dilk AJ (1987) Aviation tort litigation against the united states – judicial inroads on the pilot-in-command concept. J Air Law Commer 52:797. https://scholar.smu.edu/jalc/vol52/iss4/2

Fellner R, Zawistowski G (2021) Unmanned aircraft systems risk assessment based on SORA for first responders and disaster management. Appl Sci 11(12):5364

Goodman K et al (1997) Free flight and the pilot-in-command concept—a recipe for disaster. J Air Law Commer 62:653. https://scholar.smu.edu/jalc/vol62/iss3/5

Konert A, Kasprzyk P (2021) UAS safety operation – legal issues on reporting UAS incidents. J Intell Robotic Syst 103(3):51–66

Historical and Doctrinal Articles

Giannini A (1943) L'attività svolta del C.I.T.E.J.A. e la sua eredità. Rivista di Diritto della Navigazione 1:48

Iaccarino CM (1936) Discussioni vecchie e norme nuove sulla specialità della 'Convenzione' del capitano. Rivista di Diritto della Navigazione, ser. II:157

Maschino M (1930) La condition juridique du personnel aérien, Paris

Urban Air Mobility; Rules of Navigation and Infrastructure

Cinzia Ingratoci and Adele Marino

Contents

Abstract Urban air mobility represents the new frontier of mobility and includes operations carried out with aircrafts having vertical take-off and landing (VCA) capabilities that are employed in congested urban areas, using air and ground infrastructures integrated into a multimodal system.

The chapter will focus on the notion of Urban Air Mobility, in relation to the concepts of Advanced Air Mobility and Innovative Air Mobility.

We will then proceed with an analysis of the legislation relating to the specific operational provisions relative to the vehicles, dedicated infrastructure and flight modes.

Cinzia Ingratoci is author of Sects. 1, 2, 3, 4 and 7. Adele Marino is author of Sects. 5 and 6.

C. Ingratoci (✉)
Department of Law, University of Messina, Messina, Italy
e-mail: cinzia.ingratoci@unime.it

A. Marino
Department of Legal and Political Sciences, University of Messina, Messina, Italy
e-mail: admarino@unime.it

M. P. Rizzo, F. Franchina (eds.), *Drones in the Digital European Sky*, International Aviation Law Library 1,
https://doi.org/10.1007/978-3-032-16691-3_8

Air mobility requires ground and air infrastructures to allow VCAs to operate safely in urban centers.

International, European and national authorities are preparing the regulatory framework within which operators can invest.

Italy, through the Civil Aviation Regulatory Authority (ENAC), is investing in the use of this mobility system and on 12 June 2024 adopted a regulation on "National requirements for aircraft with vertical take-off and landing (VCA) capability and related trajectories and infrastructure".

1 Urban Air Mobility within the Framework of ITC Systems: Automation and Autonomous Vehicles

Automated and intelligent vehicles have long been the focus of particular attention from the transport industry and public policymakers (especially the European Union legislator), due to their potential to support safer and more inclusive mobility solutions. These technologies are capable of reducing major externalities—such as accidents, congestion, and pollution—while meeting the needs of a society that increasingly demands higher quality and faster services. They also play a key role in supporting growing segments of the population who require assistance with mobility.

The common framework for the implementation of intelligent transport systems in the road transport sector, as set out in Directive 2010/40/EU,[1] is of direct relevance to the regulatory regime governing interfaces with other modes of transport, including aerial mode that is expected to emerge prominently in the near future. The most recent amendments to the EU legislative text[2] aim at strengthening the shared commitment to developing an innovative intangible infrastructure that supports on-demand applications and coordinated services based on multimodal offerings (Articles 2 and 3).

The directive defines "intelligent transport systems" (hereinafter ITS) as systems in which information and communication technologies are applied in the field of road transport, including infrastructure, vehicles and users, and in traffic management and mobility management, also with regard to necessary connections with other modes of transport (Art. 4, no. 1).

When an ITS system enables users themselves (vehicles of various types, operators, and end service recipients) to interact directly by exchanging secure and reliable messages through a cooperative-type architecture, it is referred to as "Cooperative ITS (C-ITS)" (Art. 4, paragraph 1, no. 19, Directive 2010/40/EU).

---

[1] Directive (EU) 2010/40 of the European Parliament and of the Council, 7 July 2010, on the framework for the deployment of Intelligent Transport Systems in the field of road transport and for interfaces with other modes of transport.

[2] Directive (EU) 2023/2661 of the European Parliament and of the Council, 22 November 2023, amending Directive 2010/40/EU on the framework for the deployment of Intelligent Transport Systems in the field of road transport and for interfaces with other modes of transport.

Based on this definition, the core element of ITS lies in the interoperability of the technologies and processes that support it—technologies capable of ensuring real-time data exchange and providing the operator (or the vehicle, in the case of full automation or machine learning) with appropriate decisions based on constantly updated and highly detailed situational awareness.

"Multimodal digital mobility services" provide information on traffic and travel components such as the location of transport facilities, schedules, availability, or fares for multiple modes of transport. They also enable the booking or purchase of tickets, including integrated or combined ticketing solutions (Art. 4, paragraph 1, no. 24, Directive 2010/40/EU).

They define a shared functional space supporting the movement of people and goods, which underpins the concept of Mobility as a Service (MaaS). MaaS refers to a digital service that allows users to plan their journey by booking all necessary transport segments to reach their final destination through a single platform.

The organization of mobility services, based on connections between the various actors in the system and the exchange of real-time information, is referred to as *smart mobility*[3]: a set of solutions aimed at improving the efficiency, cost-effectiveness, and sustainability of travel through structural and functional innovations such as the sharing economy, on-demand rentals, low-emission and increasingly technological vehicles, micromobility, and multimodality.[4]

Vehicles (and infrastructure) can be equipped with various levels of technology—not necessarily requiring full autonomy—although the benefits offered by artificial intelligence (AI) applications form an integral part of the model.

According to the classification adopted by the U.S. National Highway Traffic Safety Administration (NHTSA) in 2016,[5] six levels of automation can be identified, starting from level "0", which refers to traditional vehicles where all driving operations are performed solely by a human driver.

At level one, driver assistance systems are present—such as adaptive cruise control or assisted braking—but a driver is always on board and remains fully responsible for vehicle operation.

Level two indicates *partial automation*, a now widespread condition in which technology assists the driver and may assume control of the vehicle in specific, limited situations.

---

[3] Communication from the EU Commission on 'Sustainable and Smart Mobility Strategy—Putting European Transport on Track for the Future', COM (2020) 789 final.

[4] Communication from the EU Commission on "*EU Green Deal* ", 11 December 2019, COM (2019) 640 final.

[5] USA Department of Transportation - National Highway Traffic Safety Administration -NHTSA, *Guidelines for the development and deployment of driverless vehicles*, 2016; Cf. pure ONU, *Economic and Social Council*, *Reference document with definitions of Automated Driving* (WP.29) and the *General Principles for developing a UN Regulation on automated vehicles*, 23 April 2018, *World Forum for Harmonization of Vehicle Regulations*and the General Principles for developing a UN Regulation on automated vehicles, 23 April 2018, World Forum for Harmonization of Vehicle Regulations. For more information see: Brodsky (2016), p. 851; Bruno (2024), p. 286; Butti (2016), p. 435; Casadei and Zanetti (2020), p. 41; Comenale Pinto and Rosafio (2019), p. 395; Crane et al. (2017); Vantin (2019), 55 ss.; Ferrazzano (2019); Pollastrelli (2020), 109 ss.; Ilková and Ilka (2017); AA.VV (2019).

Level three refers to *conditional automation*, where the vehicle can perform some driving tasks under the general supervision and control of the human driver.

Level four involves *high automation* for several driving modes. The vehicle can steer, brake, accelerate, etc., but does not make dynamic decisions, and therefore is not considered fully autonomous.

Level five, currently in the experimental phase, provides for *full automation* in all driving modes, enabling the vehicle to make autonomous decisions based on situational data. In this case, the vehicle is defined as "autonomous".

The use of such vehicles in urban environments is currently in the deployment phase in the ground transport sector, with limited application to aerial vehicles (drones) for cargo services.

However, the severe traffic congestion and environmental degradation in urban areas—now critical issues for major global cities—have challenged traditional passenger transport by road or rail, pointing to a potential solution in the aerial mode, supported by recent technological advancements in both manned and unmanned vehicles.

Urban air mobility (UAM) is therefore expected to become "an integral part of the future smart, multimodal urban mobility ecosystem, with ground and air infrastructure enabling these transport services become widespread and fully integrated".[6]

2 Definitions of *Advanced Air Mobility* (AAM), *Innovative Air Mobility* (IAM) e *Urban Air Mobility* (UAM)

Although it is still a mobility model in the process of being defined—particularly from a regulatory standpoint—it is widely believed that UAM will play a fundamental role in addressing the growing demand for urban transportation in the coming years.

The idea of using flying vehicles for intra-city travel is, in fact, not entirely new. An aerial mobility system serving short routes over inhabited areas has existed since the early twentieth century, although it has been limited to special transport services. Later, between the 1940s and 1950s, helicopters emerged as a promising mode of transport for interurban services. However, their widespread use was hindered by high costs, excessive noise, and safety concerns, which confined their application mainly to work-related and medical logistics activities. Moreover, the potential for integrating these vehicles into ground mobility systems—or their ability to perform specific segments of a multimodal journey—has been virtually non-existent.

Technical and regulatory advancements toward the goals of advanced and innovative air mobility now make it possible to support a more efficient urban air transport system.

[6]Communication from the Commission to the EU Parliament, the Council, The European Economic and Social Committee and the Committee of the Regions on 'A Drone Strategy 2.0 for a Smart and Sustainable Unmanned Aircraft Eco-System in Europe' COM (2022) 652, final, § 18.

Advanced Air Mobility (AAM) refers to air transportation that is capable of transporting people and goods between locations not currently served by conventional aviation, through the use of specialized aircraft and the automation of specific functions.

The concept, originally developed by the U.S. National Aviation Authority, was later adopted by the Federal Aviation Administration (hereinafter FAA)[7]: the Advanced Air Mobility Coordination and Leadership Act (P.L. 117–203, 136 Stat. 2227, dated October 17, 2022) defines AAM as *"a transportation system that moves people and property by air between two points in the United States (U.S.) using aircraft with advanced technologies, including electric aircraft, or electric vertical take-off and landing (eVTOL) aircraft, in both controlled and uncontrolled airspace"*.

Thus, it does not refer to a single innovation, but rather to a set of high-tech solutions applied to the aviation ecosystem. Another defining feature of AAM is its intermodal perspective, aimed at improving territorial accessibility, environmental quality, and citizen safety in the most efficient and effective way possible.

AAM constitutes the overarching architecture within which specific Innovative Air Mobility (IAM) solutions are integrated. The term IAM refers to the various components of a new mobility system designed to revolutionize transportation, by integrating next-generation aerial vehicles—such as drones and electric vertical take-off and landing (eVTOL) aircraft—into existing infrastructure.[8] IAM enables the testing of passenger and cargo air transport even in densely populated and built-up environments, thanks to automated navigation systems and alternatives to traditional aircraft that offer greater manoeuvrability and reduced environmental impact.

The *European Air Safety Agency* (EASA)[9] defines IAM as "the safe, secure and sustainable air mobility of passengers and cargo enabled by new-generation technologies integrated into a multimodal transportation system",[10] once again highlighting its multimodal dimension.

[7] Senate Bill No. 516 *(Advanced Air Mobility Coordination and Leadership Act)* of the United States Congress. See also FAA, *Advanced Air Mobility Implementation Plan,* version 1.0, June 2023, in https://www.faa.gov/sites/faa.gov/files/AAM-I28-Implementation-Plan.pdf.

[8] COM (2022) 652 final, cit., point 15.

[9] Cfr. Regulation (EU) 2018/1139 of the European Parliament and of the Council, 4 July 2018, on common rules in the field of civil aviation, establishing a European Union Aviation Safety Agency, and amending Regulations (EC) No 2111/2005, (EC) No 1008/2008, (EU) No 996/2010, (EU) No 376/2014 and Directives 2014/30/EU and 2014/53/EU of the European Parliament and of the Council, and repealing Regulations (EC) No 552/2004 and (EC) No 216/2008 of the European Parliament and of the Council and Council Regulation (EEC) No 3922/91.

[10] EASA, Opinion No 03/2023 of 31 August 2023, *Introduction of a regulatory framework for the operation of drones enabling innovative air mobility with manned VTOL-capable aircraft, the initial airworthiness of those unmanned aircraft systems operated in the specific category*, 7, in https://www.easa.europa.eu/en/document-library/opinions/opinion-no-032023#. The notion is in line with the IAM vision developed by the EU Commission in the COM (2022) 652 final, point 15.

The concept of Innovative Aerial Services (IAS) is closely related and describes the various types of activities that fall within the regulatory competence of EASA, under the provisions of the Basic Regulation on aviation safety (Regulation (EU) 2018/1139). These include operations carried out with drones (such as surveillance, mapping, and others), as well as IAM.

EASA has recently developed an IAM Hub, a digital platform that brings together all actors involved in the European air transport system—including national and local authorities, manufacturers, and operators—with the goal of facilitating the safe, secure, efficient, and sustainable implementation of IAM operations.[11]

Within the scope of IAM services, UAM represents an application that is specifically dedicated to the transport of passengers and goods in urban environments.

According to the definition adopted by FAA,[12] the concept of UAM is narrowly defined as transportation in densely populated areas and is characterized by the use of a cooperative operational environment known as Extensible Traffic Management (xTM). This system is designed to integrate the provision of traditional Air Traffic Services (ATS) with functionalities tailored to small, high-tech vehicles authorized to operate in lower airspace. A broader definition of UAM is provided in the EASA document, which describes it as "a new air transportation system for passengers and cargo in and around densely populated and built environments, made possible by electrical vertical take-off and landing aircraft (e-VTOL) equipped with new technologies such as enhanced battery technologies and electrical propulsion"[13]; it is "the subset of IAM operations conducted in, within or outside of urban environments", thus, operating not only in strictly urban environments, but also in surrounding areas, with the goal of improving connectivity both within cities and in interurban zones.

Numerous scientific studies focusing on IAM applications in urban settings—funded at the European level[14] within the framework of the Single European Sky ATM Research Joint Undertaking (SESAR-JU)[15]—are developing innovative solutions for

---

[11] The platform includes five areas: drones and e-VTOL vehicles, with information on drones; electric vertical take-off and landing vehicles authorized for operations in Europe; regulatory section; fact sheets—a repository of essential knowledge, best practices, and insights; operational information and geographical data. See the website: https://www.easa.europa.eu/en/domains/drones-air-mobility/drones-air-mobility-landscape/innovative-air-mobility-hub.

[12] *Federal Aviation Administration* (FAA), *National Aeronautics and Space Administration* (NASA), *Urban Air Mobility Concept Operation* (UAM ConOps), Version 2.0, 26 April 2023, on https://www.faa.gov/sites/faa.gov/files/Urban%20Air%20Mobility%20%28UAM%29%20Concept%20of%20Operations%202.0_0.pdf.

[13] EASA, *Urban Air Mobility*, in www.easa.europa.eu/light/topics/urban-air-mobility. EASA, Opinion No 03/2023 of 31 August 2023, cit. 7. See also Booz, Allen, Hamilton (2018); Pinto Neto et al. (2022).

[14] The FF2020, AiRMOUR, and AURORA projects, funded by the EU, have formed a consortium with the goal of developing an ecosystem of urban air mobility solutions, in www.sesar.ju.

[15] Council Regulation No 219/2007 of 27 February 2007 on the establishment of a Joint Undertaking to develop the new generation European air traffic management system (SESAR), no longer in force, repealed by Council Regulation (EU) 2021/2085 of 19 November 2021 establishing the

flights conducted in lower airspace over areas not necessarily characterized by high population density, offering a dynamic interpretation of the UAM concept.

This broader view would also include on-demand passenger and cargo services, delivered through a dedicated, self-sustaining system of vehicles and infrastructure, which incorporates communication among all the different components involved.

Within this framework, a further extension of the concept includes rural areas, where ground transportation is often difficult to access and waiting and travel times are significantly longer. In response to these challenges, air transport could offer effective solutions, particularly by improving connectivity between suburbs, peripheral zones, and nearby agricultural areas.

In summary, the various interpretations of the UAM concept can be traced back (in addition to the type of vehicles used, as discussed in the following paragraph) to different approaches regarding two key aspects: a) the sector of activities; b) the horizontal and vertical boundaries of the operational space.

Regarding point a), beyond the commercial transport of passengers and goods, innovative solutions adopted within the UAM context may also support other economically significant markets, such as surveillance services, first response, emergency assistance, aerial work, and tourism.

Indeed, several studies identify numerous activity segments in which UAM could be effectively applied.

As noted in literature, "whether these business solutions are included in the definition of Urban Air Mobility or not, their operation would still take place in urban areas, requiring the coordination and cooperation of all types of vehicles carrying out the missions".[16] Thus, a broader definition of UAM is preferable with regard to the field of activity, both from an operational and a strategic standpoint.

From an operational perspective, this broader notion allows for a unified view of all vehicles operating within a given airspace, regardless of the specific activity they perform.

From a strategic viewpoint, the existence of multiple potential markets can attract greater private investment.

Regarding point b), concerning the airspace involved, the definitions previously cited appear to support a broad interpretation of UAM—one that includes not only strictly urban routes, but also connections to and from the city. These activities would involve the movement of vehicles in lower airspace over inhabited areas, whether densely or sparsely populated, and thus also include urban peripheries, expansion zones, and connecting areas.

The concept of an "urban environment" is not univocal and may vary from country to country, as well as across different scientific disciplines.

Joint Undertakings under Horizon Europe and repealing Regulations (EC) No 219/2007, (EU) No 557/2014, (EU) No 558/2014, (EU) No 559/2014, (EU) No 560/2014, (EU) No 561/2014 and (EU) No 642/2014, as amended by Council Regulation (EU) 2023/1782 of 25 July 2023 amending Regulation (EU) 2021/2085 establishing the Joint Undertakings under Horizon Europe, regarding the Chips Joint Undertaking. For more information see Ingratoci (2023).

[16] Frank et al. (2021), p. 103111. Tojal et al. (2021), p. 4. Garrow et al. (2021); Keller et al. (2021).

Beyond the issue of definition scope, the common element among all the interpretations referenced is the necessary use of innovative vehicles and solutions, essential for carrying out aerial operations in areas characterized by specific risks, requiring adaptation at environmental, economic, and social levels.

UAM represents a strategic component of sustainability policies applied to the transport sector[17] and constitutes an integral part of the Sustainable Urban Mobility Plan (SUMP), developed according to an integrated approach. Member States are encouraged to make use of tools such as SUMPs as a mechanism to integrate alternative service delivery solutions offered by UAM into urban mobility planning, and to help address mobility challenges across the entire functional urban area, also providing for synergies with spatial, energy, and climate plans.[18]

At a functional level, the planning of UAM operations requires more direct involvement of local and regional communities, both to organize services in line with citizens' mobility needs and to better assess levels of social acceptance and integration with other modes of transport, taking into account the risk mitigation systems adopted at a territorial level and the proposed solutions to reduce noise and visual pollution·[19]

The result is a flexible and evolving notion of UAM, strongly influenced by technological progress and market experimentation, capable of employing various types of vehicles to deliver multiple services—both commercial and non-commercial—within the lower airspace, across urban and interurban geographic areas.

3 The Vehicles

UAM is supported and driven by advances in Information Technology (IT), enabling vehicles to move within the so-called "third dimension" of airspace and be integrated into a multimodal system that ensures safety, comfort, environmental sustainability, and a reduction in externalities (especially in terms of noise). These vehicles may be manned or unmanned, although special emphasis is placed—looking to the future—on fully autonomous vehicles. In any case, since they must

[17] Communication from the Commission to the European Parliament, the Council, the European Economic and Social Committee and the Committee of the Regions, *Pathway to a Healthy Planet for All EU Action Plan: 'Towards Zero Pollution for Air, Water and Soil'*, 12 May 2021, COM (2021) 400 final.

[18] COM (2022) 652 final, point 52, cit. Cfr. *Airspace, Security and Defence Industries Association of Europe* (ADS), *Urban Air Mobility and Sustainable Development, White Paper on How to Assess a contributor to sustainable development: a framework toward transitioning to sustainability driven business models*, January 2023, www.ads-europe.org.

[19] COM (2022) 652 final, point 52, cit.

operate in densely populated areas, they are characterized by their ability to take off and land vertically, without the need for a runway.

The aircraft that can be used for UAM services are vertical take-off and landing capable aircraft, known as VCA (Vertical Take-off and Landing Capable Aircraft). According to Article 2, point 8(b) of Regulation (EU) No. 1178/2011,[20] concerning provisions related to flight crews, as amended by Article 1 of Regulation (EU) 2024/1111,[21] "vertical take-off and landing (VTOL)-capable aircraft (VCA)" means a power-driven, heavier-than-air aircraft, other than aeroplane or rotorcraft, capable of performing vertical take-off and landing by means of lift and thrust units used to provide lift during take-off and landing". In this case, the reference to *manned* flights pertains to the subject matter and scope of application of the regulation.

Along the same lines, Art. 2, point 13, Reg. (EU) No. 965/2012,[22] as amended by Regulation (EU) 2024/1111, adds that *Vertical Emergencies Medical Services* (VEMS) is "a flight with a VCA that operates under a VEMS approval, where immediate and rapid transportation is essential and the purpose of which is either to facilitate emergency medical assistance by carrying one or more of the following: a) medical personnel; medical supplies (equipment, blood, organs, drugs); ill or injured persons and other persons directly involved); b) or perform any operation where a person is at imminent or anticipated health risk from the environment and either: needs to be rescued or provided with supplies; or persons, animals or equipment need to be transported to/from the VEMS operating site".

The same notion of a vertical take-off and landing vehicle is set out in Article 2, point 85(b), of Regulation (EU) No. 923/2012,[23] as amended and supplemented by Article 2 of Regulation (EU) No. 1111/2024, which also contains the definitions of rotorcraft[24] and helicopter.[25]

---

[20] Commission Regulation (EU) No 1178/2011 of 3 November 2011 laying down technical requirements and administrative procedures related to civil aviation aircrew pursuant to Regulation (EC) No 216/2008 of the European Parliament and of the Council.

[21] Commission Implementing Regulation (EU) 2024/1111 of 10 April 2024 amending Regulation (EU) No 1178/2011, Implementing Regulation (EU) No 923/2012, Regulation (EU) No 965/2012 and Implementing Regulation (EU) 2017/373, as regards the establishment of requirements for the operation of manned aircraft with a vertical take-off and landing capability.

[22] Commission Regulation (EU) No 965/2012 of 5 October 2012 laying down technical requirements and administrative procedures related to air operations pursuant to Regulation (EC) No 216/2008 of the European Parliament and of the Council.

[23] Commission Implementing Regulation (EU) No 923/2012 of 26 September 2012 laying down the common rules of the air and operational provisions regarding services and procedures in air navigation and amending Implementing Regulation (EU) No 1035/2011 and Regulations (EC) No 1265/2007, (EC) No 1794/2006, (EC) No 730/2006, (EC) No 1033/2006 and (EU) No 255/2010 (Text with EEA relevance).

[24] According to Art. 2, point 85, Reg. (EU) No 923/2012 "rotorcraft" means a power-driven, heavier-than-air aircraft that depends principally for its support in flight on the lift generated by up to two rotors.

[25] According to Art. 2, point 85a, Reg. (EU) No 923/2012, helicopter" means a type of rotorcraft supported in flight chiefly by the reactions of the air on up to two power-driven rotors on substantially vertical axes.

The various types potentially suitable for use are classified based on their design (air taxis, VTOL, fixed-wing, multirotor), their size, and the propulsion methods employed. The latter—all green technologies (electric or hydrogen-powered)—offer different levels of functionality depending on factors such as potential range, ease of refuelling, and the associated need to provide adequate support infrastructure.

In terms of usage, VCAs may be employed for airport shuttle services (or connections with other transport infrastructure), urban-suburban transport, or tourism-related services (air taxis). They may also be used for cargo transport—particularly last-mile delivery—or for emergency operations, such as the transport of patients or medical supplies.

In the EASA *Study on the societal acceptance of Urban Air Mobility in Europe* of 19 May 2021,[26] UAM vehicles are classified into three categories: Vectored Thrust, Lift + Cruise, and Wingless (multicopter). Vectored Thrust vehicles are best suited for passenger transport, and the first certified models will be manned. The second category, Lift + Cruise, appears more suitable for cargo transport, with prototypes expected to operate autonomously and carry payloads ranging from 0.7 to 200 kg. Wingless (multicopter) vehicles, on the other hand, are designed to be remotely piloted and may be used to transport emergency medical personnel to the scene of an accident. These same vehicles can also be employed in wildfire prevention efforts.

According to the findings of the AMU-LED study, conducted within the framework of the SESAR JU initiative,[27] UAM passenger services will be carried out—at least in an initial phase—using piloted e-VTOL vehicles. Unmanned vehicles, on the other hand, will be deployed in different markets, such as cargo transport, logistics, or other aerial work applications.

The simultaneous presence of different types of vehicles—manned and unmanned—in the same airspace raises the additional challenge of ensuring their safe integration within confined segments of lower airspace.

Another classification criterion for the vehicles used in UAM services concerns the risk levels associated with the specific types of operations in which they will be employed.

According to Reg. (UE) 2019/947[28] these operations are classified as "open"—freely accessible—"specific", and "certified".[29]

[26] "*Some of these air vehicle systems are already in advanced certification stages. Europe is leading with many OEMs such as Volocopter, Airbus, Lilium, Ascendance, and Pipistrel in advanced certification stages and a significant number of pilot regions and projects, for example in Frankfurt, Paris, Cologne and Dusseldorf, Linz, Helsinki, and Ingolstadt*": EASA, *Study on the societal acceptance of Urban Air Mobility in Europe* 2021, cit., 22.

[27] SESAR AMU-LED, *Large Experimental Demonstration*, in https://www.sesarju.eu/projects/AMU-LED.

[28] Commission Implementing Regulation (EU) 2019/947, 24 May 2019, on rules and procedures for the operation of unmanned aircraft.

[29] Cf. *infra* il § 4.

On this basis, vehicles are categorized as High Performing Vehicles (HPVs)—authorized for certified operations (such as air taxis) and subject to communication, navigation, and surveillance services—and Standard Performing Vehicles (SPVs), which generally operate under the open or specific category, with lower performance and regulatory requirements.

Although this is a possibility enabled by technological progress, UAM does not necessarily require advanced automation of the vehicles used, as both manned and unmanned aircraft may be employed. Nonetheless, special emphasis is placed—looking ahead—on the development of fully autonomous vehicles.

4 The Regulation of Air Traffic Circulation for VCA in the Context of Urban Air Mobility, Including Specific 'Rules of the Air' Applicable to Low-Altitude Operations

The commercial use of e-VTOL vehicles raises several operational challenges, ranging from the identification of applicable air traffic rules to the management of factors such as the direct impact of wind on flight paths and propulsion system endurance, along with issues related to social acceptance,[30] with a view to integrating urban flights into already existing smart-mobility systems.

Defining an appropriate regulatory environment is essential to ensure the reliability standards and rigour typical of commercial aviation, while at the same time providing the flexibility needed to encourage private investment in certain strategic sectors identified by the European institutions as priority areas for action.[31]

The implementation of UAM systems could, in the meantime, rely on many of the rules already established by EU legislators concerning air navigation safety[32]—particularly those related to the operation of Unmanned Aerial Systems (UAS). On the one hand, e-VTOL vehicles are classified as aircraft[33]; on the other, UAM—especially in the fields of logistics, cargo transport, and, in the future, also passenger services—will increasingly rely on unmanned systems, whether remotely piloted or autonomous, often supported by AI-based applications.[34]

At the same time, according to EASA, "it is not only the novelties in aircraft design that justify the development of specific operating requirements for VCA,

---

[30] EASA, *Study on the Societal Acceptance of Urban Air Mobility in Europe*, 19 May 2021, www.easa.europa.eu/UAM. See also COM (2022) 652, final, cit.

[31] COM (2022), 652 final, cit.§ 18.

[32] See Regulation (EU) 2018/1139 of the European Parliament and of the Council, 4 July 2018, on common rules in the field of civil aviation; Commission Delegated Regulation (EU) 2019/945, 12 March 2019, on unmanned aircraft systems and on third-country operators of unmanned aircraft systems; and Commission Implementing Regulation (EU) 2019/947, 24 May 2019, on the rules and procedures for the operation of unmanned aircraft.

[33] Art. 2, No. 8 *b* Reg. (EU) No 1178/2011. Doc. EASA, Opinion No 03/2023, cit., point 24, underlining that "VCA are considered an emerging type of aircraft that will need to develop over time".

[34] *European Union Aviation Safety Agency, Artificial Intelligence Roadmap. A human-centric approach to AI in aviation*, February 2020, easa.europa.eu. See also Taeihagh and Si Min Lim (2019).

differentiating from those applicable to aeroplanes and helicopters. This is the entire network of interconnected systems and elements that underpin the technological advancements used to boost urban air mobility (UAM), including new infrastructure solutions and new personnel competencies".[35]

This calls for careful consideration of whether a mere transposition of the rules set out in the aforementioned Regulation (EU) 1139/2018 and its related implementing and delegated provisions is adequate for UAM services.

The model has unique characteristics, as it is intended for airspace with a much higher and often less predictable density of obstacles compared to traditional cruise-phase flights, resulting in a greater risk of harm to people and property on the ground.

It is enough to consider the potential obstacles along take-off and landing trajectories, the need to adapt minimum separation distances between vehicles that are less manoeuvrable and operate within tighter spaces,[36] the impact of wind on flight paths when navigating between tall buildings (urban canyons), the requirement to define a minimum level of energy reserves,[37] or the challenges associated with GPS signal reception in areas obstructed by buildings. These specific operational factors add to the broader issues related to social acceptance of the new model, due to concerns about individual safety (such as physical security and privacy) and environmental impact (such as visual pollution and noise).[38]

In the implementation phase, which will likely be characterized by a limited number of flights operated with 'certified' vehicles,[39] UAM traffic will be manageable through the adaptation of existing regulations. In the fully operational phase, however—where higher-frequency UAM operations in congested areas will need to be coordinated within airspace shared by both manned and unmanned vehicles—the issue may prove to be significantly more complex.

Based on the guidance provided by EASA in Opinion No. 3/2023,[40] Regulation (EU) 1111/2024 has introduced new provisions into the existing regulatory framework applicable to operations involving piloted VCA or drones in urban environments, incorporating the necessary amendments to accommodate the emerging

---

[35] EASA, Opinion No 03/2023 cit., § 24.

[36] The minimum separation distance between aircraft, currently set at 5 nautical miles, would in fact be prohibitive for urban operations. A different, more flexible regulatory framework could envisage three distinct approaches: fixed separation; dynamic separation based on the characteristics of the aircraft; and a 'non-standardized' approach based on 'see and avoid' or its technological equivalent, 'sense and avoid'. The latter model presents several issues in the event of high traffic density.

[37] The need to maintain position while counteracting wind force affects the vehicle's battery life; in general, the adverse effects of weather conditions are more significant at low altitudes, also due to the lack of sufficient space to correct the flight path.

[38] While the noise levels of UAVs are generally lower than those of other means of transport, eVTOLs may have a negative impact on the quality of life of residents in densely populated urban areas. The noise generated during take-off, landing, and overflight can disrupt residents' rest, leading to physical and mental health issues, as well as reduced work efficiency.

[39] Commission COM (2022) 652 final, cit., point 58.

[40] EASA, Opinion No 03/2023 cit., §§ 9–10.

concepts of air mobility. The new Article 4 septies, inserted into Regulation (EU) No 1178/2011, sets out specific rules for type ratings for VCA vehicles, allowing applicants already holding a Commercial Pilot Licence for aeroplanes [CPL(A)] or helicopters [CPL(H)] to obtain a VCA type rating, subject to the conditions laid down in the same provision. Stricter requirements, including a minimum number of flight hours, apply to the issuance of the VCA instructor rating.

With regard to the technical requirements and administrative procedures set out in Regulation (EU) No 965/2012, Regulation (EU) No 1111/2024 introduces a new paragraph 1a in Article 1, extending the scope of the amended regulation to "innovative air mobility operations carried out under visual flight rules by day, conducted with visual contact with the surface, using manned, single-pilot aircraft with vertical take-off and landing capability as referred to in Article 2(1)(b)(i) and (ii) of Regulation (EU) 2018/1139". Article 2 is also amended to include—among other elements—the definition of "innovative air mobility (IAM) operations", described as "any operation involving an aircraft with vertical take-off and landing (VTOL) capability in both congested and non-congested areas" (Article 2, point 12, as amended).

Of particular relevance is Article 8(5) of Regulation (EU) 965/2012, introduced by Regulation (EU) No 1111/2024, according to which, with regard to flight time limitations, the IAM operator must comply with the requirements set out by the national law of the Member State in which the operator has its principal place of business, or, if the operator has no principal place of business, the Member State where the operator is established or resides.

Further amendments concern the common requirements applicable to air traffic management and air navigation service providers within the EU.[41] With regard to the organisation of such services for UAM operations, several solutions have been proposed, such as the definition of corridors based on cooperative technologies or free routes, outside of which navigation would be governed by U-Space rules.[42] The U-Space, developed by the SESAR Joint Undertaking and launched in 2015–2016, does not represent a 'passive' airspace dedicated solely to drone traffic, but rather a set of services—at least four of which are mandatory: network identification, traffic information, flight authorisation, and geo-awareness—provided in a digital and automated manner within a volume of airspace, enabling vehicles to operate safely

[41] Commission Implementing Regulation (EU) 2017/373, 1 March 2017, laying down common requirements for providers of air traffic management/air navigation services and other air traffic management network functions and their oversight, repealing Regulation (EC) No 482/2008, Implementing Regulations (EU) No 1034/2011, (EU) No 1035/2011 and (EU) 2016/1377 and amending Regulation (EU) No 677/2011. Article 5 of the aforementioned Regulation 1111/2024 provides for the insertion, in Annex IV, point ATS.TR.305, letter (a), of the said regulation, of point 7a concerning information on unmanned aircraft.

[42] See Commission Implementing Regulation (EU) 2021/664, 22 April 2021, establishing a regulatory framework for the U-Space, applicable from January 2023, which lays down rules aimed at enabling the implementation of services supporting the safety, security, and environmental sustainability of UAS operations. For more information Tapani Huttunen (2019), 69s.

below 150 metres (500 feet).[43] Implementation is primarily reserved for areas where high-density drone operations, complex and long-range UAS missions (BVLOS), and urban environment operations are expected, in order to ensure adequate separation between manned aircraft and drones. The planned use of predefined routes within cooperative areas (CAs), and the application of visual flight rules by day with visual contact with the surface—mandated for IAM operations—constitute specific safety requirements to be applied in the upcoming initial phase of UAM system implementation.[44]

The risk level inherent in flight operations involving VCA aircraft is classified based on the provisions of the aforementioned Regulation (EU) No 2019/947 and is assessed through a Specific Operation Risk Assessment (SORA), which allows for the determination of the scope of the operation and the adaptation of applicable rules, including emergency procedures. Article 3 of Regulation (EU) No 2019/947 distinguishes three categories of UAS operations, referred to as ‘open’, ‘specific’, and ‘certified’, and lays down the operating conditions for each in Articles 4, 5, and 6, respectively.

Specifically:

(a) UAS operations in the “open” category are not subject to prior operational authorisation or to an operational declaration by the UAS operator before the operation takes place;
(b) UAS operations in the “specific” category require an operational authorisation issued by the competent authority pursuant to Article 12, or an authorisation obtained in accordance with Article 16, or, in the circumstances set out in Article 5(5), a declaration to be submitted by the UAS operator;
(c) UAS operations in the “certified” category require certification of the UAS pursuant to Delegated Regulation (EU) 2019/945, certification of the operator, and, where applicable, licensing of the remote pilot.

Operations falling under the “specific” category allow drones (of any weight) to fly Beyond Visual Line of Sight (BVLOS) at all altitudes.

Other types of flight are classified as VLOS (Visual Line of Sight) and EVLOS (Extended Visual Line of Sight).

Under the current provisions, flights over assemblies of people—including those conducted in urban environments—are classified as ‘certified’ operations, meaning they may only be carried out with specific authorisation and using certified equipment and personnel (Article 6, Regulation (EU) 2019/947).

---

[43] See Regulation (EU) 2018/1139 of 4 July 2018 (Basic Regulation), Articles 55, 56, 57 and 58, as supplemented by Commission Implementing Regulation (EU) No 2019/945 and Commission Implementing Regulation (EU) No 2019/947. See also the Report of the Wise Persons Group on the future of the Single European Sky, April 2019, available on the website sesarju.eu.

[44] In this regard, the provision set out in Article 1, paragraph 1a, of Regulation 965/2012, as amended by Article 1 of the aforementioned Regulation 1111/2024.

Flights with e-VTOL vehicles, with a pilot on board, are in any case classified as "certified" operations whenever the aircraft is used for the transport of people over urban areas.

The aforementioned regulatory framework concerns VCA with a pilot on board, who is also identified as the person ultimately responsible for flight safety[45] According to a 'see and avoid' model, the human element is required to address the risks associated with flights over urban and intercity areas, through key factors such as competence, experience, and appropriate training. The pilot in command is responsible for thorough pre-flight planning, which includes defining the trajectory along a predetermined corridor, selecting take-off and landing points, and determining the necessary energy reserve, also based on a careful assessment of weather conditions throughout the duration of the flight.

The "point of commitment"[46] "… refers to the virtual decision point, identified based on the aircraft's certified minimum performance and energy reserve requirements, at which the pilot in command must verify the actual energy reserve against the planned reserve required to reach the destination vertiport. If the available reserve does not match the planned value, the pilot must proceed with an alternative pre-selected landing option. This constitutes a specific risk mitigation measure related to electric energy usage and the impact that actual flight conditions (such as wind) may have on battery endurance. For this reason, it is recommended that during the flight planning phase, the operator ensures at least two landing options are available. All safe landing options must be reachable from the decision point, while complying with the aircraft's performance limitations for that phase of flight and preserving final energy reserves.

Energy reserve monitoring must be ensured at regular intervals during cruise or automatically, through a dynamic checking process.

In its fully operational phase, the UAM system is designed to accommodate operations involving unmanned vehicles equipped with their own *Unmanned Aircraft Traffic Management* (UTM) system.

According to studies conducted by major private stakeholders (Airbus, Uber, Boeing, Amazon), UAM should benefit from the application of AI systems and blockchain mechanisms for the exchange of information in a cooperative operational environment, known as Extensible Traffic Management (xTM), designed to support traditional Air Traffic Control (ATC). By optimizing control strategies, AI would enable eVTOL vehicles to automatically reprogram flights based on real-time situational awareness through *Low Altitude Airspace Management Systems* (LAMS), taking into account both ground and airborne obstacles.

In this context, end-user terminals—such as mobile apps, smartphones, and tablets—are expected to facilitate the connection between service providers and final users accessing the UAM system to request eVTOL-related services.

[45] EASA, Opinion No 03/2023 cit., § 33.

[46] EASA, Opinion No 03/2023 cit., § 31.

The circulation of vehicles should take place within UAM corridors, which define a three-dimensional route, potentially divided into multiple segments with associated performance requirements. These would constitute a specific CA, i.e., a volume of airspace in which operations are managed cooperatively. The reference ATC unit ensures the separation of aircraft not participating in cooperative operations.

In a near future, flight rules within UAM corridors may become fully automated flight rules (AFR), reflecting technological advances and digital procedures based on the Internet of Things (IoT)—for example, through Vehicle-to-Vehicle (V2V) communication and data exchanges—and AI-based implementations capable of preventing accidents and cybersecurity threats to UAM vehicles.

As for signal reception, information technology offers significant advantages for the management of wireless communications, which are essential for continuous data exchange between vehicles and between vehicles and ground infrastructure. The UAM system will need to use a combination of communication technologies—such as 4G/5G networks, satellite, and dedicated short-range communications (DSRC)—to ensure uninterrupted contact even in shadowed or low-coverage areas.

The regulatory framework briefly outlined is expected to enable upcoming experimental use of innovative vehicles for UAM services integrated into already tested local transport systems.[47]

5 Urban Air Mobility Infrastructure: Vertiports

To enable the implementation of urban air mobility and the use of VCA, it is necessary to create specific ground infrastructure on the territory, in strategic connection points or areas of cities, the so-called vertiports.

European regulation No 1679 of 13 June 2024 on guidelines for the development of the trans-European network (TEN), classifies the vertiport among air transport infrastructure, such as "airports, including the infrastructure and equipment necessary for ground and transport operations within the airport area" (Art. 33.1 b).

A definition of vertiport can be found in EU regulation 2024/1111[48] which modifies EU regulation 965/2012 and introduces the discipline of "innovative air mobility operations" (Annex IX). Point 140 defines a **vertiport** as an "area of land, body

[47] Communication COM (2022) 652 final identifies 2030 as the year by which transport using drones and other innovative vehicles within urban areas can be adequately implemented.

[48] EASA has adopted a package of regulations on drones and vertical take-off and landing (VTOL) aircraft, which sets out the regulatory framework for the launch of Innovative Air Mobility (IAM), including air taxi services. The package comprises Commission Implementing Regulation (EU) 2024/1111 of 10 April 2024 amending Regulation (EU) No 1178/2011, Implementing Regulation (EU) No 923/2012, Regulation (EU) No 965/2012 and Implementing Regulation (EU) 2017/373 regarding the establishment of requirements for the operation of manned aircraft with vertical take-off and landing capability, and which will enter into force on 1 May 2025.

of water or structure used or intended to be used for the landing and take-off of VCA and for the movement of VCA".[49]

The regulation also contains the definition of "adequate vertiport", connected to the operational phase of the use of the VCA: "a vertiport in which the VCA may be operated, taking account of the aircraft dimensions, weight, approach and departure paths, and which is provided with services and facilities necessary for the intended operation and is available at the expected time of use".

In the operational phase of the flight it will also be possible to use other landing areas, different from the vertiports, the so-called diversion locations, or areas or infrastructure identified by the VCA operator to be used only for landing in emergency situations. The vertiport can be built inside an existing airport or can be a purpose-built structure located in strategic points of the territory.

EASA distinguishes three types of infrastructure for VTOL vehicles: vertihub, vertipad or verti-stop.

These are infrastructure that differ in size, types of equipment and interconnection with other transport systems and with different technical characteristics and safety standards compared to other air navigation infrastructure. Their qualification is linked to the type of vehicles that can be used, VCA.

Vertihubs will be structures with various take-off, landing and parking areas, as well as maintenance and repair infrastructure for eVTOL, located in crucial areas to ensure interconnection with other transport systems.

Vertibases can be positioned on the roofs of existing buildings, starting from high points, where there is not enough space on the ground and can be placed in company headquarters or in commercial districts. Vertipads and **vertistops** will be the smallest types, used for the disembarkation and embarkation of goods and passengers, with reduced equipment and limited available airspace. The latter should be, in most cases, connection points with vertiports.

Currently, there is no uniform European regulation on vertiports.

For design and construction purposes, the EASA guidelines already prepared in 2022 remain fundamental, offering local administrators, urban planners and industry the information to create a safe vertiport within the inhabited centre.

These EASA guidelines, drawn up on 24 March 2022 as "**Prototype Technical Specifications For the Design of VFR Vertiports for Operation with Manned VTOL-Capable Aircraft Certified in the Enhanced Category**", provide technical indications (PTS-VPT-DSN), not binding for States, identify the physical characteristics, the environment, and possible obstacles, lights, and signage for the construction of such infrastructure.

The guidelines are divided into 7 chapters. The first General—applicability and definitions—recalls that these guidelines are prepared for VTOLs falling into the

[49] Point 140 of Annex I to EU Regulation No. 965/2012 amended by Commission Implementing Regulation (EU) 2024/1111 of 10 April 2024 amending EU Regulation No. 1178/2011, EU Implementing Regulation No. 923/2012, EU Regulation No. 965/2012 and EU Implementing Regulation 2017/373 regarding the definition of requirements for the operation of manned aircraft with vertical take-off and landing capability.

Enhanced category, that is, which meet higher safety requirements for flights in congested urban areas and for commercial air transport operations of passengers (such as air taxis). These aircraft, with performances similar to helicopters, must have the ability to continue the flight and land safely (Continued Flight Safe Landing, CFSL) even in the event of a failure. It is also possible to certify VTLs in the basic category. These, despite having high safety standards, cannot be used for commercial passenger transport and cannot fly over congested areas.

Chapter B relating to vertiport data, in this experimental phase, is drawn up with reference to ICAO Annex 14, Volume II, relating to "Heliports", and ICAO Document 9261, Heliport Manual. It is clear, in fact, that these infrastructures are very similar to heliports and it is not excluded that in the future the regulations may be the same for both types of infrastructure.

To carry out operations safely in the urban environment, in the design phase of the infrastructure, it is necessary to imagine a space that is free from obstacles, with a funnel shape above the vertiport. This concept proposed by EASA is suitable for the operational capabilities of new VTOL aircraft, which can perform landings and take-offs in a significant vertical segment in restricted urban environments, considering the additional environmental and acoustic restrictions that may be found in the urban environment (Chapter C—Physical characteristics).

5.1 Vertiports and Urban Planning

Vertiports are infrastructure created to meet the needs of UAM that reflects the parameters of economy, efficiency and environmental compatibility. Therefore, vertiports must be integrated into the urban fabric; they are instrumental in improving the accessibility of metropolitan cities and territories using the third dimension, namely the air dimension.

UAM, together with surface, land and water mobility, will be a new segment of the movement of people and objects within the urban context. ICAO uses the expression "**urban mobility ecosystem**" (i.e. surface and air segments). Thus, it includes various services, such as: integrated traffic management (ground and air), energy grid, integrated infrastructure with ground transportation systems (e.g. intermodal hubs), information systems and ticketing".[50]

If this "ecosystem" is implemented, it will result in a change in urban mobility that will include surface, maritime and air transport, integrated infrastructure and intermodal hubs, information and ticketing systems. All these functions will have to be harmonized and interconnected.

The inclusion of new air transport in the urban context will give rise to a change in city conditions and to a change, also cultural, in the way of experiencing the city. The change will have to be "guided" by the various public or private entities

[50] In the working paper of the 41st session of the ICAO assembly of 17 August 2022.

involved; to be welcomed, it will have to prove compatible with the expectations of the communities involved.

It is evident that local authorities are the main promoters of a transformation that represents a further step towards the creation of a "smart city", that is, a "city characterised by the integration of technologically advanced structures and means, projected towards sustainable growth policies in order to obtain an improvement in the quality standards of human life".[51]

The vertiport, as an infrastructure for urban mobility, must therefore be included in the city's urban planning tools and, in particular, in **Sustainable Urban Mobility Plans** (SUMPs). According to the "Guidelines for developing and implementing a Sustainable Urban Mobility Plan" approved by the Directorate-General for Mobility and Transport of the European Commission, adopted in 2014 and updated in 2019, it is a planning tool aimed at satisfying the varied mobility demands of people and businesses in urban and peri-urban areas, aimed at improving the quality of life in cities. In the European regulation of the TEN-T networks 1679/2024, (Annex V) it is specified that the SUMP "should support [...]zero and low emission mobility and the implementation of an urban transport system, which contributes to a better overall performance of the trans-European transport network, in particular through the development of infrastructure for the seamless circulation of zero and low emission vehicles, and of multimodal passenger hubs to facilitate first and last mile connections, as well as of multimodal freight terminals serving urban nodes".[52]

With the Commission Recommendation 2023/550 of 8 March 2023 on national support programmes for sustainable urban mobility planning, the Commission urges Member States to implement programmes to support the SUMP, "pillars of European mobility policy". These represent the framework for addressing the challenges related to urban mobility and for implementing actions to ensure more efficient and less impactful movements of goods and people.

In particular, the Commission calls for greater cooperation between the different levels of governance, between cities, municipalities and urban and extra-urban areas in view of the strengthened role in EU Regulation 2024/1679 reserved for "urban nodes" which are essential for sustainable, safe, efficient and multimodal transport throughout Europe. The urban node, pursuant to Art. 3 of EU Regulation 1679/2024, "means an urban area where elements of the transport infrastructure of the trans-European transport network for passengers and freight, such as ports, including passenger terminals, airports, railway stations, bus terminals and multimodal freight terminals, located in and around the urban area are connected with other elements of that infrastructure and with the infrastructure for regional and local traffic, including infrastructure for active modes".

Therefore, considering the future use of VTOLs for UAM, it will probably be necessary to include a dedicated part in the SUMP, which interacts and coordinates with the planning adopted to address the challenges in terms of mobility for the entire functional urban area. Interaction between the vertiport and the territory is

[51] See Delle Cave (2021), p. 386.

[52] See Plötner et al. (2020); Li et al. (2018), p. 7, 264; Hietanen (2014), p. 2.

essential, to analyse its impacts not only from an environmental point of view, but also from a social, morphological and multimodal one.

As local communities are the main drivers of this transition process, the Urban-Air-Mobility Initiative Cities Community (UIC2) was created in October 2017 with the aim of guiding European cities and regions in the process of developing UAM, upholding the demands of European urban communities and promoting collaboration between the UAM sectors. In 2022, the UIC2 project merged into the broader EU CIVITAS initiative and "is one of the flagship programmes helping the European Commission achieve its ambitious mobility and transport goals, and in turn those in the European Green Deal". UIC2 is now part of the Urban Air Mobility Thematic Cluster under the CI-VITAS Thematic Area of Demand and Urban Space Management.[53]

In developing air mobility services in urban environments, several factors must be taken into consideration: safety, noise, visual pollution, wildlife protection, inclusion, economic accessibility, and privacy.

Low-altitude airspace above cities represents an extension of the public space of local authorities; it becomes an urban space, so it will be necessary to connect the subjects involved to develop a system of safe management and coordination of airspace at different altitudes. The doctrine has in fact underlined that these new forms of mobility do not belong exclusively to aeronautical bodies, but "These emerging mobility ecosystems should be a forum of cooperation between many different players and stake-holders (e.g., cities; citizens; public, urban planning entities; manufacturers; National Aviation Authorities)".[54]

6 The First Regulation on Innovative Air Mobility Adopted by Italy

Italy has decided to seize the potential of UAM to improve the liveability of Italian cities and ensure sustainable economic development, in line with European policies.

To place the State in a crucial position on the international level in terms of advanced air mobility, the National Civil Aviation Authority (ENAC) has prepared the AAM National Strategic Plan (2021–2030) for the development of advanced air mobility in Italy. This is a plan-programme that outlines the national vision with respect to the implementation of advanced air mobility, in the long term, together with mission and strategic objectives, with a "look at regulation, technology and financial aspects".

According to the programme plan, there are four main fields of use: the transport of people in urban and extra-urban environments, the transport of general goods and biomedical material, the inspection and mapping of areas and infrastructures and support for agriculture.

To carry out the planned actions, on 12 June 2024 ENAC adopted the regulation **"National requirements for operations, airspace and infrastructure for aircraft**

[53] For further information see https://civitas.eu.

[54] Andritsos et al. (2022), p. 80.

with vertical take-off and landing (VCA) capability", adopting the 2022 EASA guidelines.

The regulation outlines an initial regulatory framework for VCA operators with a pilot on board, vertiport managers, air navigation service providers and all entities that may be interested in the establishment of a VCA corridor (Art. 3).

VEMS, i.e. those emergency medical service operations carried out by aircraft with vertical take-off and landing capabilities, are excluded from the application of the regulation.

The regulation contains 56 articles divided into 5 sections.

Chapter A is composed of three articles. Art. 1 identifies the scope and object that regulates the design of airspace structures and related services, in national airspace, the navigation of VCA aircraft, mostly electric propulsion (eVTOL), as well as providing rules on the construction and operation of vertiports.

Chapter B establishes the criteria for VCA trajectories and corridors, delimited and regulated areas, according to ENAC indications, with precise restrictions, such as the obligation to maintain radio communications and to use transponders and the requirements for air navigation of these new means (Art. 6).

During navigation, VCA aircraft must follow pre-established and defined trajectories, respecting limitations on flight altitudes and adhering to specific rules for flying in congested urban areas and controlled airspace (Arts. 5–15). Chapter C specifies the requirements for the use of national airspace by VCA operators (Arts. 16–19).

Chapter D of the regulation, entitled "construction and operation of vertiports" (Arts. 26–50), includes the requirements of the vertiport infrastructure, its manager and the operations to be carried out, in five sections.

The vertiport may be located within an airport or may be an ad hoc delimited area (Art. 26), provided that it has the characteristics set out in Art. 29 "technical requirements of the vertiport". The technical characteristics and system equipment of the vertiport (Art. 30) are taken from the guidelines prepared by EASA, referred to in Annex 2 to the regulation. The infrastructure must have minimum equipment, pursuant to Art. 30, namely at least a Final Approach and Take-Off (FATO) area and the related Safety Area; b. Touchdown and Lift-Off (TLOF) area; c. Visual aids; d. works or systems set out in the current fire prevention and protection regulations where applicable. They may also have additional elements that increase the efficiency of the vertiport such as aprons; areas for the movement of goods and passengers; access and service roads; parking lots with charging stations for cars/bicycles; rooms to support the rescue and fire-fighting service; boundary fence of the site; systems for powering electric vehicles.

The last chapter, E, of the regulation (Articles 51–56) contains the final provisions relating to the sanctioning regime and the procedures to be followed in the event of possible reports of incidents. Pursuant to Art. 54, an insurance obligation is foreseen for the conduct of operations with air taxis. According to this regulation, in order to conduct operations with the VCA, it is necessary to take out third-party liability insurance that is suitable for the activity carried out based on the maximum amounts set out in the table in Art. 7 of EU regulation 785/2004. The regulation also has two annexes that are not a substantial part of it but can be modified and integrated (Art. 55). The first is a plan with general indications of the regulated areas for the corridors to be established between Fiumicino airport and the centre of Rome in the event of possible uses of VCA. In fact, Italy has equipped itself with the first vertiport, on an experimental basis, inaugurated in October 2022, inside the Leonardo Da Vinci international airport in Rome Fiumicino. Annex 2 refers to the EASA documentation of 24 March 2022 on Prototype Technical Design Specifications for Vertiports.

7 Conclusions

Vehicle traffic is the result of the behaviour of a large number of actors who collectively make individual travel decisions; in innovative urban mobility, and therefore also in UAM, such movements will have to be coordinated and coherent so that the system can function safely and efficiently.

The regulatory framework and, especially, the numerous programmatic acts of the European Union, indicate an important component of the broader integrated system of urban transport in the air modality, capable of influencing the future of the transport lines and territorial planning itself. The approach to mobility as a complex of networked services (MaaS), which governs the current vision of the system, requires multimodality, modularity and widespread accessibility, and therefore orients the planning activity towards scenarios in which air vehicles are inserted in an intelligent architecture, as it is a centre of experimentation of human connections: the idea of a smart city connects material infrastructure […] with their virtual counterparts in the digital world, integrating the human, intellectual and social capital of those who live there within a systemic vision.

Since one of the most significant advantages of UAM is time saving, it is essential that this mode is perfectly integrated with the terrestrial modalities which are active in the reference territory. For the UAM model to be successful, the customer must thus be able to interface with a single application (MaaS service provider), capable of integrating air and ground service providers, to request travel options and book the desired itinerary in real time, in a near future that will include air mobility in the broader, intermodal, urban and interurban transport system.

References

AA.VV (2019) L'automazione nei trasporti marittimi, aerei e terrestri, in Diritto dei trasporti 1

Andritsos K, Scott BI, Trimarchi A (2022) What is in a name: defining key terms in urban air mobility. J Intell Robotic Syst 80

Booz, Allen, Hamilton (2018) NASA, Urban Air Mobility market study, Final report, 21 November, https://ntrs.nasa.gov/api/citations/20190001472/downloads/20190001472.pdf

Brodsky JS (2016) Autonomous vehicle regulation: how an uncertain legal landscape may hit the brakes on self-driving cars. Berkeley Technol Law J Ann Rev 31:851–878

Bruno D, Palmieri S, Palomba R, D'Alessandro F, Bisson M (2024) Infrastrutture di mobilità intelligenti e sostenibili. Un nuovo sistema di connessioni urbane. Int J Arch Art Design 15:286–295

Butti L (2016) Auto a guida autonoma: sviluppo tecnologico, aspetti legali e etici, impatto ambientale. Riv Giur Ambiente:435–452

Casadei T, Zanetti G (2020) Tra dilemmi etici e potenzialità concrete: le sfide dell'autonomous driving. In: Smart roads e driverless cars: tra diritto, tecnologie, etica pubblica, Milano, 41 ss

Comenale Pinto MM, Rosafio EG (2019), Responsabilità civile per la circolazione degli autoveicoli a conduzione autonoma. Dal grande fratello al grande conducente in Dir. Trasp 1:395 ss

Crane DA, Logue KD, Pilz BC (2017) A survey of legal issues arising from the deployment of autonomous and connected vehicles. Mich Telecom Technol Law Rev 23:191

Delle Cave G (2021), "Comunità intelligenti", enti locali, mobilità sostenibile: le smart city al cospetto del potere pubblico. Il diritto dell'economia, 386

Ferrazzano M (2019) Dai veicoli a guida umana alle autonomous cars. Aspetti tecnici e giuridici, questioni etiche e prospettive per l'informatica forense, Torino

Frank L, Dirks N, Walther G (2021) Improving rural accessibility by locating multimodal mobility hubs. J Transp Geogr 94:103111. https://doi.org/10.1016/j.jtrangeo.2021.103111

Garrow LA, German BJ, Leonard CE (2021) Urban air mobility: a comprehensive review and comparative analysis with autonomous and electric ground transportation for informing future research. Transp Res Part C Emerg Technol 28 September, https://doi.org/10.1016/j.trc.2021.103377

Hietanen S (2014) Mobility as a service. The new transport model? ITS Transp Manage Suppl Eurotransp 12(2):2–4

Hill B (2021) UAM Vision Concept of Operations (ConOps) UAM Maturity Level (UML) 4. NASA Technical Reports Server. NASA. Retrieved 29 June 2021, https://ntrs.nasa.gov/citations/20205011091

Ilková V, Ilka A (2017) Legal aspects of autonomous vehicles – an overview. In: Proceedings of the 2017, 21st International Conference on Process Control (PC) Štrbské Pleso, Slovakia, June 6–9

Ingratoci C (2023) Entry n.136, single European sky ATM research (SESAR) in Elgar concise Enciclopedia on aviation law, by A. Masutti P. Mendez de Leon (Eds), Edward Elgar Publishing Limited, 470ss., https://www.elgaronline.com

Keller M, Hulínská S, Kraus J (2021) Integration of UAM into cities. The public view. Transp Res Procedia 59:137–143

Li S, Zhang H, Wang S, Li P, Liao Y (2018) Ethical and legal dilemma of autonomous vehicles: study on driving decision- making model under the emergency situation of red-light running behaviors. Electronics 7:264

Pinto Neto EC, Baum DM, de Almeida JR, Camargo JB, Cugnasca PS (2022) A trajectory evaluation platform for Urban Air Mobility (UAM). IEEE Trans Intell Transp Syst 23(7):9136–9145. https://doi.org/10.1109/TITS.2021.3091411

Plötner K, Al Haddad C, Antoniou C, Frank F, Fu M, Kabel S, Llorca C, Moeckel R, Moreno A, Pukhova A, Rothfeld R, Shamiyeh M, Straubinger A, Wagner H, Zhang Q (2020) Long-term application potential of urban air mobility complementing public transport: an upper Bavaria example. CEAS Aeronaut J

Pollastrelli S (2020) Driverless cars: i nuovi confini della responsabilità civile automobilistica e prospettive di riforma. In: E. Calzolaio (ed) La decisione nel prisma dell'intelligenza artificiale, Milano, 109 ss

Taeihagh A, Si Min Lim H (2019) Governing autonomous vehicles: emerging responses for safety, liability, privacy, cybersecurity, and industry risks. Transport Rev 103–128

Tapani Huttunen M (2019) The U-space concept. Air Space Law, 69s

Tojal M, Hesselink H, Fransoy A, Ventas E, Gordo V, Xu Y (2021) Analysis of the definition of Urban Air Mobility. How its attributes impact on the development of concept. Transp Res Proc 59:4

Vantin S (2019) Automobili a guida autonoma: un'inedita opportunità per le persone con disabilità fisiche. In: S. Scagliarini (ed) Smart roads e driverless cars: tra diritto, tecnologie, etica pubblica. Torino, 55 ss

Air Navigation Services and U-Space Services

Air Navigation Services

Silvio Magnosi and Chiara Vagaggini

Contents

Abstract This chapter examines the development of international regulation for air traffic management. It considers the previous 1919 Paris Convention and the relevant provisions of the 1944 Chicago Convention on International Civil Aviation, also focusing on the measures adopted by the European Union concerning ATM. In particular, the contribution examines the original 2004 European Community Regulations establishing the Single European Sky, the innovations introduced by Regulation (EC) 2009/1070 (commonly referred to as SES II, no longer in force), and, above all, the new Regulation (EU) 2024/2803 on the implementation of the Single European Sky (SES II+). Furthermore Regulation (EU) 2018/1139, with the relevant role of EASA, will also be examined.

Silvio Magnosi is author of Sects. 1–4, Chiara Vagaggini is author of Sects. 5–7.

S. Magnosi (✉)
Department of Sciences and Technologies, Parthenope University of Naples, Naples, Italy
e-mail: silvio.magnosi@uniparthenope.it

C. Vagaggini
Department of Management and Law, "Tor Vergata" University of Rome, Rome, Italy
e-mail: chiara.vagaggini@uniroma2.it

M. P. Rizzo, F. Franchina (eds.), *Drones in the Digital European Sky*,
International Aviation Law Library 1,
https://doi.org/10.1007/978-3-032-16691-3_9

1 The Birth and Spread of Air Navigation Services: International Law

Flight handling has undergone a profound evolution, involving both technical and operational aspects, as well as legal and regulatory issues. This change is connected to the growth and expansion of air transport, particularly since the Second World War. In fact, air transport has gradually shifted from being a niche, almost exclusive sector to becoming a mass phenomenon. Consequently, flight assistance has also evolved considerably from its original framework. It emerged nearly simultaneously with the advent of flight, serving both as a navigational aid and a means of monitoring and controlling airspace. In addition to the 'traditional' functions (issuing take-off, landing, and overflight authorisations; transmitting information and meteorological data, route, aircraft position, etc.), new responsibilities have been added, particularly regarding the management of aircraft movement across increasingly vast areas. In addition to ensuring flight safety, air navigation assistance services now aim to support the growing need to guarantee efficient and economical transport by making optimal use of available space.

This important change from an operational and functional viewpoint has had a considerable effect on the structure of legal regulation. In international law, this transition is clear when comparing the two earliest legal texts related to civil aviation. The Paris Convention of 1919[1] contained a single, isolated rule, but by the time of the Chicago Convention of 1944,[2] which replaced it, regulations had become much more comprehensive and detailed. Specifically, Article 25 of the Paris Convention required broad compliance with Annex D. Among the technical Annexes to that agreement, Annexe D was unique in establishing directly binding rules, mainly concerning essential safety standards for air traffic, such as beacons, signalling, maps, and rules for overflying airports and hazardous areas.[3]

The Chicago Convention dedicates, more extensively, its entire Chapter IV to "Measures to Facilitate Air Navigation", as well as Annex 11 to "Air Traffic Services (ATS)". Notably, Article 22 of the Chicago Treaty (the opening provision of Chapter IV) requires all contracting states to adopt the necessary measures to make air navigation within their jurisdiction as safe and efficient as possible. This obligation reflects the principle in Article 1 of the Convention, which states that each country exercises full and exclusive sovereignty over the airspace above its national territory and, where applicable, the territorial sea. Exercising such sovereignty also entails responsibility for the safety and efficiency of air navigation. Accordingly, the

---

[1] See Convention relating to the regulation of aerial navigation, signed in Paris on 13 Oct. 1919, no longer in force.

[2] Convention on International Civil Aviation, signed in Chicago on 7 Dec. 1944, entered into force on 4 Apr. 1947.

[3] Comenale Pinto (1999), p. 13.

organisation and provision of flight assistance services within a State's areas fall under that State's sovereignty.[4]

In this light, flight-handling services emerge and develop at the national level. These services have always operated within national borders; however, there has been, and continues to be, no shortage of tools—both technical-operational and regulatory—to achieve a high degree of standardisation and improve efficiency.[5] Chapter VI of the Chicago Convention, "International Standards and Recommended Practices (SARPs)", is particularly relevant. The aim is to commit States to work together to ensure maximum uniformity. This should be achieved by implementing rules and procedures to cover all aspects of aviation, including aircraft, personnel, routes, and above all, auxiliary systems. ICAO, of course, retains the authority to update and, therefore, modify these rules and procedures, including through the adoption of new SARPs in line with Art. 37 of the Chicago Convention.[6]

Technical uniformity, consistently pursued under the SARPs, heavily influences the provisions outlined in the aforementioned Annex 11, which is dedicated to ATS. It identifies and defines the numerous aspects related to flight-handling activities (para. 2.3). This includes the communication and exchange of flight information, traffic control, and the management of risk and alarm situations. The various control bodies are thus called upon to collaborate to ensure the safe, orderly, and efficient movement of aircraft (para. 3.1.1). Essentially, the primary aim is to prevent accidents while maintaining efficient and cost-effective transport.

2 Next: European Union Legislation, the Single European Sky (SES)

The trend towards uniformity (or, at least, standardisation) in the regulation and conduct of ATS also arises from initiatives initially undertaken by the European Community and later by the Union.

Article 100 TFEU,[7] which has always been directly applicable within the system of sources, states that the rules set out in Title VI of the Treaty (specifically in the section concerning transport) apply only to "transport by rail, road, and inland waterway". The regulation of maritime and air navigation is delegated to periodic, individual, and specific "initiatives" adopted by the European Parliament and the Council. This has led to the gradual predominance of derived European rules over the various national systems related to the maritime and aeronautical sectors.[8]

[4] Magnosi (2008), p. 14.

[5] Rizzo (2004).

[6] Ballarino and Busti (1988), p. 82.

[7] Treaty on the functioning of the European Union (TFEU), signed in Lisbon on 13 Dec. 2007, entered into force on first Dec. 2009.

[8] Munari (1996).

In the civil aviation sector, Union rules have addressed not only the specific regulation of air transport services. These services have, in fact, long been governed by principles based on the full application of liberalisation and competition—mechanisms that, as is widely recognised, were historically almost entirely absent from this particular sector. However, "European legislation" has also been extended to cover distinct but closely related aspects beyond transport strictly speaking.[9]

The objectives pursued in the civil aviation sector at both Community and Union levels have remained largely aligned with those recognised in international law, as noted. The overarching aim is to ensure the highest safety standards while improving efficiency and cost-effectiveness in air transport. Therefore, the creation of the Single European Sky (SES), together with the regulatory framework adopted by the European Parliament and the Council through the well-known set of regulations of 10 March 2004 (SES I), clearly forms part of this broader strategy.[10] In particular:

- Regulation (EC) 2004/549[11];
- Regulation (EC) 2004/550[12];
- Regulation (EC) 2004/551[13];
- Regulation (EC) 2004/552.[14]

Of these, the recent Regulation (EU) 2024/2803,[15] discussed in great detail below, retains very few provisions from the first two regulations until 2 December 2026. The third Regulation has been repealed and replaced by Regulation (EU) 2024/2803, while Regulation (EC) 2004/552 was repealed some time ago and replaced by Regulation (EU) 2018/1139,[16] which will also be discussed.

---

[9] Tuo (2008).

[10] Van Antwerpen (2002), p. 15.

[11] Regulation (EC) 2004/549, laying down the framework for the creation of the single European sky (the framework Regulation)—Statement by the Member States on military issues related to the Single European Sky, in force until 2 Dec. 2026.

[12] Regulation (EC) No 550/2004 of the European Parliament and of the Council of 10 March 2004 on the provision of air navigation services in the Single European Sky (the service provision Regulation), in force until 2 Dec. 2026.

[13] Regulation (EC) No 551/2004 of the European Parliament and of the Council of 10 March 2004 on the organisation and use of the airspace in the Single European Sky (the airspace Regulation)—Commission Statement, no longer in force.

[14] Regulation (EC) No 552/2004 of the European Parliament and of the Council of 10 March 2004 on the interoperability of the European Air Traffic Management network (the interoperability Regulation), no longer in force.

[15] Regulation (EU) 2024/2803 of the European Parliament and of the Council of 23 October 2024 on the implementation of the Single European Sky (recast).

[16] Regulation (EU) 2018/1139 of the European Parliament and of the Council of 4 July 2018 on common rules in the field of civil aviation and establishing a European Union Aviation Safety Agency, and amending Regulations (EC) No 2111/2005, (EC) No 1008/2008, (EU) No 996/2010, (EU) No 376/2014 and Directives 2014/30/EU and 2014/53/EU of the European Parliament and of the Council, and repealing Regulations (EC) No 552/2004 and (EC) No 216/2008 of the European Parliament and of the Council and Council Regulation (EEC) No 3922/91.

The resulting framework seems designed to reduce fragmentation both of spaces and the allocation of management responsibilities in the provision of flight assistance services and, more broadly, air navigation support. Through the SES, a process of harmonisation has been initiated among the various European States, which nevertheless continue to perform their respective roles according to the fundamental principles of international law applicable in this area.[17] Strict respect for national borders, although complemented by a more flexible and coordinated use of available airspace, therefore remains in place.[18]

The SES regulatory framework has inevitably undergone amendments and updates over time, all of which reflect the trend towards a more integrated approach to managing the European Union's airspace, not so much geographically as in its functional and procedural organization.[19] Comparisons with the situation in the United States of America often appear in EU documents. In the US, airspace control and related services are characterised by greater cohesion and more efficient organisation, despite the broadly similar development leading to the adoption of Regulation (EC) 2009/1070,[20] which established what is commonly referred to as SES II. Although this Regulation is no longer in force, it was followed by numerous implementing measures that significantly strengthened the safety dimension across all sectors of civil aviation, including air traffic control and management. In parallel, greater emphasis was placed on economic and performance-related aspects in the regulation of the sector than had been the case previously. This process of regulatory evolution has necessarily had implications for the various aviation bodies and authorities. The legal framework governing their respective functions and competences (and, at times, their very organisational structures) appears to reinforce the broader trend, repeatedly noted above, towards uniformity or, at the very least, standardisation.

3 The role of the European Union Aviation Safety Agency (EASA)

Regulation (EU) 2018/1139 assumes particular importance in the context described at the end of the previous paragraph. This instrument sets out general rules for civil aviation safety, including air traffic management and air navigation services. It therefore covers a much wider scope than the specific sector discussed here. It includes provisions relating to, among other things, the manufacture of aircraft and

[17] Antonini and Severoni (2009), p. 75.

[18] Trovò (2011), p. 489.

[19] Van Houtte (2017), p. 447.

[20] Regulation (EC) No 1070/2009 of the European Parliament and of the Council of 21 October 2009 amending Regulations (EC) No 549/2004, (EC) No 550/2004, (EC) No 551/2004 and (EC) No 552/2004 in order to improve the performance and sustainability of the European aviation system, no longer in force.

their individual components; their operation (including unmanned systems); recreational and sport aviation; environmental protection; aeronautical infrastructure; and air navigation support services. In all these areas, the central role assigned to the European Union Aviation Safety Agency (EASA) is clearly evident.[21] The Agency acts as a link between the European Commission and the individual National Competent Authorities (NCAs), thereby helping to establish a uniform European aviation safety system.[22] To achieve this, the Regulation ensures the adequate and continuous exchange of data and information between various national aviation authorities and EASA, which increasingly plays a key role in promoting and disseminating a shared safety culture.

Particularly significant in this regard is Chapter IV, entitled "Joint certification, oversight and enforcement system" (Articles 62 et seq.). The above-mentioned uniform safety system essentially results in a strong degree of standardisation, carried out, as noted, by the Commission, EASA, and the Member States, with respect to all aspects of certification and the monitoring of compliance with, and continued fulfilment of, the legally prescribed requirements. To this end, the Agency also has the task of establishing, "in cooperation with the national competent authorities, a mechanism for the voluntary pooling and sharing of inspectors and other personnel with expertise relevant for the exercise of the certification and oversight tasks under this Regulation".

Based on that same cooperation, the technical and professional profiles, along with the necessary experience, must be identified and defined to select the personnel to be appointed to the shared mechanism mentioned above (Article 63).

Chapter V then sets out in even more detail the EASA's functions and responsibilities. Its interaction with the Commission and the NCAs extends beyond certification and oversight, including cooperation—especially with the Commission—in drafting rules and technical measures, proposing amendments to the Regulation itself, providing appropriate scientific and administrative support, and other related tasks (Articles 75 et seq.).

The application of the Regulation to flight assistance activities is explicitly outlined in Article 2, which states that the instrument applies to air traffic management and air navigation services conducted within the Single European Sky. However, it also reaffirms the jurisdiction of the Member States over the airspace for which they are responsible. Naturally, the importance of the functions assigned to the Agency, acting as a guarantor of safety, also emerges in this area. Its responsibility for verifying compliance with the prescribed parameters and for issuing certifications extends not only to ATM/ANS but also to the training and organisation of air traffic controllers (Articles 80 and 81).

---

[21] Zunarelli and Comenale Pinto (2023), p. 42.

[22] Masutti (2021), p. 622.

Further powers are granted to EASA in relation to the implementation of the SES. These include providing technical assistance to the Commission, conducting inspections, technical audits, and other investigations. Such tasks may only be undertaken by the Agency if requested by the Commission itself.

The EASA is also tasked with assessing the performance aspects of the SES, which, as previously noted, have become increasingly important in the ongoing process of legislative reform in this sector.[23] Of particular significance in this context is Regulation (EU) 2024/2803, which will be discussed shortly. However, it should be recalled that a "performance scheme" was already established and regulated under Regulation (EC) 2004/549 (the SES Framework Regulation, cited above), aimed at improving the efficiency of air navigation services within the SES. In that regard, Article 11 assigned the Commission the duty of designating an impartial and competent body (Eurocontrol or another entity) to assess performance. The role of this assessment body involved, in practice, providing advice to the Commission and the NCAs, as well as assisting, upon request, with the implementation of the performance scheme itself. However, that provision ceased to have effect as of 2 June 2025, pursuant to Regulation (EU) 2024/2803.

The institutions of the European Union have consistently expressed their appreciation of the regulatory framework governing the (SES). It is worth noting in this regard the "Fact Sheets on the European Union. Air Transport: Single European Sky", published by the European Parliament in 2024.[24] The document once again emphasises that the enhancement of safety and efficiency levels in air navigation is necessarily linked to greater uniformity in control procedures and airspace management systems. The aim is to achieve a significant reduction in the fragmentation of airspace among the Member States, with each retaining its own jurisdiction in accordance with the foundational principles of international civil aviation.[25] The fact sheet acknowledges the progress made in terms of efficiency and cost-effectiveness in air transport but does not fail to identify the shortcomings. In particular, there remain an excessive number of operational actors, affecting both service providers and supervisory bodies. This results in recurrent delays and service disruptions in certain areas. The complete consolidation and full operational implementation of the SES therefore still appear to be some way off. Competent authorities estimate that the attainment of the highest levels of efficiency and functionality will not be realistically achievable before 2030 to 2035.

---

[23] Vagaggini (2025), p. 127.

[24] European Parliament (2024), Fact Sheets on the European Union. Air Transport: Single European Sky.

[25] Schubert (2003), p. 33.

4 The Role of the Aeronautical Authorities in the Single European Sky Reform (SES II +)

The evolutionary process regarding the SES, both in technical-operational terms and, inseparably, in terms of regulation, must therefore still be considered ongoing. This is evidenced by the package of proposals put forward by the EU institutions, beginning in 2020 and continuing through to the closing months of 2024. Regulation (EU) 2024/2803 sets out the new framework for the so-called SES II+.

The new legislative instrument reaffirms the fundamental principles set out in the 2004 package, now, as previously mentioned, repealed by the Regulation in question. It also confirms the necessity to adhere to the safety provisions mainly established in Regulation (EU) 2018/1139, briefly outlined above, although those provisions are subject to appropriate "alignment" and adjustment.

The objective was, and remains, to increase the functionality of European airspace, alongside higher safety standards and the gradual development of both economic and environmental sustainability.[26] In this context, the importance of maintaining centralised coordination of certain network functions, such as traffic flow management, is particularly emphasised.[27] This general coordination must be capable of involving the functions and activities of all operational stakeholders concerned, and it will be necessary to extend it to unmanned aircraft.

It should be noted that the new legislation also allows Member States to assign certain tasks—among those falling within the remit of the National Supervisory Authorities (NSAs)—to the National Competent Authorities (NCAs) or other entities. These tasks specifically concern assessing and oversight of the compliance of air navigation service providers with the requirements laid down in the Regulation. It follows that, in such cases, Member States must ensure that the designated authorities possess adequate resources and specific expertise, and must inform the Commission in this regard without delay.

The NSAs are, of course, required to be fully independent of air navigation service providers from the organisational, hierarchical, and decision-making points of view. Nonetheless, it is not ruled out that both entities (the NSAs and the service providers) may form part of the same ministerial body or belong to the same public administration, provided that the independence requirements are duly guaranteed.

It should be added that, in what might be described as an effort to streamline the administrative and organisational structure of the aviation sector, Regulation (EU) 2024/2803 does not exclude the possibility of merging the two national authorities—namely the NSA and the NCA—into a single entity, provided that the strict requirements and parameters of full autonomy outlined above are duly observed. Nor is it ruled out that the NSAs might be incorporated under the same conditions of independence into other national authorities not necessarily operating within the civil aviation sector. In this regard, explicit reference is made, if only as an example,

[26] Abeyratne (2014).

[27] Magnosi (2025), p. 116.

to the National Competition Authority. Furthermore, strong and continuous cooperation between the various NSAs is maintained through the establishment of a National Supervisory Authorities Cooperation Board. The Board consists of representatives (one full member and one alternate) appointed by the NSAs of the various Member States and can elect its own leadership from among its members (a Chair and a Vice-Chair). The Board's collaborative activities extend beyond the work of the NSAs themselves (such as the exchange of information on decision-making principles and the most effective procedures for implementing the Regulation), including the Performance Review Body (PRB), particularly concerning certain tasks assigned to it, such as assisting the PRB in preparing its reports and annual work programmes.

The establishment, structure, and organisation of the PRB mainly focus on performance aspects, which are explained in more detail in the following section. According to the Regulation, the PRB is a fully independent advisory body. However, a significant connection with the Commission remains, beyond the support the PRB is required to provide, especially as the Commission appoints its members. The special procedure set out in the regulations, which also allows for the inclusion of nationals from third countries with which the European Union has agreements on air traffic management, charges, and performance systems, is also worthy of note.

5 Air Navigation Services in (EU) Regulation 2024/2803

Air navigation services are governed by Chapter III, "Service Provision", of Regulation (EU) 2024/2803, which, after years of lengthy and intense negotiations, as previously noted, has reformed Single European Sky (SES) legislation,[28] implementing SES II plus. These services aim to ensure the safety and efficiency of airspace, which, regarded as a form of infrastructure in its own right, demands appropriate and carefully calibrated management proportional to the volume of traffic involved.[29] The provision of these services, closely tied to public safety needs—particularly for certain specific types of air navigation services—has, over time, justified legislation granting States strong oversight powers to ensure safe, efficient, and environmentally responsible services,[30] in line with the objectives outlined in the EU's climate legislation, especially Regulation (EU) 2021/1119.[31]

Authoritative scholarship describes these services as services of general interest: "a category that includes both market and non-market services (…) which public

[28] Van Houtte (2017), p. 447.

[29] Comenale Pinto (2007), p. 95.

[30] F. Salerno (2025), p. 73.

[31] Regulation (EU) 2021/1119 of the European Parliament and of the Council of 30 June 2021 establishing the framework for achieving climate neutrality and amending Regulations (EC) No 401/2009 and (EU) 2018/1999 (European Climate Law).

authorities regard as being of general interest and subject to specific public service obligations".[32]

Air navigation services of a non-economic nature fully include air traffic services, which are divided into air traffic control services (area, approach, and aerodrome control), flight information, alerting, and air traffic advisory services (Article 2, point 10, of Regulation (EU) 2024/2803). Given their importance for aviation navigation, these services are provided exclusively by entities designated at the discretion of Member States with regard to the airspace under their responsibility.[33]

Meteorological services (MET) may also be provided on an exclusive basis, which Article 2, point no. 44 of Regulation (EU) 2024/2803 defines as "the facilities and services that provide meteorological forecasts, warnings, briefings and observations for air navigation purposes, as well as any other meteorological information and data provided by States for aeronautical use".

Unlike air traffic services, MET services have an economic nature, as they involve technical activities not related to the exercise of public authority.[34] As a result, meteorological services are classified as services of general economic interest, subject to the provisions of Article 106(2) of the Treaty on the Functioning of the European Union (TFEU). These provisions establish their compliance with EU competition law, provided it does not hinder their specific mission. Article 10 of (EU) Regulation 2024/2803 states that: "Member States may designate, individually or collectively, a MET provider on an exclusive basis in all or part of the airspace under their responsibility, taking into account safety considerations."

In accordance with this approach, Article 11(1) of Regulation (EU) 2024/2803 allows designated air traffic service providers to purchase certain air navigation services, including MET services, on market terms, provided that the specific conditions set out in the same Article are met, including the absence of exclusive designation of those services by Member States, as established by Article 10 of the aforementioned Regulation.

Other air navigation services related to the provision of air traffic services include: communication, navigation, and surveillance (CNS) services, defined in Article 2, point 26 of Regulation (EU) 2024/2803 as "aeronautical fixed and mobile services to enable ground-to-ground, air-to-ground and air-to-air communications for ATC purposes"; aeronautical information services (AIS), described as "a service, established within a defined area of coverage, responsible for the provision of aeronautical information and data necessary for the safety, regularity, and efficiency of air navigation" (Article 2, point 2, of Regulation (EU) 2024/2803); and air traffic data services, which are newly designated as air traffic data services (ADS) in the 2024 Regulation. Article 2, point 7, of the 2024 Regulation defines these new ADS as "services consisting in the collection, aggregation and integration of operational data from providers of surveillance services, from providers of MET and AIS and

[32] Rizzo (2022), p. 86.

[33] Comenale Pinto (2022), p. 315.

[34] Rizzo (2022), p. 86.

network functions and from other relevant entities generating operational data, and the provision of processed data for air traffic control and air traffic management purposes".

The regulation of the above-mentioned air navigation services appears to differ from the rules governing air traffic and MET services. However, as noted in insightful scholarship,[35] these services, like the latter, are classified as services of general economic interest, which renders the provisions of Article 106(2) of the Treaty on the Functioning of the European Union (TFEU) applicable.

Regulation (EU) 2024/2803 introduces a new regulatory model for these services, which will be explained in more detail below. Article 11(1) of the Regulation states that designated air traffic service providers may opt to purchase CNS, AIS, ADS, or MET services on market terms, provided that the Member State has not granted exclusive designation under Article 10 of the same Regulation. This is subject to compliance with the public procurement rules set out in Directives 2014/24/EU[36] and 2014/25/EU,[37] which take precedence. According to Article 11, Member States may obtain these services through alternative arrangements (where EU directives do not apply) when market solutions are unavailable, while also considering the public interest.

6 Functions of the National Supervisory Authorities (NSAs) and the Designation of Air Traffic Service Providers

As mentioned earlier, Regulation (EU) 2024/2803 assigns the National Supervisory Authorities (NSA) the responsibility of ensuring consistent and reliable oversight of ANSPs.[38] Due to this vital role, the NSAs must operate independently of any air navigation service provider in terms of organisation, hierarchy, and decision-making processes. Separation from the ANSPs has been one of the key objectives of the SES initiative since the initial regulatory package was adopted in 2004 (Regulations (EC) No 549/2004, No 550/2004, No 551/2004, and No 552/2004), marking the start of the legislative reform process.

In accordance with Regulation (EU) 2018/1139, which establishes the competences of the EASA, and its implementing acts, Article 5 of Regulation (EU) 2024/2803 assigns the National Supervisory Authorities the responsibility of assessing and overseeing compliance with requirements relating to the financial robustness, liability, insurance coverage, ownership, and organisational structure of

[35] Rizzo (2022), p. 86.

[36] Directive 2014/24/EU of the European Parliament and of the Council of 26 February 2014 on public procurement and repealing Directive 2004/18/EC.

[37] Directive 2014/25/EU of the European Parliament and of the Council of 26 February 2014 on procurement by entities operating in the water, energy, transport and postal services sectors and repealing Directive 2004/17/EC.

[38] Magnosi (2025), p. 105.

ANSPs (Article 5(1)(a), Regulation (EU) 2024/2803). This financial certification aspect introduces a new requirement set by Regulation (EU) 2024/2803 to guarantee the economic stability of ANSPs and other air navigation service providers, whereas the issuance of safety certificates by the National Competent Authorities (NCAs) was already envisaged under Regulation (EU) 2018/1139 and Implementing Regulation (EU) 2017/373.[39] This is reflected in Article 57 of Regulation (EU) 2024/2803, "Amendments to Regulation (EU) 2018/1139," where paragraph 7(d) adds point 7, "Financial robustness, liability, insurance cover requirements, ownership and organisational structure," to Annex VIII of Regulation (EU) 2018/1139. Through this new function, the National Supervisory Authority transmits a conformity assessment to the National Competent Authority for the latter to issue the single certificate for ANSPs, in accordance with Articles 41 and 62 of Regulation (EU) 2018/1139.[40] Otherwise, the NSA may issue a recommendation for modification, limitation, suspension or revocation of the certificate (Article 5(2), Regulation (EU) 2024/2803). Article 5(1)(b) also assigns the same Authority the task of verifying compliance by ANSPs with national safety and security requirements in accordance with Regulations (EU) 2018/1139 and (EU) 2017/373. To ensure effective fulfilment of their duties, the NSAs must carry out necessary monitoring activities in cooperation with the national competent authorities, including inspections and audits, to detect any non-compliance with the requirements laid down in the aforementioned legislation by the entities under their supervision (Article 5(2), Regulation (EU) 2024/2803).

Air traffic services are supplied under an exclusive regime within designated airspace blocks, as previously established in Article 9a of Regulation (EC) 550/2004.[41] However, this requirement is no longer mandatory according to the current wording of Article 3 of Regulation (EU) 2024/2803. Article 8(1) of Regulation (EU) 2024/2803 grants Member States the discretion to designate one or more air traffic service providers, provided they meet certain requirements related to certification, principal place of business, ownership, and control (Article 8(2), Regulation (EU) 2024/2803). According to paragraphs 4 and 5 of the same Article, Member States are required to set out the rights and obligations that designated ATSPs must follow, and they must conduct periodic assessments to ensure compliance with those obligations.

In order to improve the overall performance of the European ATM system, the new 2024 Regulation promotes cooperation among certified ANSPs in accordance with Article 41 of Regulation (EU) 2018/1139, provided they meet the procurement requirements set out in Article 11 of Regulation (EU) 2024/2803. Article 8 of

---

[39] Commission Implementing Regulation (EU) 2017/373 of 1 March 2017 laying down common requirements for providers of air traffic management/air navigation services and other air traffic management network functions and their oversight, and repealing Regulation (EC) No 482/2008, implementing Regulations (EU) No 1034/2011, (EU) No 1035/2011 and (EU) 2016/1377, and amending Regulation (EU) No 677/2011.

[40] Vernizzi (2018), p. 615.

[41] Trovò (2011), p. 439.

Regulation (EU) 2024/2803 therefore confers discretionary power on the Member States regarding the designation of providers, an authority that was not retained in Commission Proposal No. 579 of 2020[42] for either en-route or terminal services.[43] It should be noted that Article 7 of the proposal reaffirms the exclusive regime for providing air traffic services within specific airspace blocks but introduces a different designation mechanism. This mechanism states that the service should be assigned to an operator, either individually or jointly designated, which will no longer be selected from one or more national providers but will be chosen through a procedure open to all compliant European providers. The Commission's proposal, which was ultimately not adopted in the final negotiations, envisaged a shift from a model where the national provider was selected by the Member State to one based on public tendering open to all eligible European providers.[44] Regulation (EU) 2024/2803 confirms that Member States retain discretionary authority in designating air traffic service providers, stating that their provision, being essential to the safety of air navigation, should be subject to designation and linked to public interest requirements. These characteristics emphasise the non-economic nature of such services and their consequent exemption from the rules on free competition established in the EU Treaties. The new Regulation also specifies that the designation process must be regulated to ensure service continuity and enable long-term investment planning by air traffic service providers. This reflects concerns raised during discussions on the aforementioned Commission Proposal No. 579/2020, whose Article 7(1)(b) sets a maximum term of 10 years for the designation of air traffic service providers, posing clear risks of market instability to the detriment of service quality and safety.

As previously noted, Regulation (EU) 2024/2803 sets out specific conditions that air traffic service providers must satisfy in order to deliver their services. In particular, Article 8(2) of Regulation (EU) 2024/2803 states that:

> Air traffic service providers shall fulfil the following cumulative conditions:
>
> (a) hold a certificate pursuant to Article 41 of Regulation (EU) 2018/1139 or a valid declaration pursuant to Article 41(5) of Regulation (EU) 2018/1139, without prejudice to Article 7(4) of this Regulation;
> (b) comply with the national security and defence requirements;
> (c) have their principal place of business located in the territory of a Member State; and.
> (d) be owned more than 50% by Member States or nationals of Member States and effectively controlled by them, whether directly or indirectly through one or more intermediate undertakings, except where otherwise provided for in an agreement with a third country to which the Union is a party.

These conditions relating to certification, national security, defence requirements, principal place of business, and ownership and control are also necessary for the

---

[42] European Commission (2020), *Proposal for a Regulation of the European Parliament and of the Council on the implementation of the Single European Sky (recast)*. COM (2020) 579 final, 22 September 2020.

[43] Masutti (2021), p. 621.

[44] Masutti (2022), p. 153.

procurement of other air navigation services. Providers intending to operate within European airspace must adhere to all of them. These standards are more rigorous than those specified in Annex IV to Implementing Regulation (EU) 2017/373, which sets out more general EU compliance criteria. The 2017 Regulation mandates that ATSPs inform the competent authorities about their legal status, ownership structure, and any arrangements that may significantly influence their control. Furthermore, providers must disclose any links with organisations not involved in providing ANSs and, more broadly, must implement all necessary measures to prevent conflicts of interest that could compromise the impartial and objective delivery of services (Annex IV—Section 1—General Requirements). The stricter framework introduced by Regulation (EU) 2024/2803 aims to uphold even higher standards for the protection of EU airspace and enhance the overall performance of the ATM system. Achieving these fundamental goals requires not only increased cooperation among air navigation service providers but also tighter coordination among the competent authorities of the Member States, which, under the new 2024 framework, are now obliged to intensify their oversight through investigations and inspections to ensure compliance with the stipulated conditions.

7 Air Navigation System (ANS) Providers: Access and Requirements

Designated ATS providers may choose to procure CNS, AIS, ADS, and MET services, but only if the Member State has not exercised the option to designate them on an exclusive basis under Article 10 of Regulation (EU) 2024/2803. They can do so either on market terms or through other forms of agreement, where Directives 2014/24/EU and 2014/25/EU do not apply, while considering public interest factors (Article 11(1), Regulation (EU) 2024/2803). Regarding terminal air traffic services (aerodrome and/or approach control), however, airport operators may only procure them on market terms with the consent of the Member State concerned, subject to prior submission of adequate justification showing anticipated service quality benefits for airspace users and assurance that the required safety levels will be maintained (Article 11(2), Regulation (EU) 2024/2803).

As previously noted, the regulatory framework in question is a significant innovation compared with the pre-existing legislative structure, partly incorporating the content of Commission Proposal No 579/2020. Article 8(1) of the proposal allowed designated air traffic service providers to purchase CNS, AIS, ADS, or MET services on market terms only if this would lead to cost-efficiency gains for the benefit of airspace users. Conversely, Article 11(2) of Regulation (EU) 2024/2803 does not adopt the rule in the second subparagraph of Article 8(1) of the Commission proposal, which would have made local tenders at airport level mandatory for the provision of terminal air traffic control services. Instead, the current 2024 Regulation specifies that Member States "may"—and not "must"—allow airport operators to procure such services on market terms, thereby granting a power rather than imposing an obligation.

This provision appears to be in line with Article 35 of Regulation (EU) 2019/317,[45] which expressly states that "Member States may decide, either before or during a reference period, that the provision of some or all of the terminal air navigation services, CNS, MET, AIS services or air traffic management ('ATM') data services provided in their charging zones established in accordance with Article 21 is subject to market conditions". A provider of CNS, AIS, ADS, MET, or terminal air traffic services (aerodrome or approach control) may therefore only be selected—and, where necessary, designated—through a public procurement process. The selection must comply with a set of cumulative conditions concerning certification, principal place of business, ownership, and national security and defence requirements in accordance with the criteria specified for exclusive designation under Article 8 of Regulation (EU) 2024/2803.

The same requirements—except for those related to certification under Article 41 of Regulation (EU) 2018/1139—apply to CIS providers that transmit essential data within U-Space airspace,[46] with the aim of ensuring the safe and efficient integration of drones with conventional air traffic. Although these services, governed by Article 12 of Regulation (EU) 2024/2803, are not classified as air navigation services in the traditional sense, such as those examined here, they nonetheless play an important role by contributing to the effective management of automated traffic in European airspace.

The legislation examined here seeks to strike a balance between the need for flexibility in a rapidly evolving sector and the necessity of implementing effective regulations to ensure high safety standards and continuous improvement in the management of air traffic in Europe.

References

Abeyratne R (2014) Aviation and climate change. In Search of a global market based measure. Springer

Antonini A, Severoni C (2009) L'organizzazione e l'uso dello spazio aereo nel cielo unico europeo. In: Rizzo MP (ed) La gestione del traffico aereo: profili di diritto internazionale, comunitario ed interno. Giuffrè, pp 71–98

Ballarino T, Busti S (1988) Diritto aeronautico e spaziale, Giuffrè

Comenale Pinto MM (1999) L'assistenza al volo. Evoluzione; problemi attuali; prospettive, CEDAM

Comenale Pinto MM (2007) Dei servizi della navigazione aerea. In: Franchi B, Vernizzi S (eds) Il diritto aeronautico fra ricodificazione e disciplina comunitaria, Giuffrè, pp 95–106

[45] Commission Implementing Regulation (EU) 2019/317 of 11 February 2019 laying down a performance and charging scheme in the Single European Sky and repealing Implementing Regulations (EU) No 390/2013 and (EU) No 391/2013.

[46] Huttunen (2019), p. 69.

Comenale Pinto MM (2022) Fornitura di servizi di controllo e responsabilità: analisi della giurisprudenza in materia di responsabilità dei controllori di volo. In: Ingratoci C, Marino A (eds) Il controllo del traffico nella navigazione. Stato dell'arte e evoluzione. ESI, pp 315–339
Huttunen M (2019) The U-space concept, air and space law XLIV-I:69–90. https://doi.org/10.54648/AILA2019006
Magnosi S (2008) Controllo satellitare del traffico aereo e regime di responsabilità. Aracne
Magnosi S (2025) Funzioni e competenze degli enti aeronautici nel processo di riforma del Cielo Unico Europeo. Rivista di diritto dell'economia, dei trasporti e dell'ambiente XXIII:105–125
Masutti A (2021) Il futuro del cielo unico europeo verso un accentramento delle competenze sul controllo del traffico aereo nell'Agenzia Europea per la Sicurezza Aerea (EASA). Diritto dei trasporti II:621–640
Masutti A (2022) Il controllo del traffico nella navigazione. Stato dell'arte e evoluzione, in Il controllo del traffico nella navigazione. In: Ingratoci C, Marino A (eds) Stato dell'arte e evoluzione. ESI, pp 153–180
Munari F (1996) Il diritto comunitario dei trasporti. Giuffrè
Rizzo MP (2004) La gestione del traffico aereo in Europa tra competenze di enti internazionali e prerogative statali, Edizioni CUST
Rizzo MP (2022) I servizi della navigazione aerea dal SES I al SES II+: qualificazione ed accesso alla fornitura. In: Ingratoci C, Marino A (eds) Il controllo del traffico nella navigazione. Stato dell'arte e evoluzione. ESI, pp 86–118
Salerno F (2025) Prospettive di riforma sul Cielo unico europeo e miglioramenti delle prestazioni climatiche e ambientali. Rivista di diritto dell'economia, dei trasporti e dell'ambiente XXIII, suppl., 73–104
Schubert P (2003) The single European sky. Controversial aspects of cross-border service provision. Air Space Law 28:32–49. https://doi.org/10.54648/aila2003004
Trovò L (2011) Il processo d'integrazione degli spazi aerei europei: dalla riorganizzazione in blocchi funzionali verso la globalizzazione dell'Air Traffic Management (ATM). Rivista di diritto dell'economia, dei trasporti e dell'ambiente IX:439–462
Tuo C (2008) Il trasporto aereo nell'Unione Europea tra libertà fondamentali e relazioni esterne. Giappichelli
Vagaggini C (2025) Il sistema delle prestazioni e la sicurezza nella gestione del traffico aereo europeo. Rivista di diritto dell'economia, dei trasporti e dell'ambiente. XXIII, suppl., 127–149
Van Antwerpen N (2002) The single European sky. Air Space Law 27:3–47. https://doi.org/10.54648/398405
Van Houtte B (2017) The single European sky: EU reform of air traffic management. In: Ortiz Blanco L, Van Houtte B (eds) EU regulation and competition law in the transport sector. Oxford University Press, pp 447–458. https://doi.org/10.1093/law:ocl/9780199671076.003.0020
Vernizzi S (2018) La certificazione dei prodotti aeronautici nella legislazione interna, internazionale ed europea. Rivista del diritto della navigazione II:615–630
Zunarelli S, Comenale Pinto MM (2023) Manuale di diritto della navigazione e dei trasporti, I, CEDAM Wolters Kluwer

U-Space Airspaces and U-Space Services

Maria Piera Rizzo and Cinzia Ingratoci

Contents

Abstract The use of drones for commercial or other purposes, already envisaged in Art. 8 of the 1944 Chicago Convention on international civil aviation, has been constantly growing for several decades. Although desirable for its positive effects on the economy, the development of the sector needs to be governed, as it could pose problems in terms of safety, security, environmental protection and privacy protection. In consideration of this, the European Union has intervened in the matter, adopting, inter alia, a system of regulations no. 664/2021, 665/2021 and 666/2021 aimed primarily at ensuring safety, put at risk in areas where a large number of simultaneous unmanned aircraft system (UAS) operations are expected or those in which UAS operate together with manned aircraft. In particular, Regulation 664/2021 contains the regulatory framework for U-space, an initiative launched in 2016 by the European Commission aimed at ensuring the safe and secure integration of drones into airspace. It provides for the designation by States of U-space airspace, in which operations conducted with drones must be assisted by mandatory U-space services. The services in question can only be provided by certified suppliers.

Starting from the definition of U-space airspace, this chapter will analyse the power/duty of States to designate the spaces in question. The survey will then focus on the certification of U-space service providers, exploring qualifying and disciplinary aspects. We will then move on to examine the mandatory U-space services and

M. P. Rizzo (✉) · C. Ingratoci
Department of Law, University of Messina, Messina, Italy
e-mail: mariapiera.rizzo@unime.it; cinzia.ingratoci@unime.it

M. P. Rizzo, F. Franchina (eds.), *Drones in the Digital European Sky*,
International Aviation Law Library 1,
https://doi.org/10.1007/978-3-032-16691-3_10

common information services with particular attention to their qualification and its impact on the applicable regulations.

1 The Designation of U-Space Airspace by States

U-space[1] is the most significant innovation recently introduced by the EU legislator in the field of air law. This initiative launched in 2016 by the European Commission is aimed at ensuring the safe and secure integration of drones[2] in airspace through a set of new services and specific procedures. It consists of a dedicated, fully digital and automated traffic management system to enable an efficient and affordable scaling up of drone services.[3]

Drone operations present significant safety risks given that they are initially flown at a very low level and, with increasing frequency, beyond visual line of sight (BVLOS). Furthermore, due to the rising use of drones, their flights will take place simultaneously and sometimes UAS will share the same airspace with manned aircraft, with appreciable risks of collision.

This considered, in 2021, the European Union adopted an innovative regulatory framework consisting of the package of regulations No. 664,[4] 665[5] and 666,[6] which establishes uniform U-space regulations, directly applicable within the Member States. However, some margins for intervention remain with national legislators. Italy has not yet legislated in this regard.

By virtue of a customary principle codified in Art. 1 of the 1944 Chicago Convention on International Civil Aviation, states are recognized as having complete and exclusive sovereignty over the airspace above their territory.[7] In accordance with the principle in question, and pursuant to Art. 3 of Regulation No. 664,

[1] See Singh and Pashchapur (2024), pp. 1–20; Rizzo (2025), pp. 257–276; Bustos Moreno (2025), pp. 489–515. See also Tapani Huttunen (2019), pp. 69–89; Marino (2023), pp. 521–524.

[2] The term "drone" is the layman's term for "Unmanned Aircraft Systems" (UAS) which means an unmanned aircraft and the equipment to control it remotely (see COM (2022) 652 final of 29/11/2022, "A Drone Strategy 2.0 for a Smart and Sustainable Unmanned Aircraft Eco-System in Europe", 1 note 5). Unmanned aircraft means any aircraft that operates or is designed to operate autonomously or be piloted remotely, without a pilot on board (Reg. 1139/2018, Art. 3, point 30.

[3] See COM (2022) 652 final, 6. See also *U-space Bluprint SESAR*, 2017, 1-2.

[4] *Commission Implementing Regulation (EU) 2021/664* of 22 April 2021 on a regulatory framework for U-space.

[5] Commission Implementing Regulation (EU) 2021/665 of 22 April 2021 amending Implementing Regulation (EU) 2017/373 as regards requirements for providers of air traffic management/air navigation services and other air traffic management network functions in the U-space airspace designated in controlled airspace.

[6] Commission Implementing Regulation (EU) 2021/666 of 22 April 2021 amending Regulation (EU) No 923/2012 as regards requirements for manned aviation operating in U-space airspace.

[7] Pursuant to Article 2 of the Chicago Convention, territory also includes territorial waters.

the designation of U-space airspace,[8] for safety, security, privacy or environmental reasons, falls within the competence of Member States. U-space airspaces are UAS geographical zones where UAS operations are subject, at least, to the mandatory U-space services.[9] Designation must be supported by an airspace risks assessment[10] which should comprise, as a minimum, hazard identification (including safety, security, privacy and environmental hazards), risk analysis and, on the basis of the latter, the definition of mitigation actions to reduce it to an acceptable level.

At this point, the question arises whether, when the conditions set out in Article 3, Paragraph 1 of Regulation No. 664 are met, Member States may establish U-space airspaces, or whether, particularly in cases where the risks are especially serious, they are instead under a duty to do so.

Indeed, the reasons for which U-space airspace is designated express superordinate values, for which Union law itself and national legal systems ensure the highest levels of protection.[11] If, in fact, there is a market (or markets), involving the use of drones, which require that the conditions for their efficient functioning are ensured and, in the absence of U-space airspace, there are reasons for possible harm to safety (also in terms of security, protection of privacy and the environment), the States "should" be considered required, and not merely allowed to designate one or more airspaces in question, within which operations are assisted at least by the so-called mandatory U-space services.

Again, Recital 10 of the Regulation in question states that "Member States should define U-space airspace and related requirements, including additional U-space services, with the aid of a risk assessment to ensure the safety of UAS operations in such U-space airspace". Recital 10 would therefore not seem to leave any margin to the states regarding as to whether it should be established, if the aforementioned safety reasons, understood in a broad sense, so require. That is, unless the States, leaving unsatisfied the requests from the market(s) (whose proper functioning they should also be called upon to guarantee pursuant to the TFEU), and disregarding the principle of proportionality, decide to prohibit operations involving the use of drones in areas[12] where they would need to be supported by

[8] See Art. 2, point 1 and Art. 3, paragraphs 1 and 2, Reg. 2021/664.

[9] Namely (a) the network identification service referred to in Article 8; (b) the geo-awareness service referred to in Article 9; (c) the UAS flight authorisation service referred to in Article 10; (d) the traffic information service referred to in Article 11. See in this volume chapter by Rizzo "U-Space Airspaces and U-Space Services", section 2.

[10] See EASA, Acceptable Means of Compliance and Guidance Material to Regulation (EU), 2021/664 for a regulatory framework for the U-space, 16 December 2022, 20.

[11] See, for environmental protection, Art. 37 of the Charter of Fundamental Rights (adopted in Nice, amended in Strasbourg in 2007, which, by virtue of Art. 6 of the TEU, has the same legal value as the Treaties) and Art. 9 and 41 of the Italian Constitution; for the right to privacy, Art. 8 of the Nice Charter and Art. 2, 15 of the Italian Constitution; for security, Art. 3 of the Nice Charter and Art. 2, 32, 41 of the Italian Constitution.

[12] For example, areas where a large number of simultaneous UAS operations are expected or where UAS operate together with manned aircraft (Recital 3 Reg,. 2021/664).

mandatory U-space services. This would mean allowing, if the conditions are met, only the few low-risk operations that are exempt from them, falling outside the scope of Regulation (EU) 2021/664.[13] In any case, for the reasons stated above, they could not do this *sine die*. Italy, and on its behalf ENAC,[14] has already taken action, and in 2024 determined a U-space airspace in Abruzzo, the first in Europe, which it reserved for subsequent publication. Point 8 of the Guidelines issued by ENAC in December 2023 states that the U-space airspace will be designated by the Authority on its own initiative or upon request of an applicant. This may be a public administration or any natural or legal person, not otherwise defined. Operators who use drones and/or their own users, service providers, etc. may be interested. The applicant identifies the geographical area and the size of the proposed U-space in relation to the activity to be carried out within it. The request is accompanied by a "Business Plan" that demonstrates the economic sustainability of the U-space (point 11).

Although it is not expressly provided for by Regulation No. 664, it seems that this path, which is moreover envisaged for the experimental phase, if it is initiated by a natural or legal person, could well constitute an implementation method for the regulation in question. In fact, there is nothing to prevent the procedure for activating a U-space airspace from being started from the bottom up, by the stakeholders. For its part, the state, which is responsible for designating the space in question—where the market (or markets) are ready for the use of unmanned technology, and where reasons of safety, security, privacy or environmental protection require it—should proceed (also) *motu proprio* to the establishment of one or more U-space airspaces, allowing operators to make use of the existing offer of U-space service provision, if adequate, and, if not, being able to intervene directly as explained in greater detail in Section 3.

[13] Pursuant to Art. 1 Para. 3 of Regulation (EU) 2021/664, the Act in question "shall not apply to operations of UAS conducted: (a) in the framework of model aircraft clubs and associations that have received an authorisation in accordance with Article 16 of Implementing Regulation (EU) 2019/947; (b) in subcategory A1 of the 'open' category of operations with an unmanned aircraft that: (i) in the case of a privately built UAS, has a maximum take-off mass, including payload, of less than 250 g and a maximum operating speed of less than 19 m/s; or (ii) is marked as class C0 and complies with the requirements of that class, as defined in Part 1 of the Annex to Delegated Regulation (EU) 2019/945; or (c) in accordance with SERA.5015 instrument flight rules of Implementing Regulation (EU) No 923/2012". For the categories of "open", "specific" and "certified" operations see, respectively, Articles 4, 5 and 6 of Regulation (EU) 2019/947 on rules and procedures for the operation of unmanned aircraft.

[14] Ente Nazionale dell'Aviazione Civile, the Civil Aviation Regulatory Authority, Art. 687 Italian C. Nav.

2 Certification of the Provider of U-Space Services and Common Information Services

In U-space airspaces, all UAS operations, except those indicated in Art. 1.3 of Regulation 664/2021,[15] shall be subject at least to the four so-called mandatory U-space services,[16] which allow, if not (the implausible) elimination of risks (from collision and/or damage to third parties on the surface, etc.), a reduction of the same to an acceptable level. These are network identification,[17] geo-awareness,[18] flight authorization[19] and traffic information[20] services. On the basis of risk assessment, states may request for each U-space airspace additional meteorological information services (Art. 12 Reg. 664) and compliance monitoring, which allows UAS

[15] See above note 13.

[16] Art. 3, Para. 2, Reg. 664.

[17] "A network identification service shall allow the continuous processing of the remote identification of the UAS throughout the duration of the flight and shall provide the remote identification of the UAS to the authorised users referred to in paragraph 4 in an aggregated manner" (Art. 8, Para. 1 Reg. 664). "The authorised users shall be: (a) the general public as regards information that is deemed public in accordance with applicable Union and national rules; (b) other U-space service providers in order to ensure the safety of operations in the U-space airspace; (c) the air traffic services providers concerned; (d) when designated, the single common information service provider; (e) the relevant competent authorities" (Art. 8, Para. 4, Reg. 664).

[18] "A geo-awareness service consisting of the following geo-awareness information shall be provided for UAS operators: (a) information on the applicable operational conditions and airspace constraints within the U-space airspace; (b) UAS geographical zones, relevant to the U-space airspace; (c) temporary restrictions applicable to airspace use within the U-space airspace" Art. 9, Para 1, Reg. 664).

[19] Pursuant Art. 10, Para 1, Reg. 664, "1. The U-space service providers shall provide UAS operators with the UAS flight authorisation for each individual flight, setting the terms and conditions of that flight, through a UAS flight authorisation service. 2. Where U-space service providers receive from the UAS operator an UAS flight authorisation request, they shall: (a) check if the UAS flight authorisation request is complete and correct and submitted in accordance with Annex IV; (b) accept the UAS flight authorisation request if the flight under the UAS flight authorisation is free of intersection in space and time with any other notified UAS flight authorisations within the same U-space airspace in accordance with the priority rules set out in paragraph 8; (c) notify the UAS operator about the acceptance or rejection of the UAS flight authorisation request; (d) when notifying the UAS operator about the acceptance of the UAS flight authorisation request, indicate the allowed UAS flight authorisation deviation thresholds".

[20] Art. 11 provides as follows "1. A traffic information service provided to the UAS operator shall contain information on any other conspicuous air traffic, that may be in proximity to the position or intended route of the UAS flight. 2. The traffic information service shall include information about manned aircraft and UAS traffic shared by other U-space service providers and relevant air traffic service units. 3. The traffic information service shall provide information about other known air traffic and shall: (a) include the position, time of report as well as speed, heading or direction and emergency status of aircraft, when known; (b) be updated at a frequency that the *competent* authority has determined. 4. Upon receiving the traffic information services from the U-space service provider, UAS operators shall take relevant action to avoid any collision hazard."

operators to verify their compliance with the requirements established by Art. 6, Para. 1 and the flight authorization (Art. 13, Reg. 664).

U-space service providers and, when designated, single common information service providers shall hold a certificate issued by the competent authority of the Member State of their principal place of business. If they have their principal place of business, are established, or reside in a third country, they can apply for a certificate from the European Union Aviation Safety Agency (Art. 14, Para. 1-2). Common information service means a service for the dissemination of static and dynamic data to enable the provision of U-space services for the management of unmanned aircraft traffic (Art. 2, Para. 4, Reg. 664). The aforementioned certificates will be issued in accordance with Annex VI and VII.

U-space service providers and, when designated, single common information service providers shall be granted certificates if they demonstrate that they have the technical, operational and financial requirements set out in Article 15[21] and they have developed a contingency plan to deal with problematic events. U-space service providers must also have an emergency management plan to assist the UAS operator experiencing an emergency and a communication plan to inform those concerned.

A U-space service provider or a single common information service provider certificate determines the rights and privileges of its holder to provide the services

[21] Art. 15 provides as follows: "1. U-space service providers and, when designated, single common information service providers shall be granted certificates if they demonstrate that they: (a) are able to provide their services in a safe, secure, efficient, continuous and sustainable manner, consistent with the intended UAS operations and in compliance with the level of performance established by the Member States for the U-space airspace in accordance with Article 3(4); (b) use systems and equipment that guarantee the quality, latency and protection of the U-space or common information services in accordance with this Regulation; (c) have the appropriate net capital commensurate with the costs and risks associated with the provision of U-space or common information services; (d) are able to report occurrences in accordance with point ATM/ANS.OR.A.065 in Subpart A of Annex III to Implementing Regulation (EU) 2017/373; (e) implement and maintain a management system in accordance with Subpart B of Annex III to Implementing Regulation (EU) 2017/373; (f) implement and maintain a security management system in accordance with point ATM/ANS.OR.D.010 in Subpart D of Annex III to Implementing Regulation (EU) 2017/373; (g) retain for a period of, at least 30 days, recorded operational information and data or longer, where the recordings are pertinent to accident and incident investigations until it is evident that they will no longer be required; (h) have a robust business plan indicating that they can meet their actual obligations to provide services in a continuous manner for a period of at least 12 months from the start of operations; (i) have in place arrangements to cover liabilities related to the execution of their tasks appropriate to the potential loss and damage; (j) where they avail themselves of services of another service provider, they have the agreements concluded to that effect, specifying the allocation of liability between them; (k) have developed a contingency plan in the case of events, including security breaches impacting the delivery of services, which result in significant degradation or interruption of their operations; 2. In addition to the requirements laid down in paragraph 1, U-space service providers shall have an emergency management plan to assist the UAS operator experiencing an emergency and a communication plan to inform those concerned".

to which it relates and will remain valid as long as the holder of the certificate complies with the relevant requirements set out in Regulation 664 (Art. 16).[22]

The aforementioned ENAC U-space Guidelines (2023) state that the application can be submitted to ENAC by a legal person who has an operational base in the national territory and can demonstrate that the person possesses the requirements set out in art. 15, which are verified by a certification team established after submission of the application. Compliance with the Acceptable Means of Compliance (AMC) and Guidance Material (GM) concerning Regulation No. 664, adopted by EASA on 16 December 2022, must also be verified. If the outcome of the verification process is favourable, the person responsible for the procedure proposes the issuing of the certificate accompanied by a surveillance plan (point 13.4) to the Director of the competent ENAC Directorate.

The requirements in question must be deducible from the applicant's declarations, reports, "descriptions" or other documentation (a solid business plan is expressly required by Art. 15.1 letter h) that may serve to provide the required proof. Although not specifically established by regulation 664 in question, even in this first phase the issuer may use the means of verification that public administrations normally have at their disposal to carry out certification activities (request for clarification, information, exhibition of documents and transmission of data, etc.). This is confirmed in the AMC and GM referred to above (p. 102). The document stipulates that during the certification procedure the applicant should provide all the necessary information to the competent authority, especially when presenting its strategy for certification purposes, in view of which the requested authority may carry out investigations on the evidence made available to it, also through on-site or remote audits, depending on the specific case. And the ENAC Guidelines, Para.13.3, state, *inter alia*, that the Authority may request the applicant to integrate or modify the documentation produced in order to be able to follow up on the application.

The evaluation of operational and financial performance is expressly provided for (as a duty) by Art. 16, Para. 3, of Regulation 664 with reference to the period of time in which the supplier already carries out its activity under the responsibility of the requested body, the competent Authority or EASA. As a result of this evaluation, the body in question may impose particular conditions to the certificate holder, amend, suspend, limit or revoke it (art. 16.4).

The provisions of Regulation 664 are not exhaustive, but need to be integrated. In fact, only the case in which the competent body issues the certificate in question is (partially) regulated, but no term is set within which the latter is required to issue the document (or reject the application), although the duty to act seems to be implied by the overall content of the relevant provisions. For this reason, the internal law of the Member State is called upon to perform a function of integrating European legislation.

[22] These certificates shall remain valid unless they have been surrendered, limited, suspended or revoked (Annex VI and VII).

In the Italian legal system, given that the procedure referred to in Articles 14–15 of Regulation No. 664 constitutes an administrative procedure, Law 241/1990 (and subsequent amendments) will apply. The commencement of activities is subject to the issuance of the certificate, which must determine the rights and responsibilities of the holder with regard to the provision of the services to which it refers (Article 14.5, Regulation cited above). Nor can Article 20 of Law No. 241 apply, which provides for the regulation of tacit consent,[23] an institution which is inapplicable in this case, given that paragraph 4 of Article 20 itself precludes this, which excludes the applicability of the provision with respect to acts and proceedings concerning, inter alia, public safety, health and public security.

3 U-Space Services and Common Information Services: Qualification and Regulations

U-space services and common information services support the flight authorisation service. Before operating in the U-space airspace, UAS operator must satisfy the requirements of Implementing Regulation (EU) 2019/947.[24] UAS operators may provide U-space services to themselves. In such cases they shall be considered as U-space services providers for the purposes of Reg. 2021/664 (Art. 6.2). If the operator is not interested in doing so, before each individual flight he must submit a request for a UAS flight authorisation to his certified provider. The latter is required to provide at least the four mandatory U-space services, as can be seen from Recital 17 of Regulation No. 664. States may require that, for each U-space airspace, additional services selected on the basis of a risk assessment, such as meteorological information services and compliance monitoring, are provided.

Pursuant to Art. 10, U-space service providers check if the UAS flight authorisation request is complete and correct and submitted in accordance with Annex IV; accept the UAS flight authorisation request if the flight under the UAS flight authorisation is free of intersection in space and time with any other notified UAS flight authorisations within the same U-space airspace in accordance with the priority rules set out in Para. 8; and notify the UAS operator as to whether the UAS flight authorisation request has been accepted or rejected. If it is not possible to issue a flight authorization in accordance with the request, an alternative flight authorization may be proposed to the operator, similar to the approach underlying the rules for the allocation of slots at European Union airports. Obviously, UAS performing special operations, or carrying out activities of public interest, have priority. If two requests for flight authorizations have the same level of priority, the first come, first served criterion applies (art. 10, paragraphs 8 and 9).

[23] "Silenzio assenso" in the Italian legal system. See Casetta (2015), p. 403.

[24] Including, where relevant, being the holder of an operational authorisation or certificate issued by the competent authority.

In U-space airspace, manned and unmanned aircraft operate together, but in U-space airspace established within controlled airspace, air traffic service providers retain responsibility for providing their services to manned aircraft. It is the responsibility of air traffic control bodies (Art. 1, Reg. 2021/665) to carry out a so-called dynamic reconfiguration[25] of the U-space airspace, to ensure that a safe distance is maintained between manned and unmanned aircraft. Given that manned aircraft that are not provided with an air traffic control service by the ANSP may also operate in U-space, such aircraft must ensure that they are constantly electronically conspicuous to the U-space service providers so that safety conditions are guaranteed (Art. 1, Reg. 2021/666).

At this point, we need to qualify the so-called mandatory U-space services, in particular the flight authorization service, also because their qualification has a significant impact on the regulations applicable to them. A similar question arises for the common information services, the provision of which Member States are required to ensure for each U-space airspace (Recital 14 Reg. 664). These are services based on data that the States themselves must make available, and include, inter alia, the horizontal and vertical limits of the U-space airspace; the UAS geographical zones relevant to the U-space airspace and published by Member States in accordance with Implementing Regulation (EU) 2019/947; static and dynamic airspace restrictions established by the relevant authorities and permanently or temporarily limiting the volume of airspace within the U-space airspace where UAS operations can take place; a list of certified U-space service providers and the services they supply (Art. 5 Reg. 664).

Common information services can be classified as services of general economic interest (SGEI), now regulated in Articles 14 and 106, Para. 2, TFEU, together with Protocol 26 thereof and in Article 36 of the Charter of Fundamental Rights of the European Union.[26] They are a category of services of general interest (SGI)[27] that the European Commission defines as "services that public authorities of the Member States classify as being of general interest and, therefore, subject to specific public service obligations (PSO)". SGEI "are economic activities which deliver outcomes in the overall public good that would not be supplied (or would be supplied under different conditions in terms of quality, safety, affordability, equal treatment or universal access) by the market without public intervention".[28] And with regard to

[25] Dynamic airspace reconfiguration means the temporary modification of the U-space airspace in order to accommodate short-term changes in manned traffic demand, by adjusting the geographical limits of that U-space airspace (Art. 2, Para. 6 Reg. 664).

[26] See above note 11.

[27] See Communication from the Commission to the European Parliament, the Council, the European Economic and Social Committee and the Committee of the Regions, A Quality Framework for Services of General Interest in Europe, 20.12.2011 COM (2011) 900 Final, 3. Services of general interest include both economic and non-economic services. See also, inter alia, Communication from the Commission to the European Parliament, the Council, the European Economic and Social Committee and the Committee of the Regions of 12 May 2004 entitled "White Paper on services of general interest", COM (2004) 374 final.

[28] See previous note.

SGEI, it has been said in the past, and also reiterated recently, that the possibility of introducing partial derogations from competition law constitutes the *raison d'être* of SGEI.[29] Indeed, it seems clear that common information services are configured as SGEI, given that Art. 5, Para. 6 of Regulation No. 664 provides that Member States may designate a single common information service provider to supply the common information services on an exclusive basis in all or some of the U-space airspaces under their responsibility, therefore applying Art. 106 TFEU.

The qualification of the mandatory U-space services seems more complicated. It is true, in fact, that Art. 7 of Regulation No. 664 presents a completely different formulation compared to that used for the common information services. The Regulation opens the supply of mandatory U-space services to the market and establishes that they are provided by suppliers, certified by competent authorities.

However, it is worth noting in this regard that, when the state designates a U-space airspace, it cannot leave the provision of mandatory U-space services exclusively in the hands of free market competition, but must monitor and ensure that such services are effectively and adequately provided by certified providers, and may intervene when the market does not function at all or functions inadequately. Article 15.1 a) of Regulation No 664 establishes that providers must demonstrate that they are "able to provide their services in a safe, secure, efficient, continuous and sustainable manner, in line with the planned UAS operations and in compliance with the level of performance established by the Member States". It is, therefore, the Union itself that states the services *de quibus* to be subject to public service obligations.[30] The fact that the services in question are mandatory, and must be provided without interruption, in a sustainable manner and in compliance with the quality requirements established by the state (Article 15) are elements that all contribute to supporting the idea that the services in question may be viewed as services of general economic interest, provided that the state concerned deems them as such and the market mechanisms are not able to guarantee satisfactory performance. This is also supported by Article 16.2 of Regulation No 664, which establishes that a certificate of provider of U-space services (or of common information services) ceases to be valid if the holder has not started the activity within six months of the issue of the certificate or if he has ceased the activity for more than twelve

[29] Trimarchi (2020), p. 53 ff.

[30] A definition of public service obligations was formulated in the late 1960s and is contained in Art. 2, Para.1 of Regulation (EEC) No. 1191 of 26 June 1969 (OJEC No. 156 of 28 June 1969). This expression refers to "obligations that the transport undertaking in question, if it were considering its own commercial interest, would not assume or would not assume to the same extent or under the same conditions". These obligations are divided into obligations to operate, obligations to carry and tariff obligations (Art. 2, Para. 2 of Regulation No. 1969/1191). The notion of public service obligations has been widely used in EU legislation on the liberalisation of maritime and air traffic. On common and specific public service obligations and EU policy instruments in the field of services of general economic interest, see the Annex to the Commission Green Paper on services of general interest, cit., 36 s. See also the Altmark judgment (ECJ, 23 July 2003, case C-280/00, Altmark Trans GMBH).

consecutive months. This is indicative of the state's marked interest in the continued provision of the services in question.

The qualification of mandatory U-space services as services of general economic interest does not preclude, but rather requires, the application of the rules protecting competition (Art. 106.2 of the TFEU). Nevertheless, the rule assigns to the state adequate margins of intervention, if the market for the supply of U-space services has not been formed, or is in any case unsatisfactory. In such circumstances, the interests of drone operators (and users) would be prejudiced: they would be prevented from accessing the spaces in which they need to be assisted by mandatory U-space services, since, in the absence of the services in question, the protection of navigation safety is not guaranteed. In fact, pursuant to Art. 106, Para. 2, the state is entitled not to apply the rules of the TFEU on competition, if their application obstructs the performance of the particular tasks assigned to the services in question. In this case, the State could establish public service obligations; where these are not assumed spontaneously by the providers present on the market, the state could assign exclusive rights to a single public or private supplier,[31] possibly providing for compensation that covers the costs associated with the burden and ensures a reasonable profit margin. Likewise, the public administration could decide to operate in-house[32] where a market for the services in question is not present and the conditions for the in-house provision of services exist.

[31] See ECJ, 7 November 2018, in C-171/17, European Commission v. Hungary, reported in Villata and Valaguzza (2021), p. 36. The Authors report that the Court's judgment was articulated in the following points: — the fact that a service is already provided on the market, but in an unsatisfactory manner and under conditions incompatible with the public interest, as defined by the Member State concerned, is capable of justifying the qualification of that service as an SGEI, in the exercise of the discretion of national public authorities; — however, allowing the exercise of an economic activity to be entrusted on an exclusive basis to a single public or private operator constitutes a restriction on the freedom to provide services; — any restriction is justified only if it responds to imperative reasons of general interest and is such as to guarantee the achievement of the objective of general interest pursued by it and does not exceed what is necessary to achieve it.

[32] In-house providing is the phenomenon of self-production by the public authority, which acquires a good or service by drawing on it from within its own organizational structure without resorting to third parties and therefore to the market (see Consiglio di Stato (section VI), judgment 3 April No 1514. In the Teckal case (18 November 1999, cause C-107/98) the Court of Justice identified the conditions that must exist if the contract is concluded between, on the one hand, an authority, and, on the other hand, a person legally distinct from the former. The Court required that "local authority exercises over the person concerned a control which is similar to that which it exercises over its departments and, at the same time, that person carries out the essential part of its activities with the controlling local authority or authorities". More recently the Court has ruled that "the control exercised over that company by the shareholder authorities may be regarded as similar to that which they exercise over their own departments in circumstances such as those of the case in the main proceedings, when: that company's activity is limited to the territory of those authorities and is carried on essentially for their benefit, and — through the bodies established under the company's statutes made up of representatives of those authorities, the latter exercise conclusive influence on both the strategic objectives of the company and on its significant decisions" (Court of Justice, SEA case,10 September 2009, cause C-573/07).

References

Bustos Moreno Y (2025) The implementation of U-space: Open challenges from the legal-private perspective. In: Pastor Sempere C (ed) Governance and control of data and digital economy in the European single market, Law Governance and Technology Series 71, 489–515, https://doi.org/10.1007/978-3-031-74889-9, 22

Casetta E (2015) Manuale di diritto amministrativo, edited by F. Fracchia, XVII ed

Marino A (2023) Entry "U-space". In: , A. Masutti, P. Mendes de Leon (eds) Eldgar Concise Encyclopedia of Aviation Law, pp 521–524

Rizzo MP (2025) I servizi U-space: dalla certificazione del fornitore all'accesso alla fornitura. Profili qualificatori e disciplinari, ATM, Drones and Digitalization, Artificial Intelligence and New Technologies for Environment. Rivista di Diritto dell'Economia, dei Trasporti e dell'Ambiente, Supplemento XXIII:257–276

Singh G, Pashchapur RA (2024) Recent trends on UAS-UTM ecosystem and integration challenges, 1–20, https://doi.org/10.1109/ICUAS60882.2024.10556851

Tapani Huttunen M (2019) The U-space concept. Air Space Law, 69–89

Trimarchi M (2020) I servizi di interesse economico generale nel prisma della concorrenza. Rivista italiana di diritto pubblico comunitario, 53 ff

Villata R, Valaguzza S (2021) Pubblici servizi, Torino

Liability Matters

Civil Liability Deriving from Artificial Intelligence Used in Air Navigation

Stefano Pollastrelli

Contents

Abstract The chapter aims to delve deeper into the topic of the civil liability deriving from Artificial Intelligence used in air navigation and to analyze the different models of responsibility. The question that lies at the centre of the debate is the source of the damage to persons or property caused by the algorithm incorporated in the device, which leads to an outcome that is unpredictable and not controllable by humans. There is a need to arrive at new forms of responsibility to guarantee adequate protection for victims of damage caused by machines equipped with artificial intelligence capable of self-learning. The issues subjected to critical examination are numerous. The work focuses on analyzing the Italian and European legislation on damages from aeronautical activities.

1 Introduction

The interrelation between artificial intelligence and law has extensively involved the navigation and transport sector, which seems increasingly characterized by the use of completely autonomous vehicles able to substitute the driver, captain and pilot of a ship or aircraft and to carry out the specific activities of the crew members.

S. Pollastrelli (✉)
Department of Law, University of Macerata, Macerata, Italy
e-mail: stefano.pollastrelli@unimc.it

M. P. Rizzo, F. Franchina (eds.), *Drones in the Digital European Sky*,
International Aviation Law Library 1,
https://doi.org/10.1007/978-3-032-16691-3_11

Within this context, which is symptomatically expressive of current technological innovations, is the sector that includes the use of UAV acronym for *Unmanned Aerial Vehicles* and more recently, UAS acronym for *Unmanned Aircraft System* or of drones, as they are commonly known.

The widespread use of drones in the diverse sectors of industry, agriculture, commerce, logistics, the environment, law and order and the military has led, in recent years, to a trend in the economic growth of companies of producers and suppliers that see important development opportunities, also in terms of employment.

Artificial intelligence applications which are progressively more sophisticated, evolved, technologically advanced and connected, make the products or machines that use them increasingly autonomous and increasingly less remote control.[1] We are witnessing the transition from an initial form of technological automation (in which the product was under human control), to a form of artificial autonomy in which the product develops self-learning pathways, through the implementation of algorithms capable of making autonomous decisions in order to acquire new knowledge and create actions independent of human beings (of their creators). They are therefore unpredictable or rather, as has been aptly stated, they have a sort of "unpredictable predictability" in that the algorithm developer is aware that the system could make unpredictable, ungovernable decisions (the phenomenon of *Machine Learning*).[2]

The technique of self-learning can also go one step further and devise new pathways using the architectures of artificial neuronal networks in its development of *Deep Learning*. These architectures have several deep, non-visible layers on a par with the human brain, and carry out nonlinear calculations originating from input signals. In giving an account of this phenomenon, it should be pointed out that the algorithms (which are an intellectual creation consisting of a mathematical formula and deemed to be intangible assets) assume a central role in the structure of artificial intelligence in that they allocate the ability to learn to the device in which they are incorporated. This is achieved through the continuous elaboration of the multiple data that they collect and the processing of a staggering amount of information (*Big Data*).

The self-learning mechanism leads the machine towards outcomes desired by humans but the internal dynamics of the device involves the ability to self-modify and adapt to the environment, arriving at autonomous decisions that depart from the original ones employed in the algorithm and that can turn into unpredictable behaviour that is outside human control (*emergent behaviour*).[3]

The product and/or the machine may thus develop different pathways, deviating in an unpredictable manner from the expected purpose for which they were initially developed and put on the market. When this occurs, it means that artificial intelligence, through its automatic learning system, has made decisions about

[1] Cf. Frontoni (2024); Razzante (2024); Ruffolo and Amidei (2024); Buyers (2023).

[2] Piergallini (2020), p. 1745 ff.

[3] Cf. Panattoni (2021), p. 317 ff.

predetermined situations. These decisions are not transparent and are difficult for humans to decipher, nor are they scientifically decryptable with the result that they remain inscrutable and obscure (the *Black Box* phenomenon).[4]

2 The Impact of New Technologies on Air Navigation

The question that lies at the centre of the debate is the source of the damage to persons or property caused by the algorithm incorporated in the device which leads to an outcome that is unpredictable and not controllable by humans. This raises new problems regarding civil liability.

The entry into the realm of aviation of products with complete autonomy, capable of self-learning and self-perfection inevitably leads to a series of reflections regarding civil liability in Aviation Law.

In this phase, marked by the fast-paced dynamic of technological and algorithmic innovation that will progressively lead to a fully automated drone market, the research to undertake should follow two paths: first to verify the validity of the traditional regulatory frameworks incorporated in the Civil and Navigation Codes, if necessary with up-to-date interpretations; second, to assess whether it is necessary to introduce new regulations to cover what we may term "algorithmic liability".[5]

Both are affected by the impact of self-learning artificial intelligence.

Hitherto legal scholars have always dealt with systems or products controlled by humans, but such an approach is now seriously outdated. Faced with machines that self-learn and decide autonomously, we need to ask who should be liable for possible damage caused to persons and property. Likewise, we need to ask who should be considered the perpetrator in cases in which the human agent has been removed from the decision-making process which has become the responsibility of an artificial agent.

The algorithm developer (its creator), the manufacturer, the producer, the trainer, the vendor, the owner and the user are all potentially liable in the event of damage to persons or property in that they are involved in the technological development process that shaped the artificial system and which uses it for the intended purposes.

The artificial system could cause harmful events that may be attributable to construction or manufacturing defects but also as a result of unexpected outputs which the system itself elaborates and learns autonomously. The basic question is the loss of control on the part of the operator, who is transformed into a supervisor with limited possibilities to interact with the system.

The problem of attributing liability is related to the degree of autonomy attributable to the system of artificial intelligence: the more autonomous (sophisticated) the system, the more difficult it will be to identify forms of liability among the legal

---

[4] Cf. Scognamiglio (2023), p. 1081.

[5] Ruffolo (2019), p. 1692.

subjects mentioned above. This is especially the case in circumstances that fall the murk field of machine learning technology, in which the programmers themselves, called upon to assess complex situations, are unable to explain the algorithmic decisions made by the machine, and remain prisoners of its intelligence.

This means that liability is attributable to the thinking machine.

But this raises further questions and stumbling blocks on a probative level.

We in fact need to question whether the rules on causality are still able to provide convincing answers in the case of harmful events caused by an artificial machine capable of self-learning. An injured party will be faced with a multitude of subjects who have taken part in the machine's various planning and production phases, but who are not able to explain the aetiological pathway that has led to the damage, nor to identify the specific cause of the damage. As has been clearly pointed out, this could result in "a jumble of alternative causative factors, which, as if this was not enough, could even be linked, thus opening up the field to a web of causation".[6]

The risk is that of creating protection gaps.

3 Various Models of Civil Liability

Art. 743 of the Italian Navigation Code defines aircraft as "*every machine intended for air transport of persons or goods*". The legislator has adopted the concept of intended use as being equivalent to that of a ship, with the exclusion of the spatial reference. The second paragraph establishes that "*remotely piloted aircraft are considered aircraft and are defined as such by special laws, ENAC regulations and, for those of the military, by Ministry of Defence decrees*". The reference is to be understood as applying to drones both for civil and commercial use.

The result, in regulatory terms, is that drones are classified as equivalent to aircraft with crews on board so that liability is applied to the former under Articles 965 (liability for damage to third parties on the surface), 966 (liability for impact damage between aircraft in flight or between an aircraft and a moving ship), 941 and 952 of the Italian Navigation Code (liability regarding the contract of carriage of persons and goods).

The subjects held accountable are the operator, pursuant to Art. 878 Italian Navigation Code, and in cases of liability regarding carriage, the air carrier (which often coincides with the operator). It also appears that the operator is held accountable, jointly and severally, both with the tortious user, in the case of use of an aircraft without his/her consent, when he/she has not exercised due diligence to avoid the damage (Art. 879 Italian Navigation Code), and with the occasional user, who has acquired the right of use of the aircraft for a duration of not more than a fortnight, when he/she causes damage to third parties (Art. 939 *ter* Italian Navigation Code).

---

[6] See, Piergallini (2020), p. 1762.

It should be pointed out from the above framework that the Rome Convention of 7 October 1952 on the subject of damage caused to third parties on the surface, which is also applied to damage caused on the national territory by aircraft registered in Italy, by rule of the extension made by Art. 965 Italian Navigation Code, attributes the liability to the pilot in command, i.e. the person using the aircraft who is in control of navigation; it should be understood that this is not the same person as the operator, namely the entity responsible for the management of the navigation, and therefore engages in a business organized with the aim of economic gain (Art. 878 Italian Navigation Code).[7]

The regulatory system described above is founded on the regulation of the operator's liability which forms part of the general legal principles regarding civil liability.[8]

The operator is liable to third parties for acts committed by members of the crew and for the obligations assumed by the captain regarding the aircraft and shipping of goods. Based on the above-stated criterion, the operator, in virtue of their supervisory role, is liable for lawful and unlawful acts committed by his/her employees or people in charge "*in the exercise of the tasks to which they are assigned*" (Art. 2049 and Art. 1228 Italian Civil Code, regarding contracts). It is a matter of strict liability for the actions of others (or *vicarious liability*)[9] without any provision of exculpatory evidence for the operator. Even if it is not absolute, it is rigorous, marked by the existence of a relationship of "*occasional necessity*", in the sense that the performance of the assigned tasks must be such as to define a situation that facilitates or makes possible commission of the offence.[10]

The "acts of the crew" insofar as they were committed in the performance of the duties assigned to them, must be considered, as regards third parties, as acts committed by the operator, who is liable for all damage, which is the concrete expression of the increased risk typically created by the process of navigation.

Art. 879 Italian Navigation Code establishes therefore a special rule and as such it prevails over that established under Art. 2049 of the Italian Civil Code. However, it does not deal exhaustively with the topic of the regulations on tort with which the operator, as legal subject and entrepreneur, must comply in the same way as with the attribution criterion. Art. 878 Italian Navigation Code attributes to the operator the legal consequences of the lawful and unlawful acts of the people in charge but gives no provision in relation to the act generating liability which remains governed by other regulations of the Civil Code among which those laid down in Arts. 2050 and 2051 Italian Civil Code applicable in the field of navigation.[11]

---

[7] Masutti (2016): "Therefore, considering the complexity of drones, it is vitally important to make a clear distinction between the person who has the authority to direct a flight (pilot in command) and is responsible for the operations of the aircraft in accordance with the rules of the air, and the legal entity operating a drone (operator)".

[8] Cf. Busnelli (1991).

[9] Ruffolo (1976); Bonvicini (1976).

[10] Cass. 10 ottobre 2014, n. 21408, in *Resp. civ. prev.*, 2015, 292

[11] Cass. 14 novembre 2014, n. 24347, in *Resp. civ. prev.*, 2015, 452 ff.

4 Artificial Intelligence and Civil Wrong

At this point, based on the attribution criterion described above, the aeronautical activities carried out by unmanned automated aerial vehicles with human operators, that cause damage to third parties, both in the case of damage to third parties on the surface and impact damage, fall within the criteria of the liability mentioned above, and may be viewed as occurring during the performance of duties of the people in charge and employees.

What is more debatable and difficult to pinpoint is the liability for damage to third parties by completely autonomous drones, where there is no remote pilot, but whose manoeuvres and behaviour are entrusted to artificial intelligence and its learning capacities (*Machine Learning*).

It is in this context questions arise regarding the concept of autonomous algorithmic liability where the subject to be held liable is the algorithm developer, who interacts with the operator and has liability under tort towards the damaged third parties. The algorithm developer is distinct from the person who incorporates the algorithm in the product or in one of its components, but also distinct from the producer, software supplier and trainer. We are dealing with distinct and autonomous liabilities that should be integrated by the traditional forms.[12]

This new awareness marks significant progress on the subject of liability in the air law sector, although problems remain. First, the operator or user may be held liable as the result of an earlier error made by the person who created the mathematical formula from which the algorithm originated. Alternatively, an algorithm capable of self-expanding and self-learning from various experiences may cause an malfunction in the product, leading to unpredictable behaviour that is the root cause of damage to persons and property.

When considering this approach, we should bear in mind the rule of causation in order to establish the scope of compensable damage.

On the level of adequate causality, in fact, the damage caused by the use of artificial intelligence would be attributable to the original programmer. However, the black box phenomenon should not be forgotten, as it produces unexpected outputs not desired by humans. Therefore, the action is not adequate to produce the expected event. In this sense, it could constitute a supervening factor capable of breaking the causal link, since it is beyond the subject's control and ability to predict. However, this must be considered an abnormal occurrence (Art. 41, paragraph 2, Italian criminal code). Whereas with reference to the theory of human causality,[13] the final unexpected outcome should not be attributable to the programmer of the original algorithm, since its ability to self-learn could lead the machine to engage in unpredictable and unusual behaviour which differs from its initial programmed instructions, thus resulting in final outcomes that humans cannot control.

[12] Cf. Ruffolo (2019), p. 1693.

[13] Cf. Antolisei (2003), p. 245 ff.

The verification of the causal link is therefore problematic, in that the action that produced the damage may derive from a programming or information error, or manufacturing defect, but also from external environmental agents or distorting phenomena that are not easy to decipher. This makes it impossible to attribute liability for damage caused by algorithms in the use of drones.[14]

In view of the perspective that we have attempted to outline, navigation law permits the application of Art. 2050 Italian Civil Code to the liability for damage caused by the exercise of hazardous activity.[15] The Italian Court of Cassation has established that the legislator does not consider aviation a hazardous activity, nor can it be deemed possible to define it as objectively hazardous. However, in reality, this danger exists every time the activity does not fall within the normal expected conditions (safety conditions, atmospheric conditions), which involve hazardous abnormal situations, and the consequent applicability of the provision of Art. 2050 Italian Civil Code to air navigation.[16]

Consequently, caselaw extends the meaning of hazardousness to encompass activities which are normally not dangerous (air navigation) but that can have dangerous aspects that exceed the normal level of risk. The notion of risk is thus extended to include aeronautical activities carried out by drones equipped with artificial intelligence. In fact, it is precisely the precondition of risk, that is intrinsic to the methods of use of products equipped with artificial intelligence self-learning, that permits civil law scholarship to suggest a criterion of attribution based on Art. 2050 Italian Civil Code which refers to the riskiness intrinsic to products of artificial intelligence.[17]

Therefore, Art. 2050 of the Italian Civil Code would appear to be the most suitable approach for regulating aeronautical activities carried out with totally autonomous drones which use self-learning artificial intelligence-systems, since they are highly likely to cause harmful events.

EU law, specifically EU Regulation 2024/1689 of 13 June 2024 on artificial intelligence classifies artificial intelligence systems based on risk. More specifically, for high-risk systems that pose significant risks for health, safety and people's fundamental rights, it establishes strict liability for operators.

Furthermore, it should be born in mind that damage may derive not only from construction flaws or production defects, but also from design flaws in the onboard software and the settings of basic algorithms (software producer) and also from communication defects in a technological and IT system of correlation and interoperability, which would not appear ascribable to the software developer nor to the owner or operator.

---

[14] Cf. Piergallini (2020), p. 1762.

[15] Cf. Querci and Pollastrelli (2023), p. 61 ff.

[16] Cass. 10 novembre 2010, n. 22822, in *Riv. dir. nav.*, 2011, 397 ff.; Cass. 18 marzo 2005, n. 5971, in *Dir. maritt.*, 2007, 1127 ff.; Cass. 19 luglio 2002, n. 10551, in *Danno e resp.*, 2002, 1215 ff.

[17] On this point, cf. Costanza (2019), p. 1688; Trimarchi (2021), p. 429 ff.; Comporti (2009), p. 172 ff.

With reference to liability for defective products, Directive (EU) 2024/2853 of the European Parliament and of the Council of 23 October 2024 on liability for defective products and repealing Council Directive 85/374/EEC, extends liability for defective digital products and the use of artificial intelligence that does not conflict with EU law in the field of artificial intelligence.[18]

5 Conclusions

The scenario outlined above, while on the one hand raising interesting points, on the other, presents inevitable application-related uncertainties regarding the allocation of liability, the identification of liable subjects and causality. In this process of technological development, increasingly propelled towards more evolved forms of artificial intelligence, it is necessary to cover modern protection needs and to redefine the boundaries of traditional civil liability frameworks established to safeguard people's fundamental rights, which might no longer be sufficient to address the unacceptable risks inherently linked with the use of machines equipped with artificial intelligence.

References

Antolisei F (2003) Manuale di diritto penale. Giuffrè, Milano

Bonvicini E (1976) La R.C. per fatto altrui. Giuffrè, Milano

Busnelli FD (1991) Illecito civile. In: Enciclopedia giuridica. XV, Roma

Buyers J (2023) Artificial intelligence. The practical legal issues. Law Brief Publishing, London

Comporti M (2009) Fatti illeciti: le responsabilità oggettive. In: Il codice civile. Commentario, fondato da P. Schlesinger, diretto da F.D. Busnelli. Giuffrè, Milano

Costanza M (2019) L'intelligenza artificiale e gli stilemi della responsabilità civile. Giur it:1688

Frontoni M (2024) AI, ultima frontiera. Roi Edizioni, Milano

Masutti A (2016) Drones for civil use: European perspective on third-party liability and insurance. Aviat Space J

Panattoni B (2021) Intelligenza artificiale: le sfide per il diritto penale nel passaggio dall'automazione tecnologica all'autonomia artificiale. Dir Inf:317 ss

Piergallini C (2020) Intelligenza artificiale: da "mezzo" ad "autore" del reato? Riv It Dir Proc Pen:1745 ss

Ponzanelli G (2025) Responsabilità da prodotto difettoso: dalla dir. n. 374 del 25 luglio 1985 alla nuova dir. n. 2853 del 23 ottobre 2024. Danno Resp:153

Querci FA, Pollastrelli S (2023) Diritto della navigazione. Cedam, Wolters Kluwer, Padova

Razzante R (2024) Manuale sull'intelligenza artificiale. Giappichelli editore, Torino

Ruffolo U (1976) La responsabilità vicaria. Giuffrè, Milano

Ruffolo U (2019) Intelligenza artificiale, machine learning e responsabilità da algoritmo. Giur It:1692

[18] Ponzanelli (2025), p. 153 ff.

Ruffolo U, Amidei A (2024) Diritto dell'intelligenza artificiale, I, II. Luiss University Press, Roma
Scognamiglio C (2023) Responsabilità civile ed intelligenza artificiale: quali soluzioni per quali problemi? Resp Civ Prev:1081
Trimarchi P (2021) La responsabilità civile: atti illeciti, rischio e danno. Giuffrè, Milano

Liability in the Event of Collisions and Damage to Third Parties on the Surface

Emilia Vermiglio

Contents

Abstract This chapter examines the legal framework governing drones and liability in the event of collisions and damage to third parties on the surface. With the increasing use of unmanned aircraft systems (UAS) for commercial, recreational, and governmental purposes, the legal landscape has evolved to address issues related to responsibility and compensation. The chapter explores the principles of liability under international, European, and national regulations, analysing the applicability of strict liability versus fault-based liability in drone-related incidents. Special attention is given to the role of airworthiness requirements, operational rules, and insurance obligations in mitigating risks. The chapter concludes by evaluating potential legislative reforms and technological solutions aimed at enhancing safety and ensuring effective compensation mechanisms for affected parties.

1 Introduction to the Regulatory Framework of Liability for UAS in the European Union

The legal framework governing liability for unmanned aircraft systems (UAS) within the European Union remains fragmented.

E. Vermiglio (✉)
University of Messina, Messina, Italy
e-mail: emilia.vermiglio@unime.it

M. P. Rizzo, F. Franchina (eds.), *Drones in the Digital European Sky*,
International Aviation Law Library 1,
https://doi.org/10.1007/978-3-032-16691-3_12

While the EU has adopted regulations concerning the operations of UAS, it has not established harmonised rules on general tort liability, nor has it introduced a dedicated liability framework for UAS.

Instead, questions of liability are primarily addressed through national legal systems, supplemented in some cases by international instruments.

Notably, liability for damage caused by UAS—such as injury to individuals or damage to property resulting from system failure—may fall within the scope of the 1952 Convention on Damage Caused by Foreign Aircraft to Third Parties on the Surface, or be adjudicated under domestic tort or product liability law.

This chapter turns its attention specifically to third-party liability, which encompasses damage inflicted on persons or property unrelated to the contractual chain.

Such liability may, for instance, result from a UAS crash that injures bystanders or damages infrastructure.

In exploring this subject, a historical perspective is necessary to understand how the broader regulatory framework regarding international aviation liability evolved.

In the early twentieth century, the rapid emergence of commercial air transport brought to light a legal vacuum. Neither domestic laws nor international agreements adequately regulated civil aviation activities. It quickly became apparent that a coherent legal structure was essential—not only to safeguard passengers' rights across borders but also to provide clarity and consistency concerning the responsibilities of air carriers. The resulting international efforts culminated in treaties that sought to unify liability standards globally, ensuring that passengers, regardless of the airline or jurisdiction, could seek compensation under predictable terms.

One of the central aims of these treaties was to establish legal certainty for air carriers. In the absence of liability limits, a single aviation accident could expose airlines to catastrophic financial consequences, threatening the viability of the fledgling industry.

Capping liability was therefore a strategic choice to promote commercial aviation, particularly at a time when safety standards were still developing.

The rationale underlying these early legal developments is instructive for today's evolving UAS sector.

As the deployment of unmanned aircraft for commercial purposes becomes increasingly sophisticated and widespread, the absence of a tailored liability regime poses similar challenges.

In order to facilitate the sustainable growth of this emerging industry, there may be a need for legal mechanisms that provide a comparable level of protection—balancing the interests of operators and manufacturers against those of individuals, consumers, and third parties affected by UAS operations.

However, the analogy with manned aviation must be drawn cautiously.

The liability rules adopted in the 1920s and 1930s responded to the technological and safety context of the time—marked by higher risk levels and a lack of robust safety mechanisms.

Today, manned aviation benefits from decades of technological advancement and strict regulatory oversight. In contrast, UAS operations currently lack equivalent safeguards and standardisation. This asymmetry underlines the necessity of treating the two sectors distinctly, while recognising their interdependence within the broader framework of civil aviation law.

Ultimately, as with other sectors shaped by rapid technological advancement, the law applicable to unmanned aviation is likely to develop incrementally, often through the negotiation and refinement of international agreements.

Such a gradual process reflects both the complexity of reconciling diverse interests and the need to ensure legal coherence across jurisdictions.

As civil aviation expanded, the risks posed to individuals and property on the ground became increasingly apparent.

The regulation of third-party liability—namely, liability towards persons who are not party to the air transport contract—emerged as a critical issue.

Much like the Montreal Convention's treatment of passenger and cargo claims, third-party liability law sought to strike a balance between two competing objectives: the protection of injured parties and the economic sustainability of air carriers. A key concern was to ensure that those affected by accidents involving foreign-registered aircraft would receive fair compensation, while also capping the extent of liability to prevent carrier insolvency or unmanageable insurance burdens.

Initial efforts to codify third-party liability culminated in the **Convention for the Unification of Certain Rules Relating to Damage Caused by Foreign Aircraft to Third Parties on the Surface**, adopted in **1933** under the auspices of the *Comité International Technique d'Experts Juridiques Aériens* (CITEJA).[1] However, the convention soon proved inadequate. A proposed amendment—the **1938 Brussels Protocol**, which aimed to expand the available defences for insurers—never came into effect due to insufficient ratifications.[2]

The onset of World War II significantly disrupted further international legal developments in this area. In the post-war period, renewed attention was given to revising the 1933 Convention. The issue was formally taken up during the inaugural session of the **International Civil Aviation Organization (ICAO)** in 1947, where its Legal Committee was tasked with updating the existing legal framework. This effort led to the adoption of the **Rome Convention on Damage Caused by Foreign Aircraft to Third Parties** in **1952**, which entered into force on **4 February 1958**, thereby superseding the earlier 1933 Convention.[3]

---

[1] Convention for the Unification of Certain Rules Relating to International Transportation by Air, Signed at Warsaw, 12 October 1929, entered into force 13 February 1933, 11 LNTS 137.

[2] Jennison (2005), p. 787.

[3] Convention on Damage Caused by Foreign Aircraft to Third Parties on the Surface, ICAO Doc. 7364/310 U.N.T.S. 182 (1952).

2 The 1952 Rome Convention: Origins, Ratification, and Limitations in Application

Despite its ambition to unify the rules on third-party liability, the Rome Convention has not achieved the same degree of global acceptance as other aviation treaties, such as the Montreal Convention.[4]

To date, the Rome Convention has been ratified by only **51 States**, and has been **formally denounced by Canada, Australia, and Nigeria**. Within the European Union, only **ten Member States** are parties to the Convention—namely Belgium, Denmark, France, Greece, Italy, Luxembourg, the Netherlands, Portugal, Spain, and Sweden.[5]

Notably, the **European Union itself is not a party** to the Rome Convention, and **no EU secondary legislation** has been enacted to incorporate its provisions into the Union's legal framework.

As a consequence, the Convention does not apply uniformly across the **Single European Sky**.

Instead, the legal landscape governing third-party liability in the EU consists of a **fragmented collection of domestic laws and overlapping international norms**, which complicates the regulatory environment and diminishes the practical significance of the Rome Convention in many jurisdictions.

The Rome Convention establishes a liability regime applicable to damage caused to persons or property situated on the surface of the earth by aircraft in flight.

Article 1 of the Convention sets out the general principle of liability, providing that any person who suffers surface damage is entitled to compensation upon demonstrating that the harm was caused by an aircraft in flight or by an object or person falling therefrom.

However, the Convention excludes liability where the damage does not arise as a **direct consequence** of the incident, or where the harm results solely from the lawful passage of the aircraft in accordance with applicable air traffic regulations.[6]

The Convention's scope is restricted to **international incidents**, mirroring the approach adopted by the Montreal Convention in the context of passenger and cargo liability. **Article 23** stipulates that the Convention applies only where damage occurs **within the territory of one Contracting State** and the aircraft involved is **registered in the territory of another Contracting State**. This territorial and registration-based requirement narrows the range of situations in which the Convention may be invoked.

With respect to unmanned aircraft systems (UAS), questions of applicability arise due to the historical context in which the Rome Convention was drafted.

---

[4] Kjellin (2008), p. 64.

[5] Scott (2016), p. 252.

[6] Masutti (2016), p. 254.

Although UAS were not contemplated in the early 1950s, contemporary consensus holds that unmanned aircraft fall within the definition of "aircraft" for legal purposes.

Therefore, if an incident involving a UAS results in surface damage—whether due to a system malfunction or the fall of cargo or passengers in vertical take-off and landing (VTOL) operations—the requirements under **Article 1** may be satisfied, assuming the UAS is in flight at the time of the incident.[7]

Nonetheless, the practical relevance of the Rome Convention in the context of UAS remains limited. The vast majority of UAS operations are conducted within national borders and therefore do not meet the Convention's internationality requirement under Article 23.

Moreover, the effectiveness of the Rome Convention as a harmonising instrument is further undermined by its relatively **low level of ratification**. With only a subset of states party to the treaty—particularly within the European Union—its application remains fragmented and inconsistent.[8]

As a result, while the Convention theoretically extends to cover certain incidents involving UAS in international contexts, its real-world impact is restricted, rendering it of limited utility in addressing the growing complexities of cross-border unmanned aviation operations.

Where the Rome Convention governs a particular incident, liability for damage caused to persons or property on the surface is attributed not to the aircraft owner or manufacturer, but rather to the **individual or entity exercising operational control** at the moment of the harmful event.

This attribution is rooted in **Article 2(1)** of the Convention, which unambiguously places legal responsibility on the **"operator"** of the aircraft.

The precise legal meaning of "operator" is further delineated in **Article 2(2)(a)**.

According to this provision, an operator is the party that is utilising the aircraft at the relevant time. Yet, if navigation of the aircraft remains under the control—direct or indirect—of a person who granted the right of use, that person may instead be regarded as the operator for liability purposes. This functional definition prioritises **control over use**, reflecting the Convention's intention to hold accountable the party best positioned to manage and mitigate operational risk.

This distinction becomes particularly relevant in the context of **unmanned aircraft systems (UAS)**. While the Convention predates the emergence of UAS, its language is sufficiently flexible to accommodate them.

Under the **EU Regulation 2019/947**, an "operator" of a UAS is defined broadly as **any natural or legal person who operates or intends to operate one or more unmanned aircraft systems**.

This broad formulation captures a diverse range of stakeholders, including commercial enterprises (e.g. cargo drone operators), private individuals engaged in

[7] Zampone (2015), p. 63.

[8] Abeyratne (2009), p. 406.

recreational flying, and potentially air mobility service providers in future passenger UAS applications.

One of the principal advantages of the **strict liability regime** under the Rome Convention lies in its procedural simplicity: victims are not burdened with the task of proving fault or causation, nor are they required to engage in complex fact-finding to identify the responsible party.

However, this procedural efficiency is contingent upon the **prompt and reliable identification of the liable operator**—typically, the individual or entity exercising control over the unmanned aircraft (UA) at the time of the incident.

Due to the **geographical separation** often present between a UA operator and the location of the incident, establishing the operator's identity becomes particularly difficult. Unlike traditional aircraft, UAs can be controlled remotely, and the operator may not even be in the same jurisdiction as the site of the damage. Requiring victims to investigate and establish this connection would **erode the efficiency and accessibility** that strict liability is designed to provide.

To avoid this, it is both **logical and necessary** to retain a presumption regarding operator identity—one that is adapted to reflect **contemporary regulatory practices**.

In this respect, the **EU's operator-based registration model** provides a compelling alternative.

Rather than requiring Member States to establish ownership-based registration systems, **EU Regulation 2019/947** mandates that UAs must be operated under a **registered operator number**, which must be visibly displayed on the aircraft. Crucially, this requirement applies irrespective of who owns the device. In other words, **legal responsibility is tied to the operator**, not the owner.[9]

This system ensures **transparency and traceability**, eliminating ambiguity about who is deemed to be operating the UA at any given time. According to this framework, the **registered operator**—whether acting directly or through agents or employees—is the individual presumed to be in control of the operation.

Accordingly, a future international liability system would benefit from adopting the **EU model as a baseline**. Legal responsibility should be assigned to the **registered operator**, who is best placed to manage the operational risk, **benefits economically** from the activity, and is in the most appropriate position to **secure insurance coverage**. Anchoring liability in this way would preserve the procedural advantages of strict liability while aligning legal responsibility with actual operational control.

In instances where liability attaches, the operator may invoke certain **defences** enumerated in the Convention; however, if liability is established, it will be subject to the **quantitative limits** prescribed in **Article 11**.

These limits were established with traditional, manned aviation in mind and were calibrated to reflect the typical risks associated with large, heavy aircraft. Applying these same thresholds to UAS—which are often significantly smaller and

[9] Scott and Hartmann (2024).

lighter—raises legitimate questions about the proportionality and adequacy of the compensation caps.

In light of this, it becomes evident that the current liability thresholds, designed for a different technological context, may not appropriately reflect the risk profiles associated with modern unmanned flight.

As UAS technology continues to evolve and integrate into civilian airspace, there is an urgent need to reassess whether legacy legal instruments like the Rome Convention offer a fit-for-purpose liability system—or whether supplementary or revised legal frameworks will be required to ensure fair and effective redress for those affected on the ground.

Under a regime of strict liability, the operator is liable for the damage irrespective of intent, negligence, or causation. While this may seem burdensome, it provides victims with a predictable path to compensation and ensures that injured parties are not left uncompensated due to evidentiary uncertainties.

A further rationale for strict liability arises from the increased autonomy of UA systems.

In instances where no identifiable human error or technical defect can be established—such as a failure arising from machine learning algorithms—traditional liability doctrines become ineffectual. Under a strict liability system, such technological opacity does not hinder a victim's ability to obtain redress.

However, this benefit is not without drawbacks. As UA technology is still maturing, software-related defects are common and may result in harm for which the operator is held strictly liable, even if the issue originates in the design or manufacture. In such cases, the operator does retain a right of recourse against the manufacturer, though this introduces a secondary layer of litigation.

Strict liability systems are typically justified in circumstances where the underlying activity is deemed inherently dangerous, regardless of the precautions taken.

This principle is embedded in legal instruments such as the Convention on Civil Liability for Oil Pollution Damage[10] and the Vienna Convention on Civil Liability for Nuclear Damage,[11] where liability is imposed due to the high-risk nature of the activities concerned.

Whether UA operations fall within this category remains a contested issue. Unlike manned aviation in the early twentieth century—then considered exceptionally dangerous—contemporary UAs vary widely in risk profile. Under the EU's risk-based regulatory approach, the level of hazard depends on factors such as the aircraft's weight, operational environment, and nature of the mission. For instance, UA activities involving hazardous materials are classified under the 'certified' category, signalling their elevated risk.

---

[10] International Convention on Civil Liability for Oil Pollution Damage (CLC), Adoption: 29 November 1969; Entry into force: 19 June 1975; Being replaced by 1992 Protocol: Adoption: 27 November 1992; Entry into force: 30 May 1996.

[11] Vienna Convention on Civil Liability for Nuclear Damage, date of adoption: 12 May 1963; Date of entry into force: 12 November 1977.

Although individual UA flights may not qualify as abnormally dangerous, the cumulative effect of mass deployment could alter the equation. With increased frequency of flights, the likelihood of ground accidents will inevitably rise, making the risk landscape more uncertain. Within the emerging U-Space framework, where autonomous technologies will play a central role, the risk profile could arguably warrant strict liability, especially as the European Commission has recognised such systems as appropriate for digital technologies operating in public environments with potential for significant harm.[12]

Finally, a strict liability framework aligns with principles of risk allocation and insurance. Those engaging in hazardous activities are often best positioned to internalise and insure against the risks they create. Operators of UAs—unlike random victims—can anticipate liability and obtain insurance accordingly. Under EU Regulation 785/2004,[13] UA operators are in fact required to carry minimum third-party liability insurance.

However, challenges may arise where UA operators are private individuals, not affiliated with larger enterprises that could absorb or distribute financial risks. Nevertheless, the possibility of insurance acquisition remains, and such mechanisms are less accessible to injured third parties, thus reinforcing the argument for placing primary liability on the operator.[14]

The operational risks associated with unmanned aircraft systems (UAS) extend beyond surface damage to include in-flight collisions, which may involve other UAS or manned aircraft.

The resulting damage can vary widely from negligible property losses to incidents involving high-value aircraft or sensitive payloads. Particularly in scenarios involving passenger-carrying UAS (e.g., PATS), the consequences of such collisions could be severe.

3 Operational Risks and Liability for Mid-Air Collisions

Although the Rome Convention of 1952 does address mid-air collisions under Article 7, its practical relevance remains limited. The Convention provides that where two or more aircraft are involved in an in-flight collision or mutual interference that results in compensable damage under Article 1, each operator is deemed jointly responsible and subject to the Convention's liability limits. This provision effectively establishes joint and several liability among the operators involved.

[12] European Commission, *Staff working document on emerging digital technologies*, 25 April 2018, SWD(2018) 137 final.

[13] Regulation (EC) No. 785/2004 of the European Parliament and of the Council of 21 April 2004 on Insurance Requirements for Air Carriers and Aircraft Operators, OJ L 138, 30 April 2004, pp. 1–6. Steer Davies Gleave, *Study on the Third-Party Liability and Insurance Requirements of Remotely Piloted Aircraft Systems (RPAS)*, Final Report 22603201 SI2.661592 (2014), 1.

[14] Mendes De Leon and Scott (2016), p. 202.

However, due to the Convention's limited ratification and its inapplicability to purely domestic flights, most incidents involving UAS mid-air collisions fall outside its ambit and are instead governed by national tort law. As of now, there is a paucity of case-law interpreting Article 7 in the context of UAS, making it difficult to predict how liability would be apportioned in such cases. The absence of precedent also reflects the novelty of UAS operations in shared airspace, further underscoring the need for legal clarity as the sector evolves.

We highlighted the partial applicability of the existing rules on international aviation liability—Rome Conventions—to the domain of unmanned aviation. Although drafted with traditional manned flight in mind, several provisions of this instrument may, by analogy or by express extension, apply to UAS.

However, the broader regulatory architecture remains incomplete. The Rome Convention, which governs third-party liability, has limited geographic reach and is not uniformly adopted across the EU. This results in a fragmented legal landscape, where the absence of harmonised standards gives rise to legal uncertainty—particularly in cases involving mid-air collisions between UAS and manned aircraft.

In practice, many of the legal gaps must be addressed through domestic tort regimes, which differ substantially across jurisdictions. The lack of consistency poses significant barriers to the cross-border scalability of UAS operations within the internal market.

At the EU level, a more coherent and future-oriented legal framework is needed. Certain rules, such as the obligation for UAS operators to maintain third-party liability insurance under Regulation 785/2004, are sensible and directly transposable to unmanned aviation. This regulation reflects the general legal presumption—common across Member States—that the aircraft "operator" bears strict liability for damages caused by aviation activities.

Looking ahead, one area that requires in-depth examination is the application of product liability law to UAS. Under Council Directive 85/374/EEC,[15] manufacturers may be held strictly liable for placing defective products on the market. This directive, once implemented into national law, provides a clear legal pathway for holding UAS producers accountable for design flaws, manufacturing defects, or failure to warn. Additionally, regulatory instruments such as the EU Toy Safety Directive[16] may apply to small or recreational UAS models, suggesting that a layered legal approach—differentiating between commercial and non-commercial use—may be necessary.

[15] Council Directive 85/374/EEC of 25 July 1985 on the Approximation of the Laws, Regulations and Administrative Provisions of the Member States Concerning Liability for Defective Products, OJ L 210, 7 August 1985, pp. 29–33. Today, the new EU Directive 2024/2853 radically modernises the product liability regime, aligning it with the digital evolution and placing specific focus on software, AI, data, and cybersecurity. It is set to enter into force on 9 December 2026, with significant impacts on businesses and consumer protection.

[16] Directive 2009/48/EC of the European Parliament and of the Council of 18 June 2009 on the Safety of Toys, OJ L 170, 30 June 2009, pp. 1–37. This has been recognised by EASA in its Concept of Operations for Drones report. EASA, 'Concept of Operations for Drones – A Risk Based Approach to Regulation of Unmanned Aircraft'.

In conclusion, while existing legal instruments provide a partial foundation, they are insufficiently tailored to the technological and operational realities of unmanned aviation. Legal reform—whether through treaty amendment, EU legislation, or soft-law instruments—will be essential to ensure that the liability system for UAS is not only fair and predictable but also conducive to innovation and public safety.

In its 2015 study on the legal implications of remotely piloted aircraft systems (RPAS), the International Civil Aviation Organization (ICAO) examined the applicability of existing international liability frameworks to these emerging technologies. With regard to the 1952 Rome Convention, ICAO observed that, notwithstanding various criticisms, its core function—to provide a rational and operational basis for assigning liability for surface damage caused by foreign aircraft, including unmanned systems—remains intact. In particular, the organization concluded that perceived shortcomings of the Convention do not detract from its effectiveness in establishing a workable system for third-party compensation involving RPAS.[17]

4 Reform Perspectives: Towards a European Liability Regime Specifically for Drones

Given this institutional endorsement, one may reasonably conclude that the Rome Convention offers a sufficient foundation for addressing ground damage caused by UAs. Its strict liability framework provides an appropriate legal response to the difficulties typically associated with proving fault and causation, particularly in technologically complex scenarios.

Nevertheless, the Convention's fixed liability limits—originally crafted with manned aviation in mind—may not reflect the specific risk dynamics of UAs.

Liability ceilings should be reconsidered in light of variables such as kinetic energy and operational environments. A more nuanced approach might involve a two-tier liability structure, balancing industry development with victim protection. Furthermore, the establishment of a compensation fund could serve as a safeguard in cases involving untraceable or uninsured operators, or catastrophic damage exceeding insurable limits.

Calls for legal harmonization become particularly relevant in the context of cross-border operations, which are expected to proliferate. A functioning internal market for UAs presupposes that operators can rely on uniform liability rules, enabling them to deploy their aircraft and personnel across Member States under consistent legal conditions. Without harmonization, the legal fragmentation across jurisdictions creates uncertainty and may deter economic actors from investing or expanding services within the EU.

UAs are likely to operate in far greater numbers and at lower altitudes, often in densely populated areas, increasing both the frequency and unpredictability of

[17] ICAO Appendix to Working paper *LC/36-WP/2-4* (n 25), para. 3.4.10

surface incidents. The EU's operation-centric regulatory model reflects this distinctive risk profile. Yet, it is acknowledged that where mixed incidents involving manned and unmanned aircraft occur, the absence of harmonized rules for both may complicate liability attribution.

Several avenues have been proposed to achieve harmonization. One approach is for Member States to incorporate the Rome Convention into domestic law, as Belgium[18] and Italy have done. Alternatively, its scope could be extended to cover domestic operations, either through unilateral declarations or a multilateral amendment process. This model is reflected in the Unlawful Interference Convention, which permits such extensions via opt-in mechanisms.

Another, more ambitious option would be for the European Union itself to accede to the Rome Convention, as it has done with the Montreal Convention, pursuant to Article 3(2) TFEU. However, this path is obstructed by the Rome Convention's own provisions (Articles 31 and 34), which do not foresee accession by supranational entities. Furthermore, the Convention's low ratification rate, perceived inadequacies, and limited liability caps render it unattractive as a basis for comprehensive EU-wide harmonization.

Given these limitations, the most pragmatic solution would be for the EU to enact its own dedicated liability instrument tailored to unmanned aviation. While civil liability traditionally falls outside EU competences, Article 114 TFEU grants authority to legislate in areas affecting the internal market. This legal basis was cited by the European Parliament in its 2017 Resolution on Civil Law Rules on Robotics, which explicitly called for EU-level rules on liability for emerging technologies, including AI and robotics.

A future legislative initiative under Article 114 TFEU could therefore serve as the foundation for an EU-specific liability regime governing UAs. This would ensure consistency, support public confidence, and facilitate commercial development while aligning with the EU's broader digital and mobility strategies.[19]

In sum, while the Rome Convention may serve as a conceptual foundation, it is neither sufficiently modern nor accepted widely enough to function as a harmonizing instrument within the EU. A bespoke EU regulatory framework is necessary to provide legal certainty, fair treatment of victims, and a conducive environment for market growth. The principal challenges ahead are not legal in nature, but rather political and procedural: achieving consensus across diverse legal systems and reconciling divergent national interests. Nonetheless, the increasing operational and economic significance of UAs renders such harmonization not only desirable, but inevitable.

---

[18] Grigorieff and De Bournonville (2019), p. 340.

[19] In this regard, in 2017, see European Parliament Resolution on Civil Law Rules on Robotics (n 184), para. 49 at 249 (Note that autonomous vehicles—including drones—are envisaged by this Resolution, in which it 'Considers that the civil liability for damage caused by robots is a crucial issue which also needs to be analyzed and addressed at Union level in order to ensure the same degree of efficiency, transparency and consistency in the implementation of legal certainty throughout the European Union for the benefit of citizens, consumers and businesses alike').

References

Abeyratne R (2009) The ICAO conventions on liability for third-party damage caused by aircraft. Air Space Law 34(6):406

Grigorieff C, De Bournonville D (2019) The 1952 Rome Convention on surface damage and its application in the case of aircraft noise emission: the example of Belgium. Air Space Law 44(4-5):340

Jennison M (2005) Rescuing the Rome Convention of 1952: six decades of effort to make a workable regime for damage caused by foreign aircraft to third parties. Rev Dr Unif 10(4):787

Kjellin H (2008) The new international regime for third party liability. Air Space Law 33(2):64

Masutti A (2016) Drones for civil use: European perspective on third-party liability and insurance. IH 2:254

Mendes De Leon P, Scott BI (2016) Drones and international air law. In: Završnik A (ed) Drones and unmanned aerial systems: legal and social implications for security and surveillance. Springer International Publishing, Cham, p 202

Scott B (2016) Key provisions in current aviation law. In: Custers B (ed) The future of drone use: opportunities and threats from ethical and legal perspectives. Asser Press, The Hague, p 252

Scott B. I. and Hartmann J. (2024), International aviation law on liability, in J. Hartmann, B. I. Scott, S. Truxal, A. Bertolini, & A. Masutti (Eds.), Civil regulation of autonomous unmanned aircraft systems in Europe, Edward Elgar Publishing, 12-30

Zampone A (2015) Riflessioni in tema di responsabilità nell'esercizio di Remotely-Piloted Aircraft System (RPAS), in. Diritto dei Trasporti 63

UAS and Criminal Law: An Analysis from the Perspective of the Italian Legal System

Giuseppina Panebianco

Contents

Abstract The chapter aims to test the limits of criminal liability in the use of unmanned aircraft systems ("UAS") in both military and civilian settings, from the perspective of the Italian legal system. The gradual introduction of intelligent systems instead of humans ends up blurring the objective and subjective link between the harmful or dangerous result and the human agent, undermining the legitimacy of using criminal law. However, today's technological structure of UAS, which can (still) be classified as semi-automatic vehicles, makes it possible to confirm the current solidity of the penal categories without excessive strain, both in the case of the intentional use of drones for the commission of crimes and in the hypothesis of the use of such instruments in the exercise of lawful yet dangerous activities. Indeed, the use of UAS does not interrupt the risk connection between human conduct and

G. Panebianco (✉)
Department of Law, University of Messina, Messina, Italy
e-mail: giuseppina.panebianco@unime.it

M. P. Rizzo, F. Franchina (eds.), *Drones in the Digital European Sky*, International Aviation Law Library 1,
https://doi.org/10.1007/978-3-032-16691-3_13

criminally relevant consequent injury, nor does it interrupt the necessary psychological link. It is, if anything, a matter of keeping the focus on the expansion of centres of responsibility in cases of complex organisations involving the collective management of the risk associated with the lawful use of drones.

1 Introduction

Whenever new interests arise that seek effective protection, or when new forms of aggression against "traditional" interests emerge, scholars of criminal law inevitably reflect on the appropriateness of resorting to punitive measures. Attention is drawn to the necessary examination of the proportionality and reasonableness of sanctions and, more generally, to concerns regarding the safeguarding of the required guarantees binding the legislator in criminal matters. This aspect is closely linked to the possible erosion of the dogmatic categories involved in attributing criminal liability should the choice fall on criminal sanctions.[1]

The issue arises particularly when established scientific knowledge is unavailable to sufficiently demonstrate the harmfulness or at least the danger of certain behaviours. A dramatic question then arises: should scientific and technological development be restrained, or should we tolerate the dreaded risk in the name of progress?[2] From traditional fields such as environmental law, agri-food safety, and product liability, the debate has expanded to encompass the emerging frontier of artificial intelligence (AI).[3] The progressive replacement of humans by intelligent systems tends to blur the essential objective and subjective link needed to attribute "criminal" responsibility: the more tasks are delegated to machines, the weaker the material and psychological connection between the harmful or dangerous consequence and the human agent. Thus, the risk increases of imputing a harmful result to a human that he/she neither intended nor could have foreseen, or worse, that he/she did not materially cause.

These considerations become especially relevant when intelligent systems operate through self-learning, accumulating data from physical experiences or from the

---

[1] For similar considerations, see Picotti (2024b), p. 293 f. The entire first issue of the year 2023 of the Revue Internationale de Droit Pénal: Picotti and Panattoni (2023) is dedicated to the topic of the relationship between the traditional categories of criminal law and AI. See also Hohenleitner (2024). For further bibliographical references, please refer to the following footnotes.

[2] In the context of the now copious literature on the precautionary principle, we limit our citation to the main Italian monographic contributions on criminal matters: Consorte 2013); Corn (2013); Castronuovo (2012); Masullo (2012). See also Beck (1986); Birger (2009).

[3] On the issues raised by artificial intelligence in criminal matters, see, among others, in addition to the literature cited in the following footnotes, D'Amico (2025); Gless et al. (2016), pp. 412–434; Hallevy (2013); King et al. (2020), pp. 89–120; Pagallo (2013); Schäfer (2024); Terrizzi (2023); Fragasso (2025).

web, and even generating new data. Self-learning implies the development of adaptive capacities by AI, which may manifest in "behavioural choices" independent of human intervention.[4] However, given the current impossibility of recreating the complexity of the human dimension using intelligent systems, criminal punitive measures must still target the person who designed or operated the device—whether intentionally preordained for harmful objectives or (more problematically) when the AI has eluded human control.[5] After all, the lack of fundamental subjective features in artificial agents—those necessary for the attribution of criminal responsibility and consequent blameworthiness—remains irreconcilable with the traditional functions of criminal law and criminal sanctions.[6] Even though some theories argue the plausibility of direct criminal liability for fully autonomous intelligent systems,[7] any such approach would still need to address the procedural rules and constitutional guarantees of criminal law.

Thus, the reflection on adapting models of criminal liability attribution in the face of the new empirical-technological reality must (continue to) concern the natural addressee of criminal sanction: the human being—and (from the Perspective of the Italian Legal System), following the framework outlined by Legislative Decree No. 231 of 8 June 2001, also legal entities.[8]

It is therefore necessary to immediately distinguish between the intentional use of unmanned aircraft systems (UAS) for causing harmful consequences that are relevant under criminal law, and the use of such tools in lawful but nevertheless hazardous activities.[9]

---

[4] Picotti (2024b), p. 295.

[5] See Piergallini (2020), p. 1763 ff., also for a summary of the theses that do not deny the possibility of establishing an autonomous punitive system and sometimes even direct criminal liability for intelligent systems. See also Salvadori (2021), p. 94 f.

[6] This is also expressed in Picotti (2023) Resolution on Traditional Criminal Law Categories and AI, p. 54 f., which rightly excludes artificial intelligence systems from having the criminal ability to act. See on this subject Picotti (2024a), p. 6 f. Salvadori (2021), p. 98 f. is also of the same opinion, but he does not exclude the introduction of direct liability for fully autonomous artificial agents in the future.

[7] See Salvadori (2021), p. 115 and literature cited therein.

[8] In the context of the now majority tendency in Italy inclined to recognise as essentially criminal in nature the liability of legal entities deriving from a crime, the reference to de Vero (2008) and de Vero (2001), p. 1126 f. remains fundamental. For a recent study on the subject see Orsina (2024), to which we also refer for the comprehensive bibliography on the subject.

[9] On the possible involvement of an AI system as a tool, as a perpetrator or as a victim of a crime see Basile (2019), p. 24 f. See also La Rosa (2023), p. 173 ff. See Mamak (2024) for an innovative analysis on robots as victims of crime.

2 The Use of Unmanned Aircraft Systems (UAS) in Military Strategy: The Issue of Targeted Killings

Although at first sight the topic concerning the use of UAS[10] for the commission of crimes may bring to mind everyday situations—particularly the unlawful capturing of images, that is related to the crime of unlawful interference with others' privacy—currently attention is mostly focused on the employment of drones in the strategic-military field, with specific regard to the practice of so-called targeted killings.[11] This situation alarms scholars because of the expansive use of such instruments, even outside recognized armed conflict zones, under the justification of the fight against terrorism.[12]

The matter appears particularly complex from the outset, considering the controversial characterization of the conflict itself, given that there are attempts to justify drone strikes against non-state actors[13] by invoking either international humanitarian law (so-called *jus in bello*) or anticipatory self-defence under Article 51 of the United Nations Charter.[14]

Even if there are serious doubts regarding the maxim "silent enim leges inter arma" ("in times of war, law falls silent"),[15] we will attempt to examine the implications of targeted killing under substantive criminal law with regard to individual responsibility. However, assuming the perspective of domestic law (that is, Italian law), it is necessary to keep in mind, on one hand, the peculiarities of the use of drones in such practices, and on the other hand, the rules regarding the extraterritorial application of substantive criminal law.

Regarding the first aspect, it must be considered that the state relating to the flag of the drone, that related to the runway, that concerning the ground pilot, and that of the target may not necessarily coincide. Under Italian criminal law, the principle of territoriality applies, under which state law applies primarily to crimes committed within its territory. As for derogations from the territoriality principle in criminal

---

[10] It should be noted that in the following, the acronym UAS and the noun 'drone' will be used interchangeably.

[11] See Droni armati in Italia e in Europa: problemi e prospettive. Tra strategie militari, esigenze di trasparenza e tutela dei diritti fondamentali. Conferenza internazionale di approfondimento sul tema dei droni armati e del loro uso per ragioni strategiche, militari, extragiudiziali, University of Milan (Italy), 25 September 2017. https://archiviodpc.dirittopenaleuomo.org/d/6399-droni-armati-in-italia-e-in-europa-problemi-e-prospettive

[12] See Dorsey (2019).

[13] See Breccia (2020), p. 278 f.; Meloni (2019), p. 15. See also Pertile (2019), p. 10, on the importance of the issue of conflict characterization in relation to the use of drones.

[14] Admittedly, nothing precludes, on the assumption of the consent of the territorial State, such practices from being regarded as law-enforcement operations, which, however, are subject to the limits of international human rights law: see Cucco and Mauri (2018), p. 68. Among other things, the large-scale undermining of human rights can even involve the commission of war crimes or crimes against humanity: see Meloni (2019), p. 16; see also, Pertile (2019), p. 8 f.

[15] In this regard, please refer to the insightful reflections of Eser (2019).

law, the law applies to acts committed abroad only in the cases expressly provided for, based on the criteria of active personality and passive personality.

Now, it may happen (and it has indeed happened) that an Italian citizen becomes the victim, by mistake, of a targeted killing carried out during a counterterrorism operation conducted by a state within the territory of another.[16]

Leaving aside the obstacles to criminal proceedings that may arise in such cases,[17] the difficulties in establishing the facts, and the complexity of reconstructing the chain of command involved in the operation[18]—difficulties certainly not eased by national governments "armed" with state secrets[19]—from the point of view of substantive criminal law, the attribution of criminal liability for the death of the collateral victim depends on whether the targeted killing itself was lawful: a controversial issue, to say the least, in the case in point. Indeed, not only is it doubtful whether such forms of counterterrorism can be classified as acts of war or as legitimate self-defence recognized under Article 51 of the UN Charter, but there is also no explicit basis in positive law that sets forth the lawfulness of homicide committed during war.[20]

Attempting to outline a framework of possible consequences—while remaining aware of the limitations on the application of criminal law due to the regime of immunities—it should be noted that the recognition of the lawfulness of the operation at the international level would reflect on the attribution of liability for the death of the collateral victim. Regardless of the fate of the designated target, responsibility would fall under negligence, provided the conditions of foreseeability and avoidability of the harmful result are met. However, given that these consequences are the result of operations deliberated and carried out within a complex multi-agent context, it is crucial to identify at what point in the chain of command the fatal error occurred. In any case, responsibility would lie with all actors involved in the decision-making and organizational process of the targeted killing operation, including intelligence agents, who would be judged under the framework of

[16] The case concerning the death of an Italian citizen killed by a US drone in the course of a targeted killing operation while he was being held hostage in Pakistan together with a US businessman, who was also killed during the anti-terrorist attack, is emblematic: on this case see Cucco and Mauri (2018), p. 65 f.; Saccucci (2019), p. 19 ff.

[17] Pursuant to Article 10 of the Italian Criminal Code (ICC), in the case of an offence (for which Italian law establishes life imprisonment or imprisonment of not less than a minimum of one year) committed abroad by a foreigner against an Italian citizen, the application of Italian criminal law is subject (in addition to the request of the Minister of Justice or the complaint of the offended person) to the presence of the offender in the territory of the State.

[18] For an attempt to piece together the chain of command, see Cucco and Mauri (2018), p. 71 f.

[19] As has rightly been said, in the case of drones, even though semi-automation is envisaged, due to the persistence of human intervention in the activation, management and control of the aircraft, there is nonetheless a depersonalisation; indeed the bureaucratic machine and above all the non-disclosure of documents make it difficult if not impossible to identify the subjects responsible for the damaging events: see Cucco (2019), pp. 307 and 313, who points out that with respect to the intended victim, targeted killing results in an execution not preceded by court proceedings.

[20] Eser (2019), p. 1108.

negligent cooperation. Consider the case in which the death of a person other than the intended target is not the result of a piloting error or a coordination failure, but rather of an authorization for the targeted killing that was issued on the basis of incorrect intelligence provided by the agents tasked with identifying the target. In such a scenario, assuming the (here not accepted) legality of the operation, negligent liability would fall on the agent responsible for the monitoring activities; the drone pilot would be exempt from liability; and other actors within the decision-making chain could be held negligently liable if it could be shown that they could have detected the mistake and faulty information upstream in the operation.

Another possible situation is that the harmful result against the unintended victim results from an authorized targeted killing, based on correct information and executed flawlessly.

Given that drone use for targeted killings is predicated on the high precision of the tool, only two possibilities arise: either the tool cannot be considered precise, calling into question the legality of the entire practice; or the collateral damage was foreseen and nonetheless accepted, leading to a qualification of intentional responsibility rather than negligence.[21]

However, assuming the legitimacy of the operation, the responsibility of those who gave the order can only arise if the order itself was unlawful, meaning not in conformity with the normative framework governing the use of drones for counterterrorism.

If an unlawful order is recognized, those who issued it would bear intentional responsibility, and the drone operator could benefit from the defence of duty fulfillment, but only if the order was indisputable and not manifestly criminal. Otherwise, the drone operator would be considered an intentional co-offender.

If, on the other hand, the practice of targeted killings was already unlawful under international law, the death of the collateral victim would imply intentional criminal liability for the decision-makers, whether the consequence was foreseen as a necessary cost of the operation or the result of an error in the use of the drone. Indeed, in the first case (planned collateral damage), any consideration of conscious negligence would be excluded from the outset due to the basic unlawfulness of the operation. In the second case (error in the performance of the operation), the consequence would fall within the scope of Article 82 of the Italian Criminal Code (ICC), according to which, if the offender injures or kills a person other than the intended target, he/she is liable as if he/she had committed the crime against the intended person.[22]

Moreover, if the targeted operation caused the death of both the designated target and an unintended victim, the Italian courts would have to consider, for sentencing purposes, the offence against the unintended victim as well, applying Article 82(2) of the ICC, which provides that if both the designated and non-designated persons

---

[21] See the perceptive reflections of Cucco (2019), p. 318, who supports similar conclusions with statistical data. See, also, Cucco and Mauri (2018), p. 78 f.

[22] See infra, footnote 42.

are harmed, the offender shall be punished with the penalty for the more serious offence, increased by up to half.[23]

This raises an important question because, for crimes committed abroad against a foreign victim, Italian law only applies under certain conditions that do not entirely coincide with those provided for offences committed against Italian citizens. Among these, Article 10 of the ICC requires that the extradition of the foreign perpetrator has not been granted or accepted by the foreign state in which he committed the crime, or by the state to which he belongs. The lack of this requirement would determine the loss of the connection between the act committed to the detriment of the designated foreign victim and Italian law, which would therefore only be applicable with respect to the offence committed against the Italian citizen.

Regarding the perpetrator of the targeted killing: the defence of duty fulfilment may still apply, but it would be difficult to claim the non-manifestly criminal nature of the order in such cases.

The situation is considerably simpler when terrorist groups employ drones to commit crimes: the intentional criminal liability is evident with regard to the offences committed.

However, the issue of drone use in targeted killings could also involve Italy at the international level. Reference is made to the unclear affair regarding the agreement between Italy and the United States for the storage of armed drones at the Sigonella military base, news of which emerged through the Wall Street Journal.[24] This agreement, subject to a high level of confidentiality, follows previous arrangements, notably the so-called Technical Arrangement on Sigonella.[25] This arrangement confirms that the Sigonella base remains under Italian command,[26] but grants full military command to the U.S. commander over U.S. personnel, equipment, and operations.[27] The U.S. commander has the obligation to inform the Italian commander beforehand only of significant U.S. activities—which do not include routine operations.[28] The Italian commander must notify the U.S. commander if the U.S. activities appear inconsistent with Italian laws[29] and, if necessary, intervenes to have the U.S. Commander immediately interrupt U.S. activities which clearly endanger life or public health.[30]

Based on the known legal framework, a targeted killing operation carried out from Sigonella with a U.S. drone would likely require prior Italian consent. Thus, Italy could incur international responsibility. Furthermore, individual criminal

[23] See infra, footnote 42.

[24] Lubold and Barnes (2016).

[25] The text of the Technical Arrangement on Sigonella is available at https://www.state.gov/06-406

[26] See Sec. VI, para. 1, Technical Arrangement on Sigonella.

[27] See Sec. VI, para. 3, Technical Arrangement on Sigonella. It has to be considered that any permanent increases of the operational component and relative support must be authorized by the Italian National Authorities: Sec. VI, para. 4, Technical Arrangement on Sigonella.

[28] See *Annex* 5, para 2, b, Technical Arrangement on Sigonella.

[29] See Sec. VI, para. 3, Technical Arrangement on Sigonella.

[30] See Sec. VI, para. 5, Technical Arrangement on Sigonella.

liability could fall on the decision-makers who authorized the operation.[31] Therefore, considerations similar to those already discussed regarding targeted killings decided, organised and carried out outside Italian territory would apply. However, in this case, Italian criminal law would be triggered by the stronger principle of territoriality, pursuant to Article 6(2) of the ICC, which adopts the ubiquity criterion for identifying the place of commission of the crime.[32]

3 Criminal Liability in the Operational and Training Use of Drones for National Defence and Security

In fact, the use of drones in the military field is not alien to Italian legislation, since Article 247 of Legislative Decree No. 66 of 15 March 2010 (Military Code, hereinafter referred to as IMC) authorizes the Italian Armed Forces to employ remotely piloted aircrafts (RPAs) in operational and training activities for national defence and security".[33] However, the same provision subordinates such use of RPAs to specific spatial and operational precautions, since the use of RPAs is limited to determined airspaces, and it is also bound by the restrictions "established in the special technical-operational document adopted by the Air Force, after consultation with the Armed Force employing the RPAs, and with the Italian Civil Aviation Authority (ENAC), in agreement with the Italian Board for Flight Assistance (ENAV), for aspects concerning air traffic management and control" (Article 247(2) of the IMC).[34] Nevertheless, these limitations do not apply "during operations on

---

[31] See Cucco (2019), p. 313.

[32] Under Article 6 of the ICC, "The offence is deemed to have been committed in the territory of the State when the act or omission constituting it has taken place wholly or in part there, or when the effect resulting from the act or omission has occurred there“. Pursuant to Article 8 of the Code of Criminal Procedure, "1. Territorial competence shall be determined in relation to the place where the offence has been committed. 2. If the criminal act results in the death of one or more persons, the court with competence shall be that of the place where the action or omission has occurred. 3. In the case of a permanent offence, the court with competence shall be that of the place where the criminal act has begun, even if such act has resulted in the death of one or more persons. 4. In the case of an attempted crime, the court with competence shall be that of the place where the latest action aimed at committing the crime has taken place". Where, on the other hand, the offence was committed "by a citizen taking part in international missions, in the territory and for the period in which they are carried out, the jurisdiction lies with the court in Rome": thus Article 19, paragraph 10 of Law No. 145 of 21 July 2016 (Rules concerning Italy‘s participation in international missions).

[33] Under Article 266 of Legislative Decree No. 66 of 2010, remotely piloted aircraft means an aircraft piloted by a crew operating from a remote command and control station. On the use of military drones see, recently Lamon (2024), p. 53 f.

[34] Moreover, pursuant to Article 248 of the IMC, "the operation of APRs weighing less than 20 kilograms, admitted to navigation and certified by the competent structure of the Ministry of Defence and entered in the relevant register, used by the Armed Forces within identified areas

national or foreign territory linked to situations of crisis or armed conflict." (Article 247(2) of the IMC).

Since the military sector and some other sectors are excluded from the application of the Italian Navigation Code regulations,[35] pilots and operators of RPAs cannot be considered perpetrators of the offences provided therein, without prejudice to their liability for the offences provided in the ICC and in the Italian Military Criminal Codes.[36]

With regard to the offences provided for in the ICC, the attribution of liability will occur according to the mental element required for the offence entailed in the particular case.

As for the military offences, not all the offences provided for in the Peacetime Military Criminal Code (hereinafter referred to as IPMCC) and relating to aircraft can be taken into account: one may think of those offences that require the condition of being on board the aircraft, or the cases concerning the breach of a commander's duty to be the last to abandon the aircraft in the event of danger (Article 112 of the IPMCC). These requirements are incompatible with RPAs.

Consequently, only the offences in which the aircraft–and thus the RPAs–constitutes the object or prerequisite of the criminally relevant conduct may apply: one may think, for instance, of the commander of an aircraft who causes collision or damage (Article 107 of the IPMCC and Article 108 for the negligent hypothesis); of the failure to use means to limit the damage in case of fire or other accident (Article 110 of the IPMCC); of the destruction or sabotage of military assets (Article 167 of the IPMCC, which also foresees the negligent hypothesis); of the loss or capture of (ship or) aircraft (Article 105 of the IPMCC and Article 106 for the negligent case); of the loss, collision, damage or abandonment of an aircraft (Article 256 of IPMCC, with reference to the cases provided for maritime pilots); of the failure to rescue or protect in the event of danger (Article 113 of the IPMCC); and possibly also of the abuse in embarking goods or passengers (Article 135 of the IPMCC).[37]

---

subject to a temporary overflight ban or outside such areas in the cases referred to in Article 247, paragraph 4, is entrusted to military personnel with appropriate qualifications."

[35] Pursuant to Article 748 of the Italian Navigation Code, the relative regulations do not apply to "military aircraft, customs aircraft, police forces and the national fire service aircraft, or to the aircraft considered in the fourth paragraph of Article 744,"i.e. "aircraft used by public or private entities, even occasionally, for activities aimed at protecting national security,"which are equated to state aircraft. Nevertheless, also for these aircraft the performance of flight operations "shall be carried out guaranteeing an adequate level of safety, identified according to the special regulations adopted by the competent State Authorities,"as well as, regarding those equated to state aircraft, in agreement with the Italian Civil Aviation Authority (ENAC). Similarly, the rules of the Navigation Code, "unless otherwise specifically provided for, do not apply to personnel, means, installations and infrastructures belonging to the Ministry of Defence and other Ministries that use State aircraft owned by them."

[36] Rivello (2018), p. 3.

[37] Pursuant to Article 273 of the IPMCC, the Rome Military Court has jurisdiction for offences committed abroad. Similarly, Article 19(1) of Law No. 145 of 21 July 2016 provides for personnel taking part in international missions, as well as personnel sent in support of the same missions, to whom the IPMCC applies.

4 Criminal Liability Relative to the Civil Use of Intelligent Aircraft: Employment of UAS for Illicit Purposes

At present, the technology on which drones are based involves semi-automation, since the start-up, management, and control of such aircraft still depend on human intervention.[38] As a consequence, the intentional use of UAS for the commission of crimes does not involve distortions of criminal law categories; nor do particular difficulties arise in terms of attributing responsibility, given that the regulatory framework makes identification of the UAS operator—meaning the person (natural or legal) who uses the drone—easy. Indeed, Article 6 of the UAS-IT ENAC Regulation (that is, the Regulation issued by the Italian Civil Aviation Authority) provides that UAV operators must be registered on the d-flight platform "also for the purposes of identification and attribution of civil and criminal liability." It is true that registration is not imposed for aircraft that weigh less than 250 grams and are not equipped with any sensor (i.e. camera); on the contrary, the obligation persists where drones (not classifiable as toys) are equipped with sensors capable of capturing personal data.[39] In fact, the criminal offence most frequently encountered appears to be that of unlawful interference in private life, committed through the illicit capture of images.[40] Another criminally relevant conduct may be identified in the use of drones for the remote monitoring of workers' activities, in violation of the provisions set forth by Article 4 of Law No. 300 of 20 May 1970 (the Worker's Statute): for such conduct, Article 171 of the Privacy Code (Legislative Decree No. 196 of 30 June 2003) stipulates that the criminal sanctions provided by Article 38 of Law No. 300/1970 shall apply.[41]

Should the intentional use of a UAS result in an outcome different from that intended by the agent—in terms of the victim harmed or the type of harmful

[38] For the categorisation of artificial agents according to the level of automation and autonomy, see Salvadori (2021), p. 92 f.

[39] See Article 14(5)(a)(ii) of Commission Implementing Regulation (EU) 2019/947 of 24 May 2019 on rules and procedures for the operation of unmanned aircraft.

[40] Under Article 615-bis of the ICC, "Whoever, through the use of visual or sound recording instruments, unduly obtains information or images pertaining to private life in the places indicated in Article 614 [that is: dwelling, other private place of abode, and belongings thereof], shall be punished with imprisonment from six months to four years. "It should be added that prosecution, which is normally referred to the complaint of the offended person, is ex officio in the aggravated hypothesis of the act committed by a public official or a person in charge of a public service, "with abuse of power or with violation of the duties inherent to his/her function or service, or by a person who also abusively exercises the profession of private detective".

[41] The case in which monitoring in the workplace is part of a preventive investigation activity, carried out by the employer's lawyer who has received a specific mandate, in the event of criminal proceedings (Article 391-novies of the Italian Code of Criminal Procedure), must be considered differently. In this eventuality, the criminal relevance of remote control with audiovisual instruments must be excluded, provided that it is an activity aimed at ascertaining a specific offence, of which there is already evidence found elsewhere, perpetrated by one or more specific employees: see Consulich (2024), p. 404 f.

consequence—the operator-pilot cannot be excused. In such cases, the legal institutions of "aberratio ictus" and "aberratio delicti", regulated by Articles 82 and 83 of the ICC, come into play.[42] One can think of a case where a drone, launched against someone else's property with the intent to damage it, due to a piloting error or another cause, strikes the property of a different person or injures or kills an unsuspecting victim nearby. In the first scenario, under Article 82 of the ICC, the agent would still be liable for intentional damage; in the second scenario, the agent would be liable for negligent personal injury or negligent manslaughter, pursuant to Article 83 of the ICC. Furthermore, if death or injuries result from an act classified by law as an intentional crime, Article 586 of the ICC will apply. This article, while referring to Article 83, also provides for increased penalties for negligent manslaughter, or negligent injuries, committed during the perpetration of an intentional crime. In this regard, one might consider an agent who, while trying to capture private moments of the victim's life with a drone, flies it so close that it causes injury or death to the victim.

However, it should be considered that the UAS operator and the pilot may not necessarily coincide. It is thus appropriate to distinguish between cases where the pilot acted in concert with the operator and cases where the pilot operated the drone without the operator's knowledge. In the case of an agreement to commit the crime, there are no particular difficulties in framing the situation within the framework of participation in a crime. If, on the other hand, the pilot committed a different crime than the one agreed upon, Article 116 of the ICC,[43] as interpreted by the Constitutional Court's judgment No. 42 of 31 May 1965, would apply. Thus, the operator would be liable for the offence other than the agreed one, only if it were a logically foreseeable development of that agreed upon.

Conversely, if the pilot employs the drone to commit an offence without the operator's knowledge, it must be verified whether, while affirming the pilot's intentional liability, the operator could be held liable for negligence, always provided that the act is also punishable as a negligent crime under law. Given the principle of individual criminal responsibility, the operator could be held liable for the pilot's act

[42] "Aberratio ictus" and "aberratio delicti" are Latin expressions used by Italian scholars to identify two types of mistakes that take place in the performance of the criminal activity; these are thus operative mistakes. Under Article 82 of the ICC (to which aberratio ictus refers), if the offender harms a person other than the one, he intended to harm because of a mistake in the performance of the crime or of another cause, he shall be considered liable as if he had harmed the victim he intended to harm. If the offender harms both the victim he intended to harm and another person, he shall be punished with the punishment related to the more serious offence, increased by up to half.

Under article 83 of the ICC (to which aberratio delicti refers), if the offender causes a result other than that he intended to cause, the offender shall be considered liable for the result that he did not want to cause, provided the committed act is an offence under law that may be committed negligently. Furthermore, if the offender caused both the intended result and another, the rule related to concurrent offences shall be applied.

[43] Under Article of 116 Italian Criminal Law, if the offence committed is different from the offence intended by one of the participants, the latter shall also be liable if the effect is a consequence of his/her action or omission. If the offence committed is more serious than the one intended, the punishment is diminished with respect to the participant who intended the less serious offence.

to the extent that it was foreseeable and avoidable under the concrete circumstances. However, it seems difficult to attribute to the operator a legal duty to prevent the pilot's crime.

4.1 Criminal Liability in the Lawful Use of UAS

The reasoning becomes far more challenging on the side of negligent liability, from which inspiration can be drawn from the related field of autonomous vehicles, on which Italian criminal law scholarship has already begun to reflect, albeit in the absence of specific regulations governing this new technological reality. Indeed, some EU countries have adopted extra-criminal regulations in this field, with France standing out for even having regulated the criminal liability profiles concerning vehicles with partial or full delegation of driving.[44] Instead, in Italy we can only quote Ministerial Decree No. 70 of 28 February 2018, which regulates the experimentation on public roads of autonomous vehicles. The decree defines such vehicles as those "equipped with technologies capable of adopting and implementing driving behaviours without active intervention from the driver, in determined road environments and external conditions".[45]

In this sector, the issue is defining the negligent liability of the human agent behind the machine when the machine, "entrusted" with driving, produces criminally relevant effects. However, as long as the vehicles are semi-automatic,[46] there is no reason to doubt the applicability of the traditional criteria concerning negligent liability, with the related limits. The first limit of negligent liability is defined as the permitted risk principle (doctrine of permissible risk). This principle assumes that there are activities that are very useful for society, but nevertheless dangerous. These are activities that are supported by a substantial framework of rules. However, it can happen that even though these activities are carried out in full compliance with the sectoral regulations as well as the ordinary precautions, harmful results occur. With respect to the latter, there is a margin of tolerance in the legal system for which criminal liability for negligence cannot be assumed. The second limit can be considered an aspect of the principle of individual criminal responsibility. This lays down that each member of society, while having to observe his/her duties of care, must be

[44] For a summary, see, Vadalà (2023), p. 6 f. See also the *reports* published in Revue internationale de droit penal 2023 94(1).

[45] Pursuant to Article 10 of Ministerial Decree No. 70 of 28 February 2018, "The on-road steering of the automated vehicle during the test is carried out by a supervisor […] The supervisor must be able to switch promptly between operating the vehicle in automatic mode and operating it in manual mode, and vice versa. The supervisor has responsibility for the vehicle in both operating modes". On the distinction between automatic agents and autonomous agents, see Salvadori (2021), p. 92.

[46] According to the levels of autonomous driving defined by the Society of Automotive Engineers, this characteristic can be found in the first three levels.

able to trust that the persons with whom he/she enters into contact will do likewise, as they are themselves capable of making responsible choices.

Regarding the first limit—that is, the extent of risk that the legal system is willing to tolerate in light of the social utility of a lawful but hazardous activity—its definition necessarily depends on the body of extra-criminal regulations governing the practice: the more extensive the regulations, the clearer the boundaries of negligence. On the other hand, in relation to novel activities for which the legal system has not yet pronounced itself regarding their social utility, it falls to the experimenter to carry out a risk assessment, refraining from engaging in activities likely to produce harmful consequences. In such a context, the sharing of know-how becomes fundamental, an aspect today increasingly promoted by the idea of Just Culture.[47]

Indeed, the framework of extra-criminal regulations concerning UAS appears nowadays comparable, in terms of abundance of rules, to that concerning road traffic, although further developments are anticipated in keeping with the advancement of intelligent technologies currently under experimentation.[48]

However, while the crucial role of extra-criminal regulation supporting the entire life cycle of intelligent systems remains undisputed, attention must focus on the degree of automation of the vehicle and the multiplicity of professional figures involved from its design to its maintenance.[49]

Nevertheless, bearing in mind the parallel experience in the field of the semi-automatic car, it must be noted that potential harmful effects can stem from a "behavioural choice" by the smart vehicle that proves erroneous when interacting with other road users, human or technological. This situation calls into question the human agent responsible for managing the vehicle. However, nothing precludes that the harmful consequence may also originate from congenital defects in the design, programming, or construction of the intelligent vehicle, bringing to the surface the difficulty of reconstructing the causal link between the conduct of the various actors involved in its production and the harmful result, especially considering the possible involvement of multiple corporate entities.[50]

In Italy, under private law, protection mechanisms are clearly available. Under criminal law, however, the tool becomes "blunt" for two main reasons: on one hand,

---

[47] With particular reference to the topic at hand, see Articles 72 and 73 of EU Regulation 2018/1139 of the European Parliament and of the Council of 4 July 2018, and Article 19 of Commission Implementing Regulation (EU) 2019/947 of 24 May 2019.

[48] Recently, the Commission Delegated Regulation (EU) 2024/1107 of 13 March 2024 supplemented the Regulation (EU) 2018/1139 of the European Parliament and of the Council "by laying down detailed rules for the continuing airworthiness of certified unmanned aircraft systems and their components, and on the approval of organisations and personnel involved in these tasks."It should be added that according to recital 50 of Regulation (EU) 2024/1689 of the European Parliament and of the Council of 13 June 2024, laying down harmonised rules on artificial intelligence (so-called *AI Act*), aeronautical vehicles can also be classified as "high risk systems" under the same regulation.

[49] See Picotti (2024b), p. 298.

[50] See Piergallini (2020), p. 1753 f.

individual liability becomes hard to attribute, given the difficulty of establishing causation between the conduct of specific individuals and the harmful result; on the other, Corporate liability under Legislative Decree No. 231 of 8 June 2001 could technically apply when the perpetrator is unidentified (under Article 8), but is limited to a catalogue of predicate offences that includes homicide and bodily injuries only when committed in violation of workplace health and safety regulations.

Moreover, the harmful consequence could result from the emergence of concurring causes resulting from intentional conducts, such as the manipulation of software, structural components, or the sabotage of the hardware system.[51] Furthermore, when conduct impacts the intelligent system, another complex issue arises: whether the AI system itself constitutes an interest deserving protection, a topic not addressed in this paper.[52]

With these premises in mind, we can draw the line at criminal liability in the lawful use of UAS. The classification of unmanned aircraft systems (UAS) clearly indicates their semi-automatic nature, and does not envisage the possibility of them operating with total autonomy. Even when the vehicle is not radio-controlled but piloted remotely, following a pre-set trajectory from take-off to landing established by the pilot, the drone remains under the constant supervision of the human operator. One might envisage a situation of quasi-total autonomy if there were a drop in the battery charge level, triggering the home-point system or even an autonomous landing in the case of a critically low battery. Nevertheless, any harmful consequence caused by a drone activating autonomous return or landing manoeuvres would still be attributable to the pilot, to the extent that the pilot should have monitored the battery charge level. In such cases, the pilot's liability could be excluded only if: a supervening causal factor intervenes, of such a quality or intensity as to overcome the originally punishable risk activated by the agent (applying Article 41(2) of the ICC);[53] or if entirely fortuitous causes intervene, producing an unpredictable harmful effect despite the observance of all required precautions in an inherently risky practice (pursuant to Article 45 of the ICC).[54]

[51] See Vadalà (2023), p. 3. On the artificial agent as the material object of the offence, see Salvadori (2021), p. 111.

[52] For a mention of this question see, La Rosa (2023), p. 174. See Mamak (2024) for an innovative analysis on robots as victims of crime.

[53] Under Article 41 of the ICC, "1. The presence of pre-existing, simultaneous or supervening causes, even though independent of the act or omission of the offender, shall not exclude a causal relationship between his/her act or omission and the result. 2. Supervening causes shall exclude a causal relationship when they were in themselves sufficient to bring about the result. If, in that case, the act or omission previously committed itself constitutes an offence, the punishment prescribed shall therefore be applied. 3. The preceding rules shall apply even when the pre-existing, simultaneous or supervening cause consists of the unlawful act of another person".

[54] Under Article 45 of the ICC, "Anyone who has committed an act through inevitable accident or force majeure shall not be punishable".

4.1.1 Notes with a View to (not Desired) Full Automation

It cannot be ruled out that in the future we will have to deal with fully autonomous UAS, for which the same issues already explored by criminal law scholarship regarding self-driving cars arise; issues which, in this context, can only be briefly mentioned. Once again, the reflection focuses on the profiles of causality and psychological connection concerning individuals whose conduct is not only non-contiguous in space and time to the harmful consequence but also appears to have been entirely surpassed by the deviant behaviour of the intelligent system, prompted by stimuli that were not foreseeable by its programmer and for which the algorithm governing the intelligent vehicle was therefore not trained. Regarding the objective element, by appealing to modern theories of objective imputation of the effect, one could envisage a hypothesis falling under Article 41(2), of the ICC,[55] whereby the causal chain initially activated by the programmer—though etiologically relevant in itself—is supplanted by a new and qualitatively different risk triggered by a decision-making system. Nevertheless, as rightly observed, the inherent unpredictability of the algorithm is not unpredictable to the programmer.[56] Based on this observation, there is scepticism about the possibility of invoking the second paragraph of Article 41[57] to exclude the causal link between the programmer's conduct and the effect caused by the intelligent system. However, it is argued that the general foreseeability of the harmful effect, inferred from the "predictable unpredictability" of the intelligent system, risks resulting in an imputation of strict liability, which is inadmissible under Italian criminal law.[58]

Yet it seems that this reflection lacks a necessary premise, which brings us back to the starting point of these brief considerations on the criminal implications of the use of UAS. As long as the use of fully autonomous systems remains in the realm of experimentation, any harmful results caused by the deviant system must be attributed, within the limits of their foreseeability and preventability, to the person who "generated" it. The fact that such an activity is, so to speak, unprecedented does not exempt the experimenter from respecting the (additional) precautions required by the still experimental practice, which inevitably fall almost exclusively to the one conducting the tests. In these terms, it does not seem that holding the programmer of the intelligent system accountable for having triggered a foreseeable risk is alien to the traditional framework of negligent liability. Subsequently, if the social utility of fully autonomous vehicles were to be recognized to such an extent as to promote their widespread use, the state's authorization would carry with it the effect of the legal system assuming the (thus tolerated) risk inherent in their circulation. Thus, harmful effects occurring despite compliance with precautionary norms provided for by law or socially approved would represent an accepted cost of modernity. In

[55] See supra, footnote 53.

[56] See Piergallini (2020), pp. 1759 and 1762.

[57] See supra, footnote 53.

[58] See Piergallini (2020), p. 1762.

such a context, the assessment regarding the sustainability of the collateral effects of the "predictable unpredictability" of intelligent systems can only fall to lawgivers, to whom it exclusively belongs—within the balancing of promoting technological development and protecting society—and it is they who would have to introduce any measures to prohibit risky activities.

4.1.2 Lawful Drone Use and Workplace Safety

A particular area in which the lawful use of drones could lead to the production of criminally relevant effects is that of work, where UAS are employed for carrying out certain activities. In such cases, it is unlikely that the operator will be the one piloting the aircraft; rather, it is foreseeable that the employer will assume the role of registered operator, while the worker will be entrusted with piloting the drone. Moreover, nothing prevents the operator from owning multiple drones assigned to different pilots. In this situation, the extra-criminal regulations framework to be considered in evaluating potential profiles of negligent liability will result from the combination of the regulations concerning UAS with the body of rules concerning the protection of health and safety in the workplace (that in Italy is regulated by Legislative Decree No. 81 of 9 April 2008).

However, the matter of identifying liabilities becomes particularly complicated, not only due to the intricate web of extra-criminal rules but also because of the high probability that the criminally relevant harmful consequence occurs in contexts involving multiple complex company organizations, each with its own set of persons bearing specific precautionary obligations. Such scenarios typically occur when specific activities are outsourced. The co-presence of the principal company and the contracting company generates not only new common risks inherent to joint activities but also interference risks arising from the intersection of activities conducted by different enterprises.[59] The emergence of new risks entails the proliferation of new safety guarantor figures, entrusted with managing them and required to collaborate to prevent harmful effects deriving from the interference of the various activities. The promotion of cooperation and coordination is entrusted to the employer, who is responsible for drafting a single risk assessment document that specifies the measures adopted to eliminate or, where elimination is not possible, to minimize the risks deriving from interference (Article 26 of Legislative Decree No. 81/2008). Moreover, it is also incumbent upon the employer to acquire certifications regarding the technical-professional suitability of the contracting company or of self-employed workers. Additionally, the employer of the contracting company bears, beyond the ordinary duties of guarantee and supervision, those concerning the safeguarding from common and interference risks; in case of subcontracting, the employer of the contracting company also bears the duties related to risks arising

[59] See Consulich (2024), p. 289.

from his own activities and those concerning common and interference risks connected with the activity of the subcontractor.[60]

On the assumption of the comprehensive UAS regulation, let us examine the profiles of criminal liability under Legislative Decree No. 81/2008 in a complex business reality. For example, imagine a multinational company entrusting a contracting company with the inspection of confined areas within a refinery using drones, and that during the inspection, a piloting error causes the injury or death of a worker belonging either to the contracting company or to the principal company.

Simplifying the situation, we can suppose three different causes underlying the accident: (a) the worker entrusted with the inspection did not possess adequate technical skills; (b) the drone employed lacked the necessary technical characteristics for that type of operation; and (c) the harmful consequence resulted solely from a piloting error by the worker-pilot.

(a) In the first case, while maintaining the pilot's responsibility, the employer of the contracting company, who would normally also be the drone operator, could be liable for culpa in eligendo (for having entrusted the piloting of the drone to a worker without the necessary skills). Moreover, the principal company could also bear liability in the case of insufficiently verified certifications.
(b) In the case where the injury occurred because of using a UAS that did not meet the technical standards required for that specific operation yet was certified as compliant, neither the pilot nor the employer-operator—who relied on the evaluation carried out by the competent certifying authority—would be liable. Thus, the principal company would also be exempt from liability.
(c) Lastly, if the worker-pilot of the contracting company—despite using a technically adequate UAS and holding the necessary special licence to pilot such aircraft—caused the harmful result by violating certain precautionary measures required by UAS regulations or workplace safety rules, the worker would bear negligent liability. The employer of the contracting company might also be liable, provided that the worker's misconduct was foreseeable and avoidable. Instead, the employer of the principal company should not be held liable. Nevertheless, it must be kept in mind that the case law is particularly strict, requiring, to exclude the liability of the employer, that "the worker's conduct falls completely outside the area of risk defined by the activity being carried out"; thus, the unwise behaviour of the worker must be interruptive "not because it is exceptional, but because it is eccentric in relation to the occupational risk that the guarantor is tasked with managing".[61] Moreover, in the situation described, the area of risk is amplified by the presence of multiple companies and by the associated common and interference risks, which could consequently also call into question the responsibility of the principal company.

---

[60] See Consulich (2024), p. 299.

[61] See Corte di cassazione, no. 49373 of 5 October 2018; among many, recently, Corte di cassazione, no. 2768 of 14 January 2025; Corte di cassazione no. 42951 of 31 October 2024; Corte di cassazione, no. 19961 of 11 May 2023.

5 Concluding Remarks

The current technological structure of UAS, which are still classified as semi-automatic vehicles, allows us to confirm the current resilience of criminal law categories without excessive strain or concerning distortions, unlike the scenarios prospectively imagined for self-learning algorithms and smart cars. At present, therefore, the risk of dangerous drifts toward forms of strict liability or even liability for others' conduct in the use of drones appears averted. Remotely piloted aircraft are still "vehicles" of criminal liability in the sense that their use does not cause an interruption in the risk connection between human conduct and the criminally relevant harmful consequence, nor does it interrupt the necessary psychological link between these two poles.

At the same time, however, attention must remain high concerning the expansion of centres of liability in cases of complex organizations that imply a collective management of the risks associated with drone use.

The interaction of multiple conducts that occur along the life cycle of the intelligent aircraft generates opposite concerns.

In the case of lawful use of UAS, the challenge lies in containing the expansion of the scope of responsibility, which tends to involve figures far removed from the criminally relevant effect. Nonetheless, – it must be reiterated—a proper management of criminal law categories allows such risks of deviation to be effectively contained.

Conversely, in the case of intentional use of remotely piloted aircraft to kill, based on claimed justifications of the military operation's legality (the plausibility of which is, at the very least, doubtful),[62] the risk arises of never being able to single out a responsible person within the labyrinth of the chain of command.

The absolute lack of transparency both regarding the material conduct of individual practices—about which the highest confidentiality is maintained—and the related regulations, which are not made public, obscures the decision-making process culminating in the production of the deliberate harmful result.

References

Basile F (2019) Intelligenza artificiale e diritto penale: quattro possibili percorsi di indagine. Diritto penale e uomo. https://dirittopenaleuomo.org/wp-content/uploads/2019/09/IA-diritto-penale.pdf

Beck U (1986) Risikogesellschaft. Auf dem Weg in eine andere Moderne. Suhrkamp Verlag, Frankfurt a.M

Birger A (2009) Das Vorsorgeprinzip im EU-Recht. Mohr Siebrek Ek, Tübingen

Breccia P (2020) Legittima difesa e targeted killings: gli Stati Uniti e il "caso Soleimani". Ordine internazionali e diritti umani:278–302

[62] See supra, §2.

Castronuovo D (2012) Principio di precauzione e diritto penale. Paradigmi dell'incertezza nella struttura del reato. Aracne, Roma

Consorte F (2013) Tutela penale e principio di precauzione. Profili attuali, problematicità, possibili sviluppi. Giappichelli, Torino

Consulich F (2024) Manuale di diritto penale del lavoro. Giappichelli, Torino

Corn E (2013) Il principio di precauzione nel diritto penale. Studio sui limiti all'anticipazione della tutela penale. Giappichelli, Torino

Cucco C (2019) La partita del diritto penale nell'epoca dei "drone-crimes". Diritto penale contemporaneo rivista trimestrale 2:304–324. https://dpc-rivista-trimestrale.criminaljusticenetwork.eu/it/archivio/rivista-trimestrale-2-2019

Cucco C, Mauri D (2018) Omicidi mirati a mezzo drone: brevi riflessioni a margine del caso "Lo Porto" tra diritto penale e diritto internazionale. Diritto penale contemporaneo 5. https://archiviodpc.dirittopenaleuomo.org/d/6019-omicidi-mirati-a-mezzo-drone-brevi-riflessioni-a-margine-del-caso-lo-porto-tra-diritto-penale-e-dir

D'Amico L (2025) La misura della (im)prevedibilità. Modelli di imputazione della responsabilità al tempo dell'intelligenza artificiale. Edizioni Scientifiche Italiane, Napoli

de Vero G (2001) Struttura e natura giuridica dell'illecito di ente collettivo dipendente da reato. Rivista Italiana di Diritto e Procedura Penale :1126–1167

de Vero G (2008) La responsabilità penale delle persone giuridiche. Giuffré, Milano

Dorsey J (2019) Towards an EU common position on the use of armed drones. https://archiviodpc.dirittopenaleuomo.org/d/6399-droni-armati-in-italia-e-in-europa-problemi-e-prospettive

Droni armati in Italia e in Europa: problemi e prospettive. Tra strategie militari, esigenze di trasparenza e tutela dei diritti fondamentali. Conferenza internazionale di approfondimento sul tema dei droni armati e del loro uso per ragioni strategiche, militari, extragiudiziali, University of Milan (Italy), 25 September 2017. https://archiviodpc.dirittopenaleuomo.org/d/6399-droni-armati-in-italia-e-in-europa-problemi-e-prospettive

Eser A (2019) Uccidere in guerra: alla ricerca di un fondamento di legittimità. Rivista Italiana di Diritto e Procedura Penale :1105–1135

Fragasso B (2025) Intelligenza artificiale e responsabilità penale. Principi e categorie alla prova di una tecnologia "imprevedibile". Giappichelli, Torino

Gless S, Silverman E, Weigand T (2016) If robots cause harm, who is to blame? New Crim Law Rev:412–434

Hallevy G (2013) When robots kill: Artificial Intelligence under criminal law. Northeastern University Press, Boston

Hohenleitner F (2024) Die strafrechtliche Verantwortung der Hersteller automatisierter und autonomer Fahrzeuge. Duncker & Humblot, Berlin

King T, Aggarwal N, Taddeo M, Floridi L (2020) Artificial intelligence crime: an interdisciplinary analysis of foreseeable threats and solutions. Sci Eng Ethics 26:89–120

La Rosa E (2023) Criminal law and artificial intelligence: which spaces for a criminal liability of the robot? In: Marino D, Monaca M (eds) Artificial intelligence and economics: the key to the future. Springer, Cham, pp 173–187

Lamon M (2024) L'impiego dei droni militari. Rivista del Diritto dell'economia, dei trasporti e dell'ambiente:XXII, 53–71

Lubold G, Barnes JE (2016) Italy quietly agrees to armed U.S. drone missions over Libya Rome allows defensive flights from Sicily in military missions against Islamic State. Wall Street J

Mamak K (2024) Robotics, AI, and criminal law: crimes against robots. Routledge, Taylor & Francis Group, London

Masullo MN (2012) Colpa penale e precauzione nel segno della complessità. Teoria e prassi nella responsabilità dell'individuo e dell'ente. Edizioni Scientifiche Italiane, Napoli

Meloni C (2019) Gli attacchi letali dei droni davanti alle Corti. https://archiviodpc.dirittopenaleuomo.org/d/6399-droni-armati-in-italia-e-in-europa-problemi-e-prospettive

Orsina A (2024) La responsabilità da reato dell'ente tra colpa di organizzazione e colpa di reazione. Giappichelli, Torino

Pagallo U (2013) The law of robots. Crimes, contracts and torts. Springer, Dordrecht
Pertile M (2019) Droni armati e diritto internazionale. https://archiviodpc.dirittopenaleuomo.org/d/6399-droni-armati-in-italia-e-in-europa-problemi-e-prospettive
Picotti L (2023) Resolution on Traditional Criminal Law Categories and AI. Revue internationale de droit penal 94:53–59
Picotti L (2024a) Categorie tradizionali del diritto penale e intelligenza artificiale: crisi o palingenesi? Sistema Penale:1–20. https://www.sistemapenale.it/pdf_contenuti/1722408015_picotti-aidp-paris-2662024-sp.pdf
Picotti L (2024b) Intelligenza artificiale e diritto penale: le sfide ad alcune categorie tradizionali. Diritto penale e processo:293–301
Picotti L., Panattoni B. (ed.) (2023), Traditional criminal law categories and AI: crisis or palingenesis? Rev Int Droit Pénal 94(1)
Piergallini C (2020) Intelligenza artificiale: da 'mezzo' ad 'autore' del reato? Rivista Italiana di Diritto e Procedura Penale :1745–1774
Rivello P (2018) Gli aspetti giuridici connessi all'uso dei droni. Il diritto penale della globalizzazione. https://www.dirittopenaleglobalizzazione.it/wp-content/uploads/2018/05/Gli-aspetti-giuridici-connessi-all%E2%80%99uso-dei-droni.pdf
Saccucci A (2019) Risarcimenti alle vittime civili degli attacchi letali dei droni: il caso Lo Porto. https://archiviodpc.dirittopenaleuomo.org/d/6399-droni-armati-in-italia-e-in-europa-problemi-e-prospettive
Salvadori I (2021) Agenti Artificiali, opacità tecnologica e distribuzione della responsabilità penale. Rivista Italiana di Diritto e Procedura Penale :83–118
Schäfer M (2024) Artificial Intelligence und Strafrecht: Zur Leistungsfähigkeit des geltenden Strafrechts im Hinblick auf die Herstellerverantwortlichkeit bei Schädigungen durch tiefe neuronale Netze. Duncker & Humblot, Berlin
Terrizzi LA (2023) Medical *devices* e diritto penale. Profili di responsabilità del produttore e dell'utilizzatore. Giuffrè Francis Lefebvre, Milano
Vadalà RM (2023) La questione penale delle auto a guida autonoma in prospettiva comparata La legislazione penale. https://www.lalegislazionepenale.eu/wp-content/uploads/2023/11/VADALA-Definitivo.pdf

UAS and Insurance

Francesca Pellegrino

Contents

Abstract This chapter focuses on the insurance issues arising from the use of unmanned aircraft, according to Italian and European regulations. In this context, the insurance issues are considered in the light, on one hand (European framework), of EU Regulation 2018/1139, which sets common rules in the field of civil aviation, supplemented by Delegated EU Regulation 2019/945 and Implementing EU Regulation 2019/947, and—on the other hand (Italian framework)—of ENAC UAS-IT 2021 Regulation. The European Regulations clarify that the operations with RPAS (Remotely Piloted Aircraft System) must be covered by adequate insurance, able to ensure that unmanned civil airborne traffic in European airspace is safe for people on the surface and in flight. The new European legislation is, in fact, based on the concept of risk of the operations. Likewise, in the Italian legal system, the ENAC Regulation requires an insurance coverage for civil liability risk, appropriate to the purpose and with maximum limits not lower than the minimum parameters set out in the table attached to Article 7 of Regulation (EC) 785/2004.

F. Pellegrino (✉)
Department of Law, University of Messina, Messina, Italy
e-mail: fpellegrino@unime.it

M. P. Rizzo, F. Franchina (eds.), *Drones in the Digital European Sky*,
International Aviation Law Library 1,
https://doi.org/10.1007/978-3-032-16691-3_14

1 Introduction

Unmanned aerial vehicles, commonly called drones, represent the new frontier of air transport for both passengers and goods.

The European drone market is growing very rapidly, reaching EUR 145 million in 2023, which represents an increase of 23% compared to previous year. Growth is expected to exceed EUR 200 million by 2030. In addition, more than 100,000 people are expected to be employed in this sector by 2035.

These particular aircraft have long been used only in specialized operations, in areas such as fire extinction, weather monitoring, aerial footage, inspection of risk zones, or agriculture.

During the Covid-19 pandemic, they were also used to deliver medicines and medical equipment, but also to disinfect public areas.[1]

In the post-pandemic era, many companies are already using drones to deliver goods and parcels, reducing delivery times and improving logistics efficiency.

But considering that unmanned aerial vehicles share the same airspace as conventional aircraft, it is crucial to ensure the safe, secure and efficient integration of drones into non-segregated airspace and aerodromes.

Therefore, the future development of this sector requires an appropriate regulatory framework at international, EU and national levels, balancing technological requirements with safety/security guarantees and liability/insurance aspects.

2 The EU Regulatory Framework

At the European level, the current regulatory framework is composed of the Basic Regulation (EU) 2018/1139,[2] laying down common rules in the field of civil aviation, supplemented by Delegated Regulation (EU) 2019/945[3] and Implementing Regulation (EU) 2019/947.[4]

---

[1] See Gaspari (2020), p. 139 ff.; Lamon (2021), p. 495 ff.

[2] Regulation (EU) 2018/1139 of the European Parliament and of the Council of 4 July 2018 on common rules in the field of civil aviation and establishing a European Union Aviation Safety Agency, and amending Regulations (EC) No 2111/2005, (EC) No 1008/2008, (EU) No 996/2010, (EU) No 376/2014 and Directives 2014/30/EU and 2014/53/EU of the European Parliament and of the Council, and repealing Regulations (EC) No 552/2004 and (EC) No 216/2008 of the European Parliament and of the Council and Council Regulation (EEC) No 3922/91 (*OJ* L 212, 22.8.2018, pp. 1–122).

[3] Commission Delegated Regulation (EU) 2019/945 of 12 March 2019 on unmanned aircraft systems and on third-country operators of unmanned aircraft systems (*OJ* L 152, 11.6.2019, pp. 1–40).

[4] Commission Implementing Regulation (EU) 2019/947 of 24 May 2019 on the rules and procedures for the operation of unmanned aircraft (*OJ* L 152, 11.6.2019, pp. 45–71). See Franchi (2018), p. 1788 ff.

These Regulations use the technical term UAS (unmanned aircraft system) to refer to both an unmanned aircraft and the equipment used to control and operate it safely and efficiently.

Regulation 2019/947 identifies three different categories of UAS operations—open, specific and certified—according to a risk-based approach.

Category A (open), in principle, includes low-risk operations conducted with light drones (*i.e.* weighing less than 25 kilograms). In this case, operations do not require any operational authorisation or declaration by the UAS operator prior to flight, although they are subject to operational limits. In fact, in this case, drones may be fly below 120 metres in altitude; transportation of dangerous goods is prohibited; the flight has to be operated within the visual line of sight (VLOS) etc.

Category B (specific) covers medium-risk operations which do not fall under the open category criteria. In this case, drones are not subject to mass limits. They can also fly out of the pilot's sight, but their use requires an 'operational authorisation', issued by the national aviation authority taking into account their risk assessment, the environment in which the operation is carried out, the territories flown over and the population living in them.

Category C (certified) includes high-risk operations, such as flights over assemblies of people and transport of people or dangerous goods. In this case, aircraft will always need to be certified, the UAS operator will need air operator approval issued by the competent authority and the remote pilot is required to hold a pilot licence.

The operations included in the last category are conducted with large drones, subject to the same operational requirements and restrictions as traditional aircraft.

There was a need to briefly and preliminarily recall this classification in order to underline that the characteristic element of the three different categories of operations is their risk level.

In fact, Regulation (EU) 2019/947 adopts a risk-based approach, superseding the traditional (and abstract) distinction between recreational or professional use of drones. Consequently, different rules may apply to the same vehicle, depending on the single operation carried out with it. Requirements shall be proportionate to the degree of risk.

The current EU legislation imposes on drone operators the obligation to take out an adequate insurance cover, in order to ensure safe and efficient operations in airspace.

In this context, 'remote pilot' *"means a natural person responsible for safely conducting the flight of an unmanned aircraft"* (Article 3, point 31, Regulation 2018/1139),[5] while 'UAS operator' is "*any legal or natural person operating or intending to operate one or more UAS*" (Article 2, point 2, Regulation 2019/947).

With regard to insurance aspects, recital 20 of Regulation 2019/947 states that "*UAS operators and remote pilots should ensure that they are adequately informed about applicable Union and national rules relating to the intended operations, in*

[5] La Torre (2024), p. 33 ff.

particular with regard to safety, privacy, data protection, liability, insurance, security and environmental protection".

In addition, in order to obtain operational authorisation from the competent national authority, the remote pilot is required to declare that the operation complies with national and EU insurance rules (Article 12 of Regulation 2019/947).

According to EU law, insurance requirements are set by the Member States. But considering that Regulation (EC) 785/2004[6] (on minimum insurance requirements for air carriers and aircraft operators) is not applicable to aircraft with a take-off mass of less than 20 kg, insurance is mandatory only for aircraft weighing more than 20 kg.

Member States are, however, free to extend this requirement to drones of lower weight. Many EU countries decided to introduce more restrictive limits in this respect.

3 The Italian Regulatory Framework

In Italy, according to Article 27 of the national Regulation UAS-IT 2021, issued by ENAC (Italian Civil Aviation Authority), all operations, regardless of the weight of the drone, must be covered by third-party liability insurance.

The insurance policy must be valid and adequate and the insurance coverage per accident must not be lower than the minimum amounts required by Article 7 of Regulation (EC) 785/2004.

As for the type of insurance policy, the above-mentioned Article 27 refers to "civil liability insurance",[7] similar to road vehicles insurance and compulsory for all drones.

Third-party liability insurance is designed to protect the insured person against the actions or claims for damages or losses caused to third parties by drones.

The mutualization of risk is the principle behind the function of any insurance coverage, including third-party liability insurance policy, which involves sharing and spreading individual risks between a group of policyholders.

As is well known, the insured risk is the key element of the insurance contract. If it is not present, the contract is null and void.

Insured risk means the "probability" that the insurable event occurs and the amount of possible damages or injuries caused by this event.

When the event occurs, the obligation to pay compensation to victims of damages caused arises.

---

[6] Regulation (EC) No 785/2004 of the European Parliament and of the Council of 21 April 2004 on insurance requirements for air carriers and aircraft operators (*OJ* L 138, 30.4.2004, pp. 1–6). See Deiana (2009), p. 209 ff.

[7] Bustos Moreno (2021), p. 889 ff.

Firstly, the event concerned must also be "harmful", *i.e.* capable of causing economically quantifiable injuries.

The occurrence concerned must also be qualified as "future", *i.e.* not existing at the time of the conclusion of the insurance contract and "uncertain" as to when it will come and whether it will come at all.

However, the concept of risk[8] already embodies the idea of uncertainty, understood in an absolute sense.

In addition, the risk must be statistically detectable so that the insurance companies are able to calculate premiums according to the estimated frequency and cost of claims.

Changes related to the insured risk in terms of probability of occurrence of the insured event may occur after conclusion of the contract. For instance, this situation arises when an operator who normally uses a drone to deliver parcels, starts to use it to transport dangerous goods, in a departure from the activities covered under the insurance contract.

These changes may also result in a breach of the contract.

All insurance policies contain their own standard terms and conditions and are subject to the 'coverage' and the 'exclusion' provided therein.

In particular, the liability insurance for drones covers unintentional incidents causing death and/or personal injury or property damage, while it does not include damage intentionally caused by the policyholder to third parties.

It should also be noted that coverage of damage caused by drones only operates if the use of the aircraft is compliant with the law and technical safety requirements provided for by current regulations.

In other words, insurance coverage is only effective if the drone is used lawfully.

For example, any operational restrictions concerning the area where the aircraft can fly should be complied with.

According to the ENAC Regulation on drones of 2013,[9] no longer in force, insurance is a condition for operating a Remotely Piloted Aircraft Systems (RPAS),[10] but nevertheless drones used for recreational and sports purposes were excluded from this obligation.

The ENAC Regulation UAS-IT of 2021,[11] currently in force, does not introduce any exemption based on the weight or different uses of drones.

The reason for these regulatory changes is that, as accident investigation has shown, even light drones, used for sport or recreation, can cause significant damage.

At present, the only exception to compulsory insurance is in the case of 'toy drones', intended as unmanned vehicles that meet all the criteria set by Directive 2009/48/EC: a) weight less than 250 grams; b) qualification as toy drones; c) label

[8] See Fanara (1976), p. 205 ff.

[9] Regulation "Mezzi Aerei a Pilotaggio Remoto", approved by ENAC (Ente Nazionale Aviazione Civile) on 16 December 2013.

[10] Panzeri (2016), p. 39 ff.; Zampone (2015), p. 63 ff.

[11] Regulation UAS-IT—Edition 1 of 4 January 2021.

on the box about minimum age recommended for use. But if the recommended user age is over 14 years, insurance will be mandatory.

Therefore, under the Italian legal system, the obligation of insurance covers all types of unmanned aircraft, except for drones qualified as toys according to Directive 2009/48/EC.

As regards the amount of compensation payable by insurers, it should be clear that the expression 'maximum compensation amount' must be understood as the highest sum that the insurance company may be required to pay for each accident.

The insured party will be liable for damages exceeding the maximum compensation amount covered by way of an insurance policy. The excess sum (so-called "deductible") is directly deducted from the amount refunded by the insurance company.

Although the weight of drones is irrelevant for the purpose of compulsory insurance, the maximum compensation amount is established on the basis of the maximum mass of the unmanned aircraft, including cargo and fuel, referred with the acronym MTOM (Maximum Take-Off Mass) or MTOW (Maximum Take-Off Weight).[12]

Moreover, it is also necessary to define the meaning of the expression "minimum compensation amount", considering that it is essential to respect this limit in order not to incur possible sanctions.

According to Regulation (EC) No. 785/2004, the insurance coverage per accident shall not be lower than the minimum compensation amount set by Article 7. The latter is the minimum sum, set by law, that the insurance company must be paid per accident, but Member States are however free to establish higher amounts.

According to the amounts shown in the table in Article 7 of Regulation 785/2004, different minimum amounts, based on weight of the drone, and not a single amount, must be taken into account in determining the "minimum compensation amount".

For example, for an aircraft weighing less than 500 kilograms the minimum compensation amount is 750,000 Special Drawing Rights (SDRs).[13]

In accordance with the above-mentioned minimum compensation amounts, at a national level, Article 27 of the current Italian Regulation on drones allows model aircraft clubs and associations, recognized under Article 16 of Regulation (EU) 2019/947, to take out cumulative insurance policies in order to cover damage caused to third parties during sport practices, events, competitions, etc.

Another aspect which deserves attention is contained in the first sentence of Article 27, paragraph 2, of the current ENAC Regulation, which provides that: "*In accordance with Article 743 of the Italian Navigation Code, Article 1015 of the same Code also applies to aircraft subject to this regulation*".

[12] According to Regulation (EU) 945/2009, for example, subcategory A1 includes drones with a CE mark of C0 (up to 250 grams) or C1 (up to 900 grams).

[13] Special drawing rights (SDRs) refer to an international type of monetary reserve currency created by the International Monetary Fund (IMF) in 1969

Article 743 of the same Code equates unmanned aircraft to traditional aircraft.[14] Consequently, article 1015 of the same text entitles the injured party to take direct action against the insurer, by taking the place of the debtor in the contractual relationship.

Article 1234 of the Navigation Code provides for a penalty of between 50,000 and 100,000 euros in the case of drone operations carried out without compulsory insurance cover.

Italian Legislative Decree No. 197/2007[15] provides for financial penalties in the event of infringement of the above-mentioned EU Regulation 785/2004 requirements. In particular, Article 4 of this Decree provides for a financial penalty of between €30,000 and €60,000.

4 Final Remarks

Finally, I would like to make some closing remarks.

Firstly, some coordination difficulties arise between the current ENAC Regulation and the European Regulations governing this sector. It should be noted that the minimum compensation amounts set in the table of Article 7 of Regulation 785/2004 depending on the weight of the aircraft do not correspond to the drones open category listed in Implementing Regulation (EU) 2019/945.

The reference in the current ENAC Regulation to EU Regulation 785/2004 for all types of drones (whatever their weight) also seems questionable, considering that this European legislation expressly excludes from its scope aircraft with a MTOM of less than 20 kilograms (Article 2).

In addition to these legal remarks, general considerations must also be made.

In order to effectively address the application of emerging technology in aviation, insurance companies should abandon the traditional, reactive (*ex post*) approach and instead emphasise a proactive and predictive (*ex ante*) approach.

According to the principle of mutualization of risk, when taking out insurance, each policyholder is part of a risk pool and is reciprocally responsible for others' risks.

Today, the function of insurance coverage is linked not only to solidarity with the victims of accidents, but also to the need to prevent new potential risks deriving from some emerging technologies.

In this scenario, a continuous adaptation of the insurance policies to the European and national regulations governing this sector and to the needs of stakeholders, is required. Therefore, it is necessary to offer various types of specialized policies,

[14] La Torre (2022), p. 469 ss.

[15] Italian Legislative Decree of 6 November 2007, No. 197 containing sanctions for violation of the provisions of Regulation (EC) No. 785/2004 on insurance requirements applicable to air carriers and aircraft operators (*GU* n.261 del 9.11.2007).

tailored to the different drone operations, which—in addition to third-party liability insurance—include the management of other risks.

In fact, the introduction of compulsory third-party liability insurance does not prevent UAS operators from voluntarily taking out additional policies, on the basis of a cost-benefit analysis and a rigorous risk assessment, taking into account the various drone operations.

For example, considering that remote pilots are not classified as flight personnel, an insurance policy that offers coverage for injuries suffered by pilots during the use of drones could be required.

Another additional coverage could provide financial protection in the event of temporary disruption of flight operations, due to equipment failure or other unforeseen events.

Insurance policies may also be concluded to cover damage suffered by the aircraft and/or their equipment or goods on board, such as cameras or other sensors. These policies are usually required by operators of commercial drones, used for specialized operations, such as aerial photography.

Another additional form of coverage could be devoted to protect aircraft against damage caused by extreme weather events, collisions,[16] explosions etc.

Furthermore, since these vehicles may unintentionally capture images or produce videos, a privacy invasion policy that aims to protect drone operators from potential violation of privacy rules[17] may prove necessary.

It is also important to offer cyber risk policies, specially designed to protect operators from cyber-attacks, cyber threats and similar illegal activities.

In conclusion, the insurance market must demonstrate its ability to collect and use properly all the information necessary to correctly calculate the level of risk and effectively manage it, through a careful risk assessment that takes into account essential factors, such as the pilot's experience, the type of aircraft and the operating environment, contributing ultimately to the sustainable development of the sector.

References

Brignardello M (2018) Collisioni tra mezzi aerei senza equipaggio e aeromobili tradizionali: misure di prevenzione e responsabilità in caso di drone "strike". Rivista del Diritto della Navigazione 2:439–469

Bustos Moreno Y (2021) La irrupción de los drones (sistemas de aeronaves no tripuladas, UAS) y la responsabilidad civil. El futuro de los UAS autónomos Cuestiones clásicas y actuales del Derecho de daños: Estudios en homenaje al profesor Dr. Roca Guillamón / coord. por Joaquín Ataz López, José Antonio Cobacho Gómez; Juan Roca Guillamón. Adolfo Díaz-Bautista Cremades 1:889–950

[16] Brignardello (2018), p. 439 ff.

[17] Merla (2016), p. 29 ff.; Finn and Donovan (2016), p. 47 ff.; Damiani (2012), p. 157 ff.; Finn and Wright (2016), p. 325 ff.

Damiani E (2012) Privacy e utilizzo dei droni in ambito civile. Eur J Priv Law Technol 1:157–179
Fanara E (1976) Le assicurazioni aeronautiche. Editori Meridionali Riuniti, Reggio Calabria
Finn RL, Donovan A (2016) Big data, drone data: privacy and ethical impacts of the intersection between big data and civil drone deployments. In: Custers B (ed) The future of drone use. Opportunities and threats from ethical and legal perspectives. Springer, pp 47–67
Finn RL, Wright D (2016) Privacy, data protection and ethics for civil drone practice: a survey of industry, regulators and civil society organisations. Comput Law Secur Rev:577–586
Gaspari F (2020) La regolazione multilivello degli aeromobili a pilotaggio remoto e la disciplina «speciale» dell'ENAC nel contesto della pandemia covid-19. Rivista del Diritto della Navigazione 1:139–192
La Torre U (2022) Spunti sulla nozione di aeromobile. Rivista del Diritto della Navigazione 2:469–517
La Torre U (2024) "Pilot in command" e pilota remoto fra tradizione e nuove tecnologie. Rivista del Diritto della Navigazione 1:33–74
Lamon M (2021) La rivoluzione aeronautica dei sistemi aerei a pilotaggio remoto e il loro esercizio nella lotta alla pandemia da Covid-19. Il Diritto marittimo 2:249–266
Merla L (2016) Droni, privacy e tutela dei dati personali. Informatica e diritto 1:29–45
Panzeri S (2016) I sistemi aerei a pilotaggio remoto (SAPR): profili giuridici. Rivista di Diritto dell'Economia, dei Trasporti e dell'Ambiente:39–60
Zampone A (2015) Riflessioni in tema di responsabilità nell'esercizio di "remotely-piloted aircraft system (RPAS) operations". Diritto dei trasporti 1:63–89

UAS and Data Protection

Emilia Vermiglio

Contents

Abstract This chapter offers systematic reflections arising from the study of the legislation on data protection, applied to the use of remote-piloted aircraft. In particular, it analyses how the principles from EU GDPR Regulation No 1679/2016 intersect with the sector's regulatory framework for drones, especially with reference to EU "basic" Regulation No 1139/2018 and Implementing Regulation No 947/2019. After having addressed the legal notion of drone, declined in the "technical-static" sense of aircraft, the chapter examines data protection, both from a public law perspective, as a cross-cutting interest that guides the Member States' powers to demarcate portions of airspace, and in terms of private law, by examining how UAS operators can pre-emptively foresee risks and related solutions for possible personal data breaches.

1 Data Protection as a Fundamental Right in the EU Framework

It is now well established, both in terms of legislation and case-law, that the protection of personal data has acquired the status of a fundamental human right.

E. Vermiglio (✉)
University of Messina, Messina, Italy
e-mail: emilia.vermiglio@unime.it

M. P. Rizzo, F. Franchina (eds.), *Drones in the Digital European Sky*,
International Aviation Law Library 1,
https://doi.org/10.1007/978-3-032-16691-3_15

Article 8 of the Charter of Fundamental Rights of the European Union,[1] entitled *"Protection of personal data,"* explicitly affirms that *"Everyone has the right to the protection of personal data concerning him or her".* This provision, which holds primary legal status within the EU legal order, outlines the fundamental principles governing the lawful processing of personal data: fairness, purpose limitation, the existence of a legal or contractual basis, or the freely given consent of the data subject.

Correspondingly, within the framework of the European Convention on Human Rights (ECHR), the right to personal data protection—although not expressly enshrined in the Convention—is consistently interpreted by the European Court of Human Rights as an inherent component of the right to respect for private life, as protected by Article 8 ECHR.

The normative framework underpinning this right is both complex and of relatively recent origin. At the European level, the cornerstone is Regulation (EU) 2016/679, commonly referred to as the General Data Protection Regulation (GDPR).[2] This Regulation forms part of a broader legislative reform agenda, prompted by the Union's recognition of the need to govern the implications of technological, economic, and digital transformation—a transformation that unavoidably involves issues of personal data.

The legal basis for this legislative initiative lies in Article 16 of the Treaty on the Functioning of the European Union (TFEU), which now explicitly confers upon the Union competence in the domain of personal data protection.[3]

In the aftermath of the GDPR's adoption, it is important to underscore that data protection is no longer equated with privacy understood solely as the *right to be let alone*. Rather, the GDPR introduces a paradigm shift towards a modern conception of data protection as the individual's right to exercise control over the processing and dissemination of information concerning them in a digital environment.

In synthesizing the relevant legal framework, the GDPR defines *personal data* as any information relating to an identified or identifiable natural person.

Consistent with the provisions of the Charter of Fundamental Rights, data processing is permissible under the GDPR only if it adheres to a set of foundational principles. Chief among these is the principle of lawfulness. Pursuant to Articles 5(1)(a) and 6 GDPR, processing is lawful only if it satisfies one of the specific legal bases enumerated in Article 6. These include: the data subject's consent; the

[1] Rossi Dal Pozzo (2020), p. 71 ff.

[2] Regulation (EU) No 2016/679 of the European Parliament and of the Council of 27 April 2016, on the protection of natural persons with regard to the processing of personal data and on the free movement of such data.

[3] Article 16 TFEU (formerly Article 286 EC) empowers the European legislator to adopt, through the ordinary legislative procedure, rules relating to the protection of natural persons with regard to the processing of personal data and the free movement of such data by the institutions, bodies, offices, and agencies of the Union, as well as by the Member States when carrying out activities within the scope of Union law. The Article further provides that compliance with these rules shall be ensured by independent supervisory authorities.

necessity of processing for the performance of a contract; compliance with a legal obligation incumbent upon the controller; protection of vital interests; performance of a task carried out in the public interest or in the exercise of official authority; and the pursuit of the legitimate interests of the controller or a third party, provided such interests are not overridden by the fundamental rights and freedoms of the data subject—particularly where vulnerable categories such as minors are concerned.

The principle of transparency, which is intrinsically linked to lawfulness, is codified in Articles 5(1)(a), 12, 13, and 14 of the GDPR. Transparency requires that the data subject be clearly and comprehensively informed about the identity of the data controller, the purposes of the processing, and the legal basis underpinning such activities.

Transparency operates both ex ante, through the requirement of prior consent or a demonstrable legal basis, and ex post, through the obligation to ensure that the data subject has access to their data and can verify its retention and use, insofar as such access is consistent with the purposes of processing.

The principle of purpose limitation, set forth in Articles 5(1)(b) and 6, imposes an obligation on the controller to ensure that personal data is collected only for specified, explicit, and legitimate purposes, and that it is not further processed in a manner incompatible with those original purposes. The stated purpose provides the legal justification for processing. Nonetheless, the Regulation permits subsequent processing for different purposes under certain conditions—particularly where consent or another suitable legal basis exists and where the new purpose is necessary and proportionate.

Closely related is the principle of data minimisation, which requires that personal data be adequate, relevant, and limited to what is necessary in relation to the purposes for which it is processed. This principle applies not only to the volume of data collected, but also to the scope of processing, duration of storage, and extent of accessibility.[4]

In practice, this means that, by default, personal data should not be made accessible to an indefinite number of persons without the express intervention of the data subject.

A practical manifestation of this principle is the concept of pseudonymisation, defined under Article 4(5) GDPR as a process by which personal data can no longer be attributed to a specific data subject without the use of additional information. It thus constitutes a safeguard mechanism to ensure that individuals cannot be directly identified. Operational extensions of these principles are found in the concepts of privacy by design and privacy by default.[5]

These refer to technological and organisational measures—often software-based—that automatically obscure or restrict access to personal identifiers. Such mechanisms, according to prevailing academic opinion, may result in shifting liability to the system designer or technology provider in cases of non-compliance.

---

[4] Gentili (2022), pp. 47–57.

[5] Foresta (2024), pp. 129–156.

2 Data Protection Challenges Posed by UAS Operations

Within this complex and articulated regulatory framework, the use of unmanned aerial vehicles (UAVs) or remotely piloted aircraft systems (RPAS) poses a significant risk of undermining—or even entirely negating—the individual's legitimate right to control the flow of their personal data, due to the technical and structural features of such devices. These characteristics enable the potential capture and processing of large volumes of personal data in ways that may be difficult to monitor or regulate.[6]

The privacy risks associated with drone operations are closely linked to their capability for real-time video surveillance and data acquisition while in motion—not only of visual images, but also of other types of information that, even if indirectly, may lead to the identification of natural persons. These may include data such as thermal emissions, audio recordings, or contextual cues that, when combined, allow for re-identification of individuals.

Although the traditional safeguards applicable to fixed video surveillance systems may, in theory, be extended to drone operations, in practice such protections prove limited or otherwise difficult to implement, particularly with respect to the information obligations imposed on data controllers. These obligations require that data subjects be properly and clearly informed when they are subject to video capture, typically through visible signage or symbols—an approach that is often unfeasible or ineffective in the context of aerial surveillance conducted by drones.

It is therefore necessary to identify a point of reconciliation between the general framework on personal data protection and the specific regulatory regime governing UAVs, in order to achieve a fair balance between the competing interests at stake. Drones may be deployed for a range of legitimate public purposes—including environmental monitoring, public health protection, civil protection, and emergency response—but their use must be harmonised with the overarching principles of lawfulness, necessity, and proportionality under data protection law.[7]

Recital 4 of the GDPR expressly clarifies that the right to the protection of personal data is not an absolute prerogative, but must be interpreted in light of its social function and balanced against other fundamental rights, in accordance with the principle of proportionality.

Unmanned Aircraft Systems (UAS), too, may serve a legitimate social function, contributing to objectives such as enhanced mobility, environmental sustainability, and the efficiency of transport, made possible by the advancement of emerging technologies. Accordingly, the processing of personal data through drone operations must remain proportionate and intrinsically linked to the purpose for which the drone is deployed. This proportionality is central to the reconciliation of fundamental rights and reflects the balancing act required by EU data protection law between

---

[6] Dei and Kutynska (2023), pp. 39–155.

[7] Damiani (2021), pp. 157–179.

the rights of data subjects and the legitimate aims pursued through the use of such technology.

It is important to note, however, that drones may also be operated for recreational or personal purposes, potentially giving rise to a perceived regulatory vacuum with respect to personal data protection. This is particularly relevant in light of Recital 18 and Article 2(2)(c) of the GDPR, which exclude from the Regulation's scope the processing of personal data by a natural person in the course of a purely personal or household activity, thereby exempting non-commercial or non-professional uses.

Nevertheless, such a legal vacuum must now be regarded as merely apparent. The Court of Justice of the European Union (CJEU) has, over time, adopted a progressively narrower interpretation of this exemption.[8] Case-law has confirmed the applicability of the GDPR even in personal contexts, particularly where the data processing involves the systematic capture of images or footage of public spaces or streets, thereby potentially impacting the rights and freedoms of others.

Moreover, images or videos originally acquired for personal or recreational purposes may subsequently be disclosed—for example, by being shared on social media platforms—thereby exceeding the scope of the personal-use exemption and falling within the material scope of the GDPR. In such cases, the individual becomes a data controller and is subject to the full range of obligations imposed by the Regulation.

It is necessary, first and foremost, to clarify that the legal classification of drones as aircraft, insofar as they are vehicles intended for transportation, is not relevant for the purposes of the present analysis.

What is instead relevant to the issue at hand is the qualification of the drone as an aircraft in structural and aerodynamic terms, as provided by the so-called *Basic Regulation*, which defines it as *"an apparatus that is capable of sustaining flight in the atmosphere by reactions of the air other than the reactions of the air against the earth's surface"*.

This definition aligns with the international standard adopted in ICAO Annex 7 to the 1944 *Chicago Convention on International Civil Aviation.*[9]

Such regulatory definitions reflect a predominance of the so-called "technical-static" perspective, which defines the drone as an aircraft based on its structural and aerodynamic characteristics, rather than on its functional purpose, i.e., as a vehicle intended for the carriage of persons or goods—as is the approach taken in the Italian Navigation Code.[10]

[8] Court of Justice of the European Union, judgment in František Rynes, 11 December 2014, Case C-212/13, and European Data Protection Supervisor, Opinion of 26 November 2014 addressed to the European Commission.

[9] In the definition set out in ICAO Annex 7 to the 1944 Chicago Convention, "*aircraft*"is understood as: "Any machine that can derive support in the atmosphere from the reactions of the air other than the reactions of the air against the earth's surface". A similar definitional approach emerges from EU technical aviation law, in particular Article 3(28) of Regulation (EU) 2018/1139. For an overview of doctrinal positions on the definition of aircraft, see: Vernizzi (2020).

[10] Vernizzi (2020).

From this functional standpoint, the prevailing academic view is persuasive. According to this view, the reference made in Article 743 of the Navigation Code should be interpreted not as an act of strict legal classification, but rather as a form of assimilation—a "legal fiction", that is, a legal technique used by the legislator to extend a specific legal regime to an object that is similar, but not identical, to the one originally contemplated.[11] Thus, drones are assimilated to aircraft for the purposes of regulatory application, rather than being fully identified as such.

This clarification is useful for our purposes here, since the need to protect personal data is not dependent on whether the drone is technically or legally designated for the carriage of persons or property. Such a functional classification is, in fact, irrelevant in the context of data protection.

What is determinative, rather, is whether the structural configuration of the drone includes the installation of sensors capable of capturing images, thermal signatures, or other forms of data that may lead to the identification of a natural person. If so, the device becomes a data processing system within the meaning of the GDPR, and the operation may involve the collection and processing of various types of personal data, triggering the full application of data protection obligations.

As is well known, Regulation (EU) 2018/1139, commonly referred to as the *"Basic Regulation,"* establishes the overarching regulatory framework for unmanned aircraft systems (UAS) and simultaneously institutes the European Union Aviation Safety Agency (EASA) as the competent authority in the field of aviation safety.[12]

Recital 49 of the Regulation contains an express reference to the GDPR, explicitly affirming that the provisions laid down in Regulation (EU) 2016/679 are fully applicable within the scope of UAS operations. The integration of data protection principles into the aviation domain is thus not merely indirect or analogical, but formally and substantively incorporated into the regulatory logic of unmanned aircraft operations.

This connection is further reinforced in Annex IX of the same Regulation, which, in addressing the design requirements applicable to UAS, stipulates that such systems must be equipped with specific functionalities and technical characteristics that take into account data protection principles from the very design phase (privacy by design) and by default settings (privacy by default). The objective is to mitigate risks associated with drone use, particularly in relation to safety, privacy, personal data protection, security, and environmental impact.

The GDPR's principles—especially pseudonymisation, data minimisation, and default restrictions on data accessibility—are thus embedded at the level of

[11] La Torre (2008), p. 96 ff.

[12] Regulation (EU) No 2018/1139 of the European Parliament and of the Council of 4 July 2018, on common rules in the field of civil aviation and establishing a European Union Aviation Safety Agency, and amending Regulations (EC) No 2111/2005, (EC) No 1008/2008, (EU) No 996/2010, (EU) No 376/2014 and Directives 2014/30/EU and 2014/53/EU of the European Parliament and of the Council, and repealing Regulations (EC) No 552/2004 and (EC) No 216/2008 of the European Parliament and of the Council and Council Regulation (EEC) No 3922/91, published in OJ L 212/1 of 22.8.2018.

technical requirements, and become essential safety criteria for unmanned aerial systems as defined by EU law.

In addition, the Regulation expressly acknowledges the possibility for Member States to establish exemptions or restrictions to certain rights and obligations under the GDPR, especially in cases involving the processing of personal data relating to remote pilots. Such processing is deemed necessary to facilitate effective inter-state cooperation concerning certification procedures and the monitoring of pilots' physical and mental fitness.

This legislative intent is clearly articulated in the final part of Recital 49, which affirms that, *"where appropriate, it is necessary to supplement or clarify the principles laid down in Regulation (EU) 2016/679 within this Regulation."* This indicates that the reference to the GDPR is not purely declaratory, but substantively integrated, with specific GDPR principles being elaborated upon and adapted to the particular regulatory context of UAS operations. As a result, data protection within this field operates on multiple levels—legal, technical, operational, and institutional.

Most significantly, the protection of personal data within the UAS sector emerges as a matter of overriding public interest, potentially affording Member States greater regulatory discretion, similar to the discretion recognized for concerns related to public order or national security.

This reading is confirmed by Article 56(8) of the Basic Regulation, which authorizes Member States to adopt national rules imposing conditions on the operation of unmanned aircraft, where necessary, for reasons including public safety, privacy protection, and data protection, in accordance with EU law.

In line with this provision, Recital 18 of Implementing Regulation (EU) 2019/947 reiterates that Member States retain competence to adopt binding measures designed to safeguard privacy and data protection as interests of general importance. This includes the power to designate UAS geographical zones (as defined in Article 2(4) of the Implementing Regulation), within which the national competent authority may set limits or conditions on UAS operations to address risks related to safety, privacy, data protection, security, or the environment.

Moreover, under Article 15 of the same Regulation, Member States may prohibit certain UAS operations, or impose prior operational authorisation requirements, regardless of the category of the drone, where deemed necessary to protect confidentiality and privacy.

Consequently, as further highlighted in Recitals 20 and 21 of Implementing Regulation 2019/947, UAS operators and remote pilots are required to be adequately informed of the applicable national and EU-level rules, particularly with regard to safety, privacy protection, data protection, civil liability, insurance obligations, and environmental protection.

This emphasis is also reflected in Annex IX to Regulation 2018/1139, which outlines the "Essential Requirements for Unmanned Aircraft", and specifies that such aircraft must possess capabilities ensuring compliance with restrictions, prohibitions, or operating conditions, especially when flying in designated geographical zones.

Taken as a whole, these legislative instruments indicate that the protection of personal data in the context of UAS operations not only qualifies as a fundamental individual right, but also as a public interest of a supra-individual nature, capable of guiding Member States' regulatory discretion, even toward restrictive measures, on a par with the interests protected in the context of public order or national security.

Annex IX of the Basic Regulation stipulates, inter alia, that unmanned aircraft must be equipped with features and functionalities that ensure easy identification of the aircraft, as well as clear indication of the nature and purpose of its use.

Recital 31 of Implementing Regulation (EU) 2019/947 establishes a clear link between personal data and the need to register unmanned aircraft, underlining the obligation to develop national registration systems for both aircraft and their operators. These systems must ensure compliance with data protection and confidentiality requirements, and the data must be stored in easily accessible systems.

From a data protection perspective, the registration of drones and their operators represents a crucial interface between aviation regulations and the GDPR framework. The registration system is managed and supervised by the competent national authority, and imposes pre-authorization obligations on operators, requiring them to provide information regarding the aircraft in use and the planned flight path. The competent authority then exercises oversight aimed at identifying and managing the main risks associated with the operation.

The registration mechanism thus functions as a preventive safeguard, obliging the operator to comply with a range of regulatory requirements, which are then subject to supervisory checks by the competent authority.

Implementing Regulation (EU) 2019/947, building on the Basic Regulation, sets out more explicit rules regarding the mandatory registration of unmanned aircraft operators. In Recital 14, it is stated that registration is required for operators whose drones are capable of transferring to a human body kinetic energy in excess of 80 joules upon impact, or whose operation poses risks to privacy, personal data protection, safety, or the environment.[13]

On the basis of the literal wording of the provision, it is evident that operator registration is required whenever drone operations could potentially compromise privacy or personal data protection, regardless of the drone's weight or impact energy.

Recital 16 further specifies that registration is mandatory for operators of unmanned aircraft equipped with sensors capable of collecting personal data—thus establishing that the existence of data-capturing sensors is the decisive structural

[13] Pursuant to this provision, UAS operators are required to register: a) when operating within the "open"category using unmanned aircraft with a mass greater than 250 grams, or that, in case of impact, can transfer kinetic energy exceeding 80 joules to the human body, or when operating unmanned aircraft equipped with sensors capable of capturing personal data, unless the aircraft complies with Directive 2009/48/EC (on toy safety); b) in all cases, when operating within the "specific"category, regardless of the aircraft's mass. Article 18 further outlines the duties of the competent authority, including, under letter (m), the establishment and maintenance of registration systems for: UAS subject to certification, and UAS operators whose operations may pose a risk to safety, including risks related to security, privacy, personal data protection, or the environment.

element for triggering GDPR applicability, even independent of the aircraft's mass or energy capacity.

Exempt from this registration requirement are drones already covered by Directive 2009/48/EC on the safety of toys. Under this directive, compliance is presumed when the drone is lighter than 250 g and either lacks a camera or sensor or is certified as a toy, even if it includes basic imaging features. In this case, the device is considered incapable *de iure* of compromising personal data, and thus falls outside the scope of GDPR-related drone regulation.

This position is reinforced in Article 14, titled *"Registration for Risky Operations"*, which confirms the criteria outlined above.

3 Specific Category UAS Operations: Authorisation, Compliance and Operator Responsibility

Special provisions are made for UAS operating in the 'specific' category. Pursuant to Article 12 of Regulation 2019/947 (*"Operational Authorisation – Specific Category"*), flight authorisation is required, to be issued by the competent authority, which undertakes a comprehensive risk assessment of the intended operation.

The authority evaluates the risk profile and the adequacy of the mitigation measures proposed by the UAS operator, and grants authorisation only when it is satisfied that the operation can be carried out safely, taking into account all identified risks, both on the ground and in flight.

As part of the authorisation request, the operator must provide a declaration of compliance with relevant Union and national law, with particular reference to: privacy protection, data protection, civil liability, insurance coverage, operational safety, and environmental safeguards.

In relation to this declaration, Annex B of Regulation 2019/947 expressly imposes a specific responsibility on the operator to ensure that all operations are conducted in compliance with Regulation (EU) 2016/679 (GDPR) concerning the protection of natural persons with regard to the processing of personal data and the free movement of such data.

For drones meeting the aforementioned technical requirements, it is clear that registration of the operator (more precisely, "operator registration") represents the principal mechanism through which the legislator seeks to ensure data protection compliance, by allowing the competent authority to identify the responsible party—a crucial aspect in the event of damage to third parties.

A different system applies, however, to drones operating within the 'specific' category.

In such cases, while registration remains necessary, it is not sufficient: the operator must also obtain specific operational authorisation, following submission of an ad hoc request that includes a declaration of compliance with data protection rules.

The operator is thus required to guarantee compliance with personal data protection rules in advance; only upon such assurance—along with satisfaction of other regulatory conditions—may the competent authority grant operational authorisation.

This authorisation is issued on the basis of the operator's self-declaration of conformity with national and EU legislation on privacy and data protection (as well as other relevant legal fields). Annex B of Regulation 2019/947 expressly attributes responsibility to the UAS operator to ensure full compliance with the General Data Protection Regulation (GDPR). Therefore, any personal data breach remains legally attributable to the operator who has signed the compliance declaration. The competent authority merely exercises discretionary risk assessment powers regarding the flight operation as a whole and does not carry out a substantive evaluation of the data protection risks, which remain entirely within the operator's sphere of responsibility.

Based on the wording of the regulation, it appears that the authority's role in granting authorisation is limited to verifying the existence of the declaration of compliance, without conducting a full analysis of the data-related risks involved.

As a result, even in the specific category, there is no actual preventive control mechanism carried out by the competent authority with respect to the protection of personal data. In both open and specific category operations, the current regulatory structure relies on self-certification by the operator. Although registration facilitates the identification of the responsible party, it does not in itself provide a sufficient safeguard against potential data breaches or unauthorised processing.

4 Concluding Reflections on Multi-Level Data Protection in UAS Operations

To address these shortcomings, the application of preventive measures provided by the GDPR becomes essential.

In this regard, central importance should be given—once again—to the principles of privacy by design and privacy by default, which must be integrated into both the design and default configuration of the drone. This is in line with Article 5 of the GDPR, which enshrines the principle of data minimisation.

This approach is also reflected in the ENAC Regulation, specifically in Article 29 (renumbered Article 33 in the draft version under revision as of February 2025), which stipulates that drones must be designed to collect only those data strictly necessary and proportionate to the intended purpose, and must include automated systems for obfuscation or filtering of identifiable features, as well as automatic deletion mechanisms for superfluous data.

Although these technical measures are useful, in practice, personal data may still be compromised, as obfuscated or filtered data can, in some instances, still lead to the indirect identification of individuals.

Accordingly, it may be appropriate to consider two additional tools under the GDPR that could be applied to this context:

1. Data Protection Impact Assessment (DPIA)

   Regulated under Article 35 of the GDPR, the DPIA is mandatory in certain circumstances—particularly where data is processed on a large scale or in public spaces—and requires the operator to map out the nature, scope, context, and purpose of the data processing activity, identify potential sources of risk, and determine technical and organisational measures to mitigate them.[14] Through the DPIA, the operator gains a comprehensive overview of how proportionate the data processing operation is, and how to implement appropriate safeguards such as security protocols, data minimisation tools, and barriers against unauthorised access. The operator must also identify the legal basis for processing, ensure transparency, and declare whether data will be shared with third parties.

   As such, the DPIA represents a proactive mechanism for identifying privacy risks and establishing solutions before the operation begins.
2. Codes of Conduct under Article 40 of the GDPR

   These offer a form of co-regulation, allowing industry actors to develop sector-specific standards.[15] Under Article 24, adherence to such codes—or to certification mechanisms under Article 42—may serve as evidence of compliance with the controller's legal obligations. As recognised by EASA, Codes of Conduct are intended to assist UAS operators and remote pilots in carrying out professional services while minimising their impact on privacy. They enable companies to adopt internal procedures, train personnel, and ensure alignment with GDPR requirements. For a Code of Conduct to be fully operative, it must be supervised by a Monitoring Body, designated under Article 41, which ensures compliance by the signatories.

   This approach suggests that Codes of Conduct, more than certification schemes, may offer a practical and flexible solution—providing an effective form of public-private co-regulation capable of ensuring that technologically complex norms are properly implemented, rather than remaining merely aspirational.[16]

References

Amram D (2023) Comparing EU initiatives on data: addressing risks and enhancing harmonisation opportunities. Opin Juris Comp 1:1–2

Chiara P, Galli F (2024) Normative considerations on impact assessments in EU Digital Policy. MediaLaws 1:86–105

[14] Chiara and Galli (2024), pp. 86–105.

[15] Amram (2023), pp. 1–25.

[16] Pollicino (2022), pp. 1051–1068.

Damiani E (2021) Privacy and the use of drones in the civil sector. Eur J Priv Law Technol 1:157–179

Dei M., Kutynska A. (2023), Legal Regulations of the Use of Drones: Human Rights and Privacy Challenges, in Journal of International Legal Communications, 39–155

Foresta D (2024) Pseudonymisation and anonymisation of personal data contained in judicial decisions. Persona e Mercato 1:129–156

Gentili G (2022) The principle of data minimisation and the threshold of compensable damage under Article 15 of the Italian Privacy Code. Giur It 1:47–57

La Torre U (2008) UAVs: unmanned aerial vehicles. In: Leali RT, Rosafio EG (eds) Security, navigation and transport, p 96 ff

Pollicino O (2022) Codes of conduct between "self-regulation" and "hard law": is there truly a third way for digital regulation? The case of the European strategy against online disinformation. Riv Trim Dir Pubbl 4:1051–1068

Rossi Dal Pozzo F (2020) The case law of the court of justice on the processing of personal data. Annali AISDUE I:71 ff

Vernizzi S (2020) The aircraft: technical and functional data. Static and Dynamic Profile, Rome

Innovation and Sustainability

European Union Air Navigation Services and Digitalization

Federico Franchina

Contents

Abstract The "digitalisation" of the Single European Sky plays a fundamental role in the imminent development of the new architecture of airspace management and flight assistance service providers, and perhaps in the air transport model of the coming decades, given the numerous implications that will derive from it.

The new "functionality" assigned to European airspace is the further evolution of a process that has been underway for some time.

In strictly legal terms, the experience started with Reg. 219/2007 and then continued with Reg. 721/2014, and was completed in Reg. 2085/2021 and in the consequent renaming of the SESAR 3 Joint Undertaking.

The latest reform reaffirmed some principles and objectives that have historically characterised the SESAR joint undertaking, while also broadening the scope of action through the grafting of additional purposes deriving both from technological development and from alignment—also of the deployment activity financed at the EU level—with the new values that the European Union pursues. Foremost amongst these is that of wider environmental sustainability, with the most recent legislation also extending to air transport.

F. Franchina (✉)
Department of Law, University of Messina, Messina, Italy
e-mail: federico.franchina@unime.it

M. P. Rizzo, F. Franchina (eds.), *Drones in the Digital European Sky*,
International Aviation Law Library 1,
https://doi.org/10.1007/978-3-032-16691-3_16

In particular, a new deadline (2035) has been established, and SESAR is called upon to provide technological solutions for high-performance air traffic management. This reaffirms one of the founding objectives of the Joint Undertaking and the SES initiative since 2004: to allow non-congested operation.

Reg. 2085/2021 recalls the technical aspects of the first Masterplan adopted by Council Decision 2009/320/EC. SESAR is divided into three interconnected, continuous, and evolving collaborative processes that define, develop, and disseminate innovative operating procedures and technological systems. These processes are the basis of the European digital sky.

In this interpretative framework, SESAR is now required to develop a research and innovation ecosystem that thoroughly covers the U-space air traffic management and airspace value chains, thereby enabling the construction of the digital European sky defined in the European ATM modernisation plan.

The chapter aims to explore this new approach, highlighting the effects and consequences of regulations that will need to be issued.

1 Introduction

The air transport liberalisation process initiated in the early 1990s, following wide-ranging American deregulation, immediately brought to light the "limits" of the physical and legal configuration of European airspace.[1]

The opening of land borders with the Schengen Agreement did not, in fact, remove the legal obstacle linked to the persistence of the principle of national sovereignty[2] over the airspace of the individual Member States of the Community (later the Union). The logical consequence of this—the fragmentation of aerial borders—prevented the full realisation of the idea of a "European airspace," which the single market mechanism (and principle) had managed to achieve in other areas such as air licences and other services.[3]

On the other hand, the growth of civil aviation at the European level had to contend with the structure of the airport system of the Member States, which was based on strictly national and, in some cases, even local planning approaches, thereby constituting a sort of physical limit to the orderly development of air transport.[4]

Therefore, these were pre-existing critical issues upon which a model of deregulation was superimposed. With liberalisation and competition, the consolidation of low-cost air transport, and the ever-increasing push for global interconnection (with its related traffic pressures), this model ultimately revealed the insufficiency of airspace.

---

[1] Kahn (1970–1971); Kahn (1978a, b, c); Kahn (1988); Kahn (2008); Ebke (1991).

[2] Böckstiegel (1995); Kotaite (1995).

[3] See Regulation (EC) No 1008/2008 of the European Parliament and of the Council of 24 September 2008 on common rules for the operation of air services in the Community.

[4] Adkins (2001); A High-Level (2015); Balfour (1995, 2008); Belobaba (2015).

This evidence becomes even clearer when one considers that the massification of air transport seems to have granted the passenger the legal status of a consumer (Regulation 261/2004),[5] thereby transferring further obligations, mainly of a contractual nature, onto operators (companies, managers, service providers, etc.). These obligations are not always compatible with the risk and complexity factors that—in any case—continue to characterise air navigation.

This context, which seems to present a picture with relatively static variables—given that the principle of national sovereignty over airspace has remained non-negotiable, as have the principles of freedom and competition in the context of intra-community air services, along with the constant growth in demand and the difficulty of increasing infrastructural supply—left the European Commission with no other solution than to intervene on the principal component susceptible to flexibilisation: the management of air traffic at the community level according to an innovative paradigm.

Air traffic management plays a primary role in the aviation system, ensuring that all flights are conducted safely and in order.

Given the necessary interconnection between national airspaces, the capacity of Air Traffic Management (ATM) systems to respond to the growing demand for air transport is a determining factor in the proper functioning of the entire sector.

When this capacity proves inadequate, however, safeguard mechanisms are triggered. While preserving safety, these mechanisms generate cascading dysfunctions (delays, cancellations, etc.), compromising both economic and environmental efficiency.

Furthermore, it cannot be ignored that such inefficiencies translate into a failure to meet the legitimate expectations of airspace users (passengers, carriers, airports).

It is therefore within this framework that the Single European Sky[6] (SES) initiative is situated. As will be clarified below, it has undergone a significant evolution due to its continued status as perhaps the only element capable of absorbing and addressing the ever-increasing and complex challenges of air transport.

2 The Evolution of Regulations on the Single European Sky

The "digitalisation" of the Single European Sky plays a fundamental role not only for the now imminent development of the new architecture for airspace management and air navigation service providers, but perhaps for the air transport model of the coming decades, given the numerous implications that will derive from it.[7]

[5] Colangelo (2019).

[6] European Court of Auditors Special Report Number 18 on the "*Single European Sky: a changed culture but not a single sky*", https://eca.europa.eu/Lists/ECADocuments/SR17_18/SR_SES_EN.pdf, 2017.

[7] European Court of Auditors (2017); Calleja and Fenoulhet (2011); Button and Neiva (2013); Rizzo (2006, 2008, 2009, 2022).

The new "functionality" assigned to European airspace constitutes the further evolution of a long-standing process.

As is well known, in 2004 the European Commission, acknowledging the progressive increase in air transport flows (also in light of the liberalisation process) and, consequently, the equally progressive reduction of airspace concretely usable by airlines, initiated an ambitious reform project (Single European Sky—SES I) aimed, among other things, at pooling the airspaces of European countries according to the logic of functional blocks.

This initiative, however, as is known, proved to be partly ineffective, since the States showed particular reluctance to share the management of their airspace, which they viewed as the ultimate manifestation of the concept of national sovereignty.

Leaving aside the objections regarding the validity of such a "justification" in light of the perhaps more pertinent (and realistic) issue of the heterogeneity of tariffs for air traffic services (ATS), the European Union did not, in any case, abandon the project initiated in 2004, also in light of the unstoppable growth of demand/supply in air transport.

Thus, in 2009, a new package of regulations, the so-called SES II, was issued. This sought to overcome the critical issues that had emerged by creating the figure of the network manager, preparing a performance and charging system, and establishing new requirements for functional blocks.

The regulatory framework was also completed by other implementing rules to ensure the systems' interoperability.

Once again, the importance of creating the so-called functional blocks and the need to overcome the fragmentation of European skies were emphasised.

However, despite the evident need to achieve a new, more modern, and more responsive airspace configuration to meet traffic growth needs, the Commission's efforts, completed with the second intervention in 2009, did not garner particular support.

In 2013, therefore, the European Union returned to the subject, formulating a reform proposal called SES II+.

The new reform attempt was articulated in the identification of specific objectives such as improving the performance of air traffic services in terms of efficiency and the use of air traffic management capacity, as well as operational objectives determined in compliance with the principle of transparency in the provision of air navigation services and according to market logic, strengthening the role of national supervisory authorities, and consolidating the performance review system of the services offered.

The proposal also returned to the need to reorient the strategic value of functional blocks, of which it was noted—once again—that they had not been established (i.e., operated) despite their original provision.[8] This would grant Member States greater flexibility to align the performance of air navigation service providers with the objectives set by the Single European Sky performance system.

[8] On this aspect, see Fox (2016), pp. 87–119.

The economic crisis (2008–2011) and, perhaps, the evolution of the air transport market and airport systems, together with the persistent opposition of Member States still entrenched behind the issue of sovereignty, led to the substantial abandonment of this proposal.

Only in 2019, faced with the now inevitable need for reform (given the traffic levels that reached new records year after year), did the European Commission entrust a group of experts with drafting a new and further reform proposal for the SES through the Directorate-General for Mobility.

Therefore, in that year, the report of the Wise Persons' Group suggested developing a whole series of interventions aimed at adapting the technical and regulatory context to the changed context of air transport.[9]

In this context, the focus was on the need to expand the role of the Network Manager, integrate airports into the network management system, develop a new concept of Air Traffic Management services that took into account technological development and the ever-increasing presence of automation systems, and establish a "seamless European upper airspace system".

The report in question finally stressed the need to achieve a "digital single sky", so that the air transport system—in its various and diverse components—could balance the supply/demand ratio and react to any endogenous and exogenous factors likely to compromise the continuity of the provision of air navigation services.

Shortly thereafter, however, the storm of Covid-19 delayed the start—at least in the institutional forums of the European Union—of the discussion on reform.

Despite this, in 2020, the EU Commission, with COM 577 and COM 579, presented a proposal for SES reform based on some points that, in intention, would perhaps have achieved the long-sought attempt to create a "single European sky."

The 2020 reform proposals, in addition to reaffirming some fundamental principles such as respect for national sovereignty over airspace (also due to the obligations arising from the 1944 Chicago Convention), went so far as to advocate for a reform of route charges along with the concentration of the functions of the performance review body for air navigation service providers at the European Union Aviation Safety Agency (EASA), as well as an increased role for the network manager.

It is worth noting here that this latest attempt by the European institutions to innovate airspace management did not elicit positive reactions from operators—especially airlines—who had hoped to see more ambitious models.

This is all the more true when considering that the new regulatory framework adds further "goals" to the already complex mission of the Single European Sky, which is now also directed towards the objectives of reducing emissions and thus the greater environmental sustainability of air transport.

Therefore, the reform proposed by the European Commission in 2020 was not met with particular enthusiasm, so much so that it was significantly scaled back in

---

[9] See the report at https://www.sesardeploymentmanager.eu/news/sesar-deployment-alliance-initial-statement-on-wise-persons-group-report

its objectives and found a synthesis in Regulation 2803/2024,[10] in response to the nonetheless pressing needs for regulatory innovation.

This legislative text reaffirms the aims of the European ATM system in terms of safety, efficiency, and sustainability, providing that Member States shall ensure that air navigation services are provided in conditions of safety, regularity, and sustainability, optimising the use of airspace, and contributing to the reduction of emissions.

Furthermore, the Member States maintain the power to designate an independent national supervisory authority to ensure consistent and reliable surveillance of the provision of air navigation services. In contrast, air navigation service providers are now called upon to cooperate with other providers to improve the overall performance of the European ATM system.

3 The SESAR Programme as "Collateral" to the Single European Sky

Parallel with the various aforementioned reform attempts, the European Union, as early as Regulation 219/2007, began to consider the research and development activities that would need to be supported and incentivised in the aviation sector, particularly in air traffic management.

This initiative, indeed, responded to the need to address the lack of common technologies to ensure interoperability between the various systems used for traffic management and to create a common procedure for the certification of the components integrating these systems.

On the other hand, and several years later, as will be explained in detail below, such a technical-normative process perhaps underground created the minimum conditions for collaboration among the various stakeholders of air transport who, primarily due to the increasingly complex challenges, now seem irreversibly (in a positive sense) linked (also from a legal point of view) to the achievement of common objectives.

Thus, Regulation 219/2007 created the SESAR Joint Undertaking, which is characterised by the need to modernise the European ATM system and involve stakeholders in developing technological projects and their subsequent deployment.[11]

The objectives set in 2007 were multifaceted, involving a whole series of strictly industrial aspects.

This programme's activity, which was supposed to be completed by the end of 2016, was then extended with Regulation 721/2014, which launched the SESAR 2020 initiative to align development programmes with the Horizon 2020 activities.

These latter provisions already expressed a clear need to tackle the challenge of technological evolution with greater vigour.

[10] Regulation (EU) 2024/2803 of the European Parliament and of the Council of 23 October 2024 on the implementation of the Single European Sky.

[11] Lawless (2014).

This need became even more evident in light of the difficulties, as mentioned earlier, encountered by the Union in creating the SES and the ever-constant growth in demand for air transport.

If, therefore, on the one hand, we have witnessed the almost absolute impossibility of achieving the creation of the SES as imagined initially by the EU in 2004, on the other hand, the increase in air transport and the physical and infrastructural limit linked to the location of airports have renewed the idea that intervention on the air traffic management system is considered the only lever capable of improving the efficiency of the entire sector as well as responding to ever-changing and contingent needs.

From a strictly operational point of view, SESAR's activities, or rather the objectives that the joint undertaking is called to achieve, are synthesised in the ATM Masterplan, subsequently approved by a Council Decision.

The Masterplan, containing the European plan for modernising air traffic management, is the planning tool for air traffic management throughout Europe. It links ATM research and innovation activities with deployment scenarios to achieve the performance objectives of the Single European Sky.

In other words, this document represents the roadmap agreed upon between stakeholders and regulators. It connects the research and development activities of technological and technical regulation solutions with practical use scenarios to achieve the SES performance objectives.

It is perhaps of interest to note the particular mechanism that links the various components at play: the harmonisation of normative instruments (the Regulations establishing the SES and SESAR) with the more strictly operational ones (the Masterplan), identifying the connecting link in the aforementioned Decision by the Council, constitutes a positive example of synthesis of the interests involved (public and private), as well as the achievement of objectives on a European scale that would otherwise be unattainable.

In this context, since achieving the SES through direct regulations has proven difficult, and given the strong political will of the Member States, efforts have been made to ensure a minimum level of uniformity that improves the efficiency of air traffic management by sharing common technological solutions among stakeholders. As a result, 'collateral' initiatives have emerged that help implement the final goals of the SES programme.

In this sense, as mentioned, the process initiated with Regulation 219/2007 and then continued with Regulation 721/2014 found its latest synthesis in Regulation 2085/2021[12] and the consequent renaming of the joint undertaking to SESAR 3.[13]

[12] See Council Regulation (EU) 2021/2085 of 19 November 2021 establishing the Joint Undertakings under Horizon Europe and repealing Regulations (EC) No 219/2007, (EU) No 557/2014, (EU) No 558/2014, (EU) No 559/2014, (EU) No 560/2014, (EU) No 561/2014 and (EU) No 642/2014.

[13] Masutti (2011, 2021); EUROCONTROL (2022, 2023); ICB (2019); Joint Stakeholder Declaration on Future of the Single European Sky (2019); Schubert (2017); SESAR Joint Undertaking (2019); Van Houtte 2017

Based on the latest "update," some principles and objectives that have historically characterised the SESAR joint undertaking were reaffirmed. On the other hand, the scope of action was expanded through the inclusion of further purposes deriving both from technological development and from the alignment—also of the deployment activity financed at the community level—with the new values that the European Union pursues and, in particular, that of environmental sustainability extended, with the most recent legislation, also to air transport.

In particular, a new deadline (2035) was established, by when SESAR is called to provide technological solutions for high-performance air traffic management, reaffirming one of the founding objectives of the same joint undertaking and the SES initiative since 2004: to allow uncongested operation.

The new discipline then links the traditional purposes to the new ones that have emerged more recently. This is because it requires modelling air traffic management based on greater respect for the environment and climate in line with the European Green Deal and European climate legislation.

On the other hand, and on a more strictly operational level, Regulation 2085/2021, recalling the technical aspects of the first Masterplan adopted by Council decision 2009/320/EC for which SESAR is articulated into three interconnected, continuous, and evolving collaborative processes that define, develop, and disseminate innovative operational procedures and technological systems, places these same processes at the basis of the digital European sky.

The theme, or rather, the aim of "digitalisation" was reaffirmed when the Regulation in question entrusted SESAR with the task of accelerating the sector's digitalisation and making it more resilient and, responding to one of the indications from the Wise Experts Group of 2019, triggering the scalability of the airspace management system according to traffic fluctuations.

Associated with this aspect is also the provision for the inclusion of unmanned aerial mobility in the SES architecture, as well as the renewed and ever-present need—in compliance with the founding principles of the European Union—to strengthen, through innovation, the competitiveness of manned and unmanned air transport and air traffic management services, in order to support economic growth and recovery.

Finally, the further consideration that the new joint undertaking should be able to develop and validate technical contributions, assist the Commission in regulatory activities concerning air traffic management by preparing technical documentation for common projects, conduct technical studies, or support standardisation activities is not insignificant.[14]

Examining more closely the provisions of Regulation 2085/2021 regarding the objectives that are added to those already proper to previous legislative provisions, the particular density of their content is immediately evident. Although outlined in just two articles, it implicitly refers not so much to an explanatory document, but

[14] See *Recital* no. 89 of Reg. 2021/2085.

instead to an approach that now inevitably seems to characterise the intimate connection between technical development and regulation.

In fact, their interpretation requires going beyond the textual data of the norms and delving deeper—also by resorting to transversal skills—into the "merit" of the research projects that are initiated and then, precisely under the aegis of the described scheme, examining their relative deployment.

In this interpretative framework, SESAR is now required to develop a research and innovation ecosystem that fully covers the value chains of air traffic management and U-Space air navigation services. This will allow the construction of the digital European sky defined in the European air traffic management modernisation plan.

Such a result should, therefore, allow for the necessary collaboration and coordination between air navigation service providers and airspace users to ensure a single harmonised EU air traffic management system for manned and unmanned operations.

Likewise, the joint undertaking must now also take on the tasks of a) developing and validating air traffic management solutions that support high levels of automation, b) developing and validating the technical architecture of the digital European sky, c) supporting an accelerated market deployment of innovative solutions through demonstrators, d) coordinating the definition of priorities and the planning of the Union's air traffic management modernisation efforts, based on a consensus-driven process among air traffic management stakeholders, and finally, e) facilitating the development of standards for the industrialisation of SESAR solutions.[15]

What is relevant, also for this work, is the fact that such objectives are not limited to research and development activities but, as mentioned, play a decisive role in providing the technical basis that is then "incorporated" into the legal norm.

Article 143 of Regulation 2085/2021, in fact, provides that the joint undertaking must facilitate an accelerated market deployment of SESAR solutions by: a) organising and coordinating large-scale demonstration activities; b) implementing close coordination with the European Union Aviation Safety Agency (EASA) to allow for timely development by this Agency of regulatory measures falling within the scope of Regulation (EU) 2018/1139 and its implementing rules, and c) supporting the related standardisation activities, in close collaboration with standardisation bodies and EASA, as well as with the entity established to coordinate the tasks of the SESAR deployment phase in line with Commission Implementing Regulation (EU) No 409/2013.[16]

From the examination of the framework within which the theme of the Digital European Sky develops—as will be explained in detail below—two preliminary aspects of particular importance seem to emerge.

[15] See also art. 143, Reg. 2021/2085.

[16] Commission Implementing Regulation (EU) No 409/2013 of 3 May 2013 on the definition of common projects, the establishment of governance and the identification of incentives supporting the implementation of the European Air Traffic Management Master Plan.

On the one hand, the centrality of the joint undertaking is reaffirmed not only in the phase of identifying technical solutions but also in their development, which, in light of the complexities given by technological evolution, calls for the necessary involvement of the most representative and most authoritative group of stakeholders.

On the other hand, and with a significant innovation compared to the repealed discipline, the outcomes of the activity carried out by the joint undertaking become the basis for the subsequent elaboration of both technical standards (with the evident logical consequences in terms of industrial application) and regulation at the European Union level.

This consideration, as mentioned above, should push us to investigate in more detail not so much the essence of the normative texts, which appears increasingly cryptic, but rather the path taken by SESAR during the research, development, and application phase through the programming document (Masterplan), the various projects, and related development activities.

4 The Architecture of the Digital European Sky

Article 142, paragraph 3, of Regulation 2085/2021 contains the definitions of "digital European sky" and "architecture of the digital European sky" which, as can be seen, do not identify a legal concept in the strict and traditional sense, but rather, as mentioned before, underpin an approach that links technological development activity with purely legislative activity, suggesting the existence (present and future) of a whole series of initiatives functional to enabling the air transport system to manage future growth in a safe, efficient, and sustainable manner.[17]

In other words, it is a list of principles rather than a true definition capable of allowing interpreters to easily perceive the *res extensa.*

Therefore, and as mentioned, this requires finding the content of these "definitions" elsewhere, in order to try to better understand their meaning and, above all, to identify the themes and issues that European legislators will pursue in executing the objectives established under law.

Indeed, the 2020 Blueprint, published by the SESAR joint undertaking and the Directorate-General for Mobility of the European Commission, already sets some fundamental points that will guide the reconfiguration of the air traffic management system until 2040.

The document in question identifies seven areas of intervention in which the future air traffic management system will develop.

The first area concerns the connection of ATM services, which, according to the text, must provide hyper-connectivity between all interested parties (vehicle-to-vehicle, vehicle-to-infrastructure) through high-bandwidth and low-latency fixed and mobile networks.

[17] Masutti (2011, 2021).

Furthermore, the operation of highly automated systems is envisaged, allowing numerous subjects to interact with each other seamlessly, and making the scalable system more secure.

A second aspect concerns the relevance of ground infrastructures for interaction with remotely piloted vehicles.

In this respect, the hoped-for (indeed, prescribed, by virtue of Regulation 2803/2024) integration of unmanned flight activities in manned airspace has led to attention also being focused on aspects related to the security of connections and the capacity of the ground infrastructure to offer and receive information.

From another perspective, however, the Blueprint identifies in the development of new technologies the opportunity to access a dynamic reconfiguration of airspace that takes into account the need, especially in cases of maximum intensity of air movements, to activate cross-border air traffic control services, thereby allowing increasing capacity and, therefore, the broadest possible use of physical resources without prejudice to carriers.

A fourth objective is the now mature—from a strictly technological standpoint—possibility of separating the provision of services from the physical infrastructure, allowing air traffic and service providers, regardless of national borders, to connect their operations where necessary in a secure manner.

Technological evolution will always be the driver for further development of the air traffic management system, as the Blueprint considers the increasingly significant appearance in the aeronautical sector of machine learning, deep learning, and big data analysis.

According to this document, the acquisition of more data and the quality of the consequential processing will contribute to improving the ATM system.

The progressive affirmation of new forms of air mobility and their impact on urban systems has been considered in the Blueprint. As a sixth objective, the document contemplates the need for a digitally native traffic management system capable of ensuring the safe integration of drones into the airspace, especially in urban areas, taking into account new and existing aerial vehicles and autonomous operations.

One of the most challenging use cases of U-Space will be enabling urban air mobility, which should advance autonomous technologies in several areas.

Finally, there is an increasing need to promote civil/military interoperability and coordination.

Dual-use technologies such as those for communications, navigation, and surveillance and other solutions that allow the exchange of trajectory information in real time will improve, according to the text in question, the predictability of military operations and the network's overall capacity.

Concurrently with the aforementioned Blueprint and at an even more detailed level in terms of operational and technical regulation aspects, the 2020 Air Traffic Management Masterplan has also intervened.

This text traces a series of guidelines along which the air traffic management system will develop and evolve.

Some points of particular importance can be noted regarding the aspects that allow us to ascertain the content of the expression "digital European sky."

The 2020 Masterplan, indeed, emphasises that digital transformation is not an objective in itself, but rather a means to accelerate the implementation of the SESAR vision, which goes far beyond the simple "transition from paper to digital" and aims to improve the overall performance of the aviation system in terms of safety, efficiency, and cost.

At a strictly operational level, the 2020 Masterplan identifies four evolutionary phases of the "Digital European Sky", not failing to underline how the transition to a digitised air traffic management system involves significant challenges not only from a technological point of view, but also from a regulatory and governance perspective.

In particular, in "Phase A", the objective is to adopt an architecture of air navigation services that enables and promotes aeronautical activity based on the efficiency of the flight trajectory (TBO).

"Phase B" focuses on service and infrastructure efficiency, providing for the development of open standards and introducing a common service layer through ATM data service providers.

From a strictly regulatory point of view, such a result will be linked to the adaptation of certification regulations for new virtualised services and to the obvious criticalities that the transition from physical to virtual infrastructures will raise regarding the allocation of responsibilities in case of malfunctions or incidents.

The third step, "Phase C," will realise the defragmentation of European skies through virtualisation and the integration of increasing levels of automation and connectivity.[18]

This should (use of the conditional is necessary, due to the not always successful outcomes of attempts at service communion) lead to the possibility for service providers to provide services regardless of national borders (so-called "geographical decoupling"), which would probably require a revision of the regulations on certification and liability of service providers as well as—if this objective is achieved—the opportunity for a new legal framework to establish responsibilities when services are provided by a provider from a country other than that in which the flight takes place.

The 2020 Masterplan is then completed in "Phase D," regarding "digitalisation," which envisages an integrated digital ecosystem characterised by distributed data services and a high degree of automation.

In this last step, the technological development of ATM services must be accompanied by adequate rules regarding the limits of automation and human responsibility, the development of new approaches to certify systems in which a large part of the decisions is delegated to machines, a new governance of integrated mobility, and constant attention to pollution limits.

[18] Comenale Pinto (2004, 2007).

The objectives set by the 2020 Masterplan in the four distinct phases are harbingers of further profiles of legal relevance, which it will inevitably need to tackle.

Indeed, if on the one hand the document explicitly recognises the need to fully respect the sovereignty of Member States over their airspace, on the other hand, a plurality of factors promotes greater integration, especially where the virtualisation of services will be completed.

This should, perhaps, lead to the drafting of a supranational governance model for information management as well as new legal mechanisms for the delegation of services across national borders.

The transition from a nationally fragmented system to an integrated digital ecosystem will, therefore, require managing integration and national sovereignty in a balanced way, new liability regimes for virtualised and cross-border services, the regulation of automation and artificial intelligence in safety-critical systems (both in the safety and security versions), as well as the discipline of new entrants, in particular drones and urban air mobility.

In anticipation of the update of the ATM Masterplan, the consultations among stakeholders that took place at the beginning of 2024[19] had the merit of highlighting further aspects that, dictated by impressive technological development, have launched new challenges, especially from a regulatory perspective.

The results of discussions emphasise that the aviation of the future will, first and foremost, be characterised by a radically new approach, aimed at minimising the environmental impact in all its forms, both in terms of CO2 emissions and other factors (noise pollution).

The air traffic management (ATM) system should become extremely precise and optimised, as it will be based on each aircraft's individual performance, user preferences, real-time traffic, and weather conditions.

In this sense, the airspace is expected to be configured in real time according to traffic demand.

In the new scenario, the human role will evolve towards more complex tasks, as most routine activities will be managed through machine-to-machine applications.

The "digital European sky" will include higher levels of automation, incorporating digitised and automated services; artificial intelligence-enabled systems will be fundamental for processing advanced parameters related to climate and aircraft performance.

The man-machine relationship should move towards a "teaming" situation where the aircraft crew could be reduced to a single pilot who will be called to manage on-board automation and collaborate with digital assistants.

Of particular interest is the evolution of the role of air traffic control, which will develop a variable interaction with automation and artificial intelligence systems according to tasks and objectives.

[19] A summary of the consultation work was carried out during the European ATM MP Stakeholder Consultation Workshop held in Brussels on 22–23 April 2024. Detailed information is available at https://www.eurocontrol.int/article/european-atm-master-plan-and-eurocontrols-role-wider-atm-transformation

All these aspects had been found a specific assessment in the ATM Masterplan 2025.

As we have seen the 2020 Masterplan represented the zenith of a pre-pandemic paradigm. Its principal impetus was a foreseeable, linear "capacity crunch" resulting from the consistent rise in traffic. Its fundamental vision aimed to establish a "high-performing" system focused on facilitating airspace users to operate along their "preferred trajectories." The implementation framework, founded upon nine "Essential Operational Changes" (EOCs) and a four-phase research and development roadmap, was characterised by an academic, sequential, and technology-driven approach.

The 2025 Masterplan is a strategic document developed in response to what it describes as a "formidable challenge. " It is characterised by three new, urgent drivers: (1) The Political Mandate: The "twin green and digital transition" now serves as the main guiding principle, raising sustainability from merely an operational advantage to the primary political goal of the system, with a new emphasis on non-CO_2 emissions; (2) The Geopolitical Reality: The "Russian war against Ukraine" is explicitly cited, introducing a new security and resilience imperative that redefines the purpose of civil-military cooperation and the dynamics of airspace; (3) The Technological Urgency: The plan shifts from a conceptual "digital transformation" to a concrete "service-oriented architecture (SOA) delivery model" and from "automation support" to "human-machine teaming" and artificial intelligence.

The most notable change, however, is the implementation framework. The 2025 plan replaces the R&D-led EOCs with ten "Strategic Deployment Objectives" (SDOs). This indicates a vital and urgent shift from research to deployment, establishing an investment and regulatory pathway aimed at speeding up the adoption of mature solutions and finally recognising that "innovation and the deployment of new ATM systems are not up to speed".

The 2025 Masterplan, published in December 2024, entirely redefines this vision. The new aim is to make Europe the "most efficient and environmentally friendly sky to fly in the world" by 2045.

This is a significant re-purposing. The aim has shifted from simply enabling the user's path to actively directing that path to achieve a shared, societal aim. The 2025 plan's goal is to "avoid any unnecessary fuel burn" and, most importantly, to "improve performance on non-CO_2 emissions, noise, and local air quality."

The system now needs to be designed to "minimise the total impact of aviation on the climate". This introduces a new and fundamental tension. The 2020 airline-preferred trajectory (chosen for fuel and cost efficiency) may differ from the 2025 climate-preferred trajectory (aimed at avoiding contrail formation and high non-CO_2 impact areas).

The 2025 vision foresees a future where the ATM network, in support of the EU's Green Deal, must supersede the 2020 user-focused vision. The system will prioritise a new, network-driven and climate-oriented approach, rather than an individual airline's business case.

The 2025 plan replaces the 2020's broad concept with a detailed, two-part blueprint for reaching the digital sky. It brings the 2020 vision into action.

The 2025 plan is based on "five technological levers for transformational change": (1) Trajectory-based operations (TBO): Building on the 2020 concept, TBO now depends on "data-enriched flight plans" that facilitate highly precise, fuel-efficient, and climate-optimised routes; (2) Increased data volumes: This serves as the fuel for the new system, enabling "machine learning, artificial intelligence (AI), and big data analytics" to operate more intelligently and safely; (3) Elevated levels of automation: This marks a significant progression from 2020. The vision, extending to 2045, is that "voice communication will no longer be the primary means of communication as most routine tasks will be managed through machine-to-machine applications"; (4) Human–machine teaming: An advanced new concept replacing the simpler "automation support" of 2020; (5) Dynamic airspace: Now a security necessity, this will enable "near-real-time configuration of airspace".

Conversely, the 2025 plan requires adopting a "data-driven and cloud-based service-oriented architecture (SOA) delivery model". This SOA approach signifies a major shift from owning assets (the traditional ANSP model of monolithic, sovereign systems) to consuming services (a shared platform or marketplace of digital ATM services).

This new architecture is the technical solution to the new contextual drivers.

It offers scalability and resilience: A cloud-based SOA enables the system to "dynamically and collaboratively scale capacity up or down within minutes," addressing post-pandemic volatility. It also delivers rapid innovation, as the plan states this model "shifts the focus from assets to services, enabling the quicker deployment of new features."

From a regulatory perspective, this model will "facilitate the development of a technical regulatory framework focusing on developing or updating specific services rather than overhauling and certifying the entire system.

Moving beyond automation, the 2025 plan introduces the concept of "Human–machine teaming". This is a far more sophisticated and integrated idea, suggesting a collaborative partnership between humans and AI. In this model, the machine has a greater level of agency. As the plan states, "machine-to-machine applications" will handle "most routine tasks", with the human (controller, pilot) working alongside the machine "to deliver the highest quality of service", likely by managing exceptions, strategic decisions, and complex, non-routine events.

This is not merely a theoretical objective, as the 2025 Masterplan explicitly states that it "aligns SESAR's automation strategy with EASA's artificial intelligence 2.0 roadmap." This alignment demonstrates a mature, coordinated, and regulator-endorsed strategy aimed at transcending basic automation and progressing toward a future of collaborative human-AI air traffic management.

In the unmanned domain, the 2020 plan regarded the "booming drone industry" as a "significant and complex challenge in terms of ATM. " The entire framework was devised to address this challenge by isolating it. U-space was characterised as an "ecosystem that is very different from ATM but seamlessly integrated with it. ".

The 2025 plan fundamentally alters this paradigm. Motivated by substantial commercial and political pressures to develop the drone economy, U-space and

Innovative Air Mobility (IAM) are reconceptualised as a central strategic opportunity.

This is most evident in the new implementation framework. This area is officially recognised as one of the "10 Strategic Deployment Objectives": SDO 10—Enable innovative air mobility (IAM) and drone operations.

Along with the 2020 Masterplan, the joint undertaking also published—in the same year—the Strategic Research and Innovation Agenda (SRIA[20]), which describes in detail the research and innovation roadmaps to realise the digital European sky, in line with the ambitions of the "European Green Deal" and the "Europe fit for the digital age" initiative.

The SRIA reaffirms the necessary and urgent rethinking of the ATM system in from a digital perspective, through the creation of an integrated environment based on distributed data services, in which digital technologies do not represent a mere support tool, but rather the driving force of a profound transformation of the entire sector.

This should facilitate the birth of a fully scalable ATM system, capable of responding to the needs of both traditional and unmanned aviation, further raising safety standards through closer integration between flight and ground systems.

However, the scenario outlined by the 2020 Masterplan and the modifications in the 2025 edition leave open a series of legal and regulatory problems of no minor importance.

To support this technological transformation, an adequate regulatory framework is necessary.

The certification regime will have to evolve to allow for an accelerated transformation while maintaining the necessary guarantees, thereby perhaps requiring the updating of regulations such as the regulation on the licensing and certification of air traffic controllers (EU) 2015/340[21] and the ATM/ANS regulation (EU) 2017/373.[22]

Likewise, it would perhaps be appropriate to adapt the regulatory framework in light of the new models of human-machine collaboration, both in relation to the static phase (certification) and the dynamic-operational phase (especially in the "transitions" between automation and human control) and from the perspective of liability.

---

[20] https://www.sesarju.eu/sria

[21] Commission Regulation (EU) 2015/340 of 20 February 2015 laying down technical requirements and administrative procedures relating to air traffic controllers' licences and certificates pursuant to Regulation (EC) No 216/2008 of the European Parliament and of the Council, amending Commission Implementing Regulation (EU) No 923/2012 and repealing Commission Regulation (EU) No 805/2011.

[22] Commission Implementing Regulation (EU) 2017/373 of 1 March 2017 laying down common requirements for providers of air traffic management/air navigation services and other air traffic management network functions and their oversight, repealing Regulation (EC) No 482/2008, Implementing Regulations (EU) No 1034/2011, (EU) No 1035/2011 and (EU) 2016/1377 and amending Regulation (EU) No 677/2011.

At the same time, the implementation of a dynamic airspace configuration, adaptable in real time, might require a redefinition of national jurisdictions and the competencies of control authorities, perhaps through the creation of a cross-border legal regime that overcomes the current limitations based on national borders, through binding multilateral agreements and also the elaboration of harmonised normative standards for decision-making delegation to automated systems.

5 The Digital European Sky and the European Green Deal

In addition to the significant progress regarding adapting the air traffic management system to changed needs, the European Union has, since 2020, included the air transport sector in the broader strategy aimed at CO2 reduction,[23] assigning a priority role to the reform of the Single European Sky.

This consideration is of fundamental importance as it shows the change—from a political perspective—in the approach to the issue of the Single European Sky.

The grafting of this issue onto the broader and horizontal environmental dimension involves adding a further lever for achieving the objectives of reducing climate impact. At the same time, it affects the development and implementation of the specific and original purposes of the "Single European Sky" project.

In 2021, EUROCONTROL and EASA published a joint document aimed at identifying the obstacles to achieving a uniform approach to managing the path towards sustainable aviation in the historical problems of the SES.[24]

The need to link the implementation of the Digital European Sky to the environmental sustainability of air transport is thus highlighted. The applicable Euro-union regulatory framework here identifies the adoption of new solutions on the technical and regulatory level of air traffic management as a further tool for reducing emissions.

Specifically, the document in question reaffirms that, since 2004, the regulatory framework has identified the implementation of the SES as a factor capable of reducing CO2 emissions by 10%.

At the same time, the mandatory implementation of Common Project 1 (CP1) emphasises how trajectory-based flight operations and the establishment of a digital infrastructure for the SES are capable of contributing to a 2% reduction in emissions per flight compared to the 2012 baseline.

Beyond the benefits, the text is of interest because it does not leave in the background the need to identify adequate parameters to measure, monitor, and manage the environmental benefits deriving from improvements in air traffic control services, suggesting the need for a more complete regulatory framework to assess the

---

[23] Abeyratne (2014, 2016); Rosafio (2020); Salerno (2017); Tellarini (2018); Vagaggini (2021); Budd et al. (2013); Button (2009).

[24] See EUROCONTROL and EASA, *Five Pillars for a Green Single European Sky, Joint no-Paper* (2021), www.eurocontrol.int.

environmental performance of the ATM system. On the other hand, it also underlines the possible overlap (or perhaps, better, conflict) regarding the international programme launched by ICAO which is based on market-based measures such as CORSIA (Carbon Offsetting and Reduction Scheme for International Aviation) and the EU emissions trading system (ETS), which complement intra-sectoral measures to address the climate impact of aviation.

For these reasons and in order to address old and emerging issues (and objectives), particularly within the framework of a principle of climate neutrality, EUROCONTROL and EASA have proposed the need to extend the effects of the Single European Sky updates to other sectors (noise pollution), to develop "green trajectories" for airspace users, as well as to provide incentives to encourage efficient flight trajectories.

The addition of the further environmental theme to the "tasks" that the SES system has long been called to perform, if on the one hand, is appreciable and aligns all subjects involved in air transport with the horizontal objective (sustainability), on the other hand, it leaves unresolved a whole series of problems of which, perhaps, it amplifies the scope.

The transition to a "more intensive ATM data ecosystem," as envisaged by the document, raises legal questions of fundamental importance that the current regulatory framework does not seem able to address adequately.

Data sharing in real time between different stakeholders, a central element of the future ATM system, requires clear rules on data ownership, access, use, and protection.

One could, perhaps, hypothesise that a specific legal framework for the governance of ATM data is necessary, which balances the need for maximum sharing for system optimisation with the legitimate needs of protecting sensitive data and operators' commercial interests.

In the absence of such a framework, the risk is that the distrust of the system's actors regarding the sharing of their data could compromise the innovative potential of new technologies.

At the same time, the lack and insufficiency of tools (and rules) to preside over the monitoring and evaluation—in terms of metrics—of emissions by the new air traffic management system certainly does not contribute to assessing its effects in terms of environmental benefits.

6 The Role of Artificial Intelligence in the Digital European Sky. Points for Reflection *de iure condendo*

The considerations made so far must, however, also be read in light of the parallel development—at the Euro-union level—of horizontal legislation concerning new technologies.

In April 2021, the European Commission, in fact, presented a proposal for harmonised rules on artificial intelligence (AI).

The text, definitively approved in June 2024, was published in the Official Journal in the form of Regulation 1689/2024 on 12 July 2024.[25]

The regulation (also known as the EU AI Act) aims to provide a general regulatory framework for deploying this new technology, which, according to the proposal itself, can "support socially and environmentally beneficial outcomes and provide key competitive advantages to European businesses and the economy."

As far as is of interest for this work, the provision establishes rules for AI through a risk-based approach and considers aviation as a high-risk sector,[26] indirectly affected when AI systems are used or are part of a "safety component" that performs a safety function for a product.[27]

Based on these assumptions, any introduction of AI in the field of aviation should follow certain principles established by the regulation in question.

This implies, first of all, that high-risk AI systems must be designed and developed in such a way as to ensure that their operation is sufficiently transparent to allow users to interpret the system's output and use it appropriately.

The text also states that high-risk AI systems must be resilient concerning errors, failures, or inconsistencies that may occur within the system or the environment in which the system operates, particularly due to their interaction with natural persons or other systems.

Furthermore, the regulation in question provides that the design and development of AI must also be carried out through the lens of human-machine interface tools and supervision by a "natural person" during its use.

In this case, human supervision is entrusted with the specific objective of preventing or minimising risks to health, safety, or fundamental rights that may arise when a high-risk AI system is used in accordance with its intended purpose or under conditions of reasonably foreseeable misuse.

Along with all this, human supervision is required to fully understand the AI system's capabilities and limitations and to duly monitor its operation in order to detect and address any signs of anomalies and dysfunctions.

It is, therefore, envisaged that the human being using and/or supervising the AI system must: (a) be aware and sufficiently understand the relevant capabilities and limitations of the high-risk AI system and be able to duly monitor its operation, so that signs of anomalies, dysfunctions, and unexpected performance can be detected and addressed as soon as possible; (b) remain aware of the possible tendency to automatically or excessively rely on the output produced by a high-risk AI system ("automation bias"), particularly for high-risk AI systems used to provide

[25] Regulation (EU) 2024/1689 of the European Parliament and of the Council of 13 June 2024 laying down harmonised rules on artificial intelligence and amending Regulations (EC) No 300/2008, (EU) No 167/2013, (EU) No 168/2013, (EU) 2018/858, (EU) 2018/1139 and (EU) 2019/2144 and Directives 2014/90/EU, (EU) 2016/797 and (EU) 2020/1828

[26] See *Recital* no. 49.

[27] Pilon (2024); Kumar (2022); Kornilakis et al. (2023); Cheng et al. (2016).

information or recommendations for decisions to be made by natural persons; (c) be able to correctly interpret the output of the high-risk AI system, taking into account in particular the characteristics of the system and the available interpretation tools and methods; (d) be able to decide, in any particular situation, not to use the high-risk AI system or otherwise ignore or reverse the output of the high-risk AI system; (e) be able to intervene on the operation of the high-risk AI system or stop the system via a "stop" button or a similar procedure that allows the system to stop in a safe state, unless human interference increases the risks or negatively affects performance in consideration of the generally recognized state of the art.

The European regulation on AI seems to shift from a human-centred approach to a human supervision approach, leading to different outcomes and raising various questions, especially for the aviation sector, which had recently achieved unanimous agreement on placing the human being at the centre of the activity.[28]

The introduction of AI into the aviation environment could involve a variety of actors, including natural persons, air carriers, air navigation service providers, states, and manufacturers, not to mention the multifaceted hypotheses of liability that this would entail.

These problems would be exacerbated if it were not possible to trace—as should be "normal"—the decision-making process that the "machine" adopted to reach the output, starting from an input datum.

There are many ways this technology can be incorporated into routine tasks, particularly in air traffic control. However, it also brings a range of complex issues—though not all of them are listed here—that will require legal experts to find definitive solutions.

Beyond these questions, the impact of AI on the air transport system and—to a large extent—as already highlighted, on the air navigation services sector led EASA to set up, in July 2024, a task force with the specific task of identifying the necessary modifications to a vast compendium of regulations in the aeronautical field.

7 Conclusions

The analysis of the normative and structural evolution of the Single European Sky, from its original conception to the current configuration of the Digital European Sky, highlights a significant change in the Euro-union regulatory approach.

There has been a shift from a model based predominantly on direct normative instruments (the regulations of the SES I and II packages) to a more complex paradigm that integrates technological development, governance tools, and compatibility profiles with the Union's other transversal objectives.

[28] See in this sense the EUROCONTROL FLY AI Report (www.eurocontrol.int) and EASA AI Roadmap (www.easa.eu)

This change reveals the adoption of a "regulation by layers" strategy, which, facing the irreducible principle of national sovereignty over airspace, has sought alternative ways to achieve the objective of overcoming the structural fragmentation of European skies.

In this context, the SESAR programme, in its successive evolutions up to the current SESAR 3, has assumed a pivotal role not only as a research and development tool but also as a genuine mechanism of participatory governance capable of coordinating the interests of the various stakeholders of air transport and, downstream, promoting regulatory and legislative initiatives at various levels.

The digitalisation of the air traffic management system, crystallised in the definition in Article 142 of Regulation 2085/2021, is today configured as the primary enabling factor for achieving the historical objectives of the Single European Sky, to which new imperatives related to environmental sustainability and the integration of innovative forms of air mobility have been added.

From a legal point of view, this transformation raises questions of considerable complexity that require in-depth reflection on multiple aspects.

The virtualisation of ATM services and the progressive "geographical decoupling" between the provision of services and physical infrastructure impose the creation of a cross-border governance system that overcomes the limits of the current FABs (Functional Airspace Blocks), which have proven ineffective, or, alternatively, enhances, with the appropriate modifications, the role already held by EUROCONTROL as network manager.

This evolution would require a revision of the current certification systems (Regulation 2017/373) and an elaboration of new models of civil and administrative liability that take into account the distributed and transnational nature of the services.

On the other hand, the implementation of artificial intelligence systems in the critical domains of aviation, as foreseen by phases C and D of the Digital European Sky and, more generally, by the EU AI Act, would impose a rethinking of the normative paradigms on aviation safety.

In this respect, the current regulatory framework, founded on the principle of the "human-centered approach" expressed in ICAO technical standards and EASA regulations, will need to evolve towards a model that contemplates the concept of "human supervision" introduced by Article 14 of the EU AI Act, with relevant implications for aspects of professional liability regarding air traffic controllers (Regulation 2015/340) and pilots (Regulation 1178/2011).

In this context, the parameters of professional diligence and the relative standards of care will need to be redefined, going beyond the current dichotomy between fault-based liability and strict liability to achieve a more articulated system that considers the role of automation in decision-making processes.

The integrated digital ecosystem envisaged by phase D of the Digital European Sky presupposes an intensive sharing of operational, meteorological, and traffic data among public and private subjects.

This scenario requires the elaboration of a specific legal framework for the governance of ATM data that addresses the various issues, from ownership to the right of access, as well as respect for the principles of interoperability and standardisation, balancing security needs and commercial interests.

This is further supported by the fact that integrating climate objectives in the context of the Digital European Sky calls for applying innovative regulatory models that overcome the traditional command-and-control approach.

The transition towards "green trajectories," which consider the environmental impact with probable positive feedback from carriers and consumers—since reducing polluting emissions should lead to lower fuel consumption and, therefore, a lowering of air transport prices—requires a solid legal basis that harmonises environmental performance objectives with those of economic efficiency without prejudice to flight safety.

In this context, the experience gained with the emission trading schemes (EU ETS) and CORSIA can provide useful indications for developing a regulation system based on market mechanisms and incentives, rather than rigid prescriptions, in line with the principles of better regulation of the European Union.

The considerations made so far present the Digital European Sky as a complex socio-technical system whose implementation requires an equally sophisticated approach that integrates traditional normative instruments, technical standards, and participatory governance mechanisms.

The challenge for the Euro-union legislator lies in balancing the need for a harmonised regulatory framework with the flexibility required by technological evolution.

In this process, SESAR 3's role is emerging as central, not only as the subject in charge of deployment but also as a facilitator of a regulatory dialogue between the various stakeholders.

The success of the Digital European Sky will ultimately depend on the ability to overcome the sectoral approach that has so far characterised aeronautical regulation, in favour of an integrated vision that considers the interconnections between the different domains of the air transport ecosystem, also through a change of perspective that emphasises the services to be provided and their relative modalities, rather than on the technologies to be implemented.

Only in this way will it perhaps be possible to achieve that "digital transformation" which, in the words of the ATM Masterplan 2020, goes "far beyond the simple transition from paper to digital" to become a true paradigm shift in the management of European airspace.

References

A High-Level (2015) Vision for achieving the single European sky. Industry Consultation Body, Brussels. https://ec.europa.eu/transport/sites/transport/files/modes/air/single_european_sky/doc/icb/2015-01-22-icb-high-level-vision-for-achieving-ses.pdf

Abeyratne R (2014) Aviation and climate change: in search of a global market based measure. Springer, Cham

Abeyratne R (2016) Competition and investment in air transport: legal and economic issues. Springer, Cham
Adkins B (2001) Air transport and E.C. Competition Law, European Competition Law Monographs. Sweet & Maxwell, London
ATM Masterplan 2020 and ATM Masterplan 2025 are available at www.sesarju.eu
Balfour J (1995) European community air law. Butterworths, London
Balfour J (2008) EC external aviation relations: the community's increasing role, and the new EC/US Agreement. Common Mark Law Rev 45(2):443–466
Belobaba P, Odoni A, Barnhart C (eds) (2015) The global airline industry, 2nd edn. John Wiley & Sons, Chichester
Böckstiegel K-H (1995) Current challenges in the legal regulation of civil aviation. Ann Air Space Law 20:135–148
Budd L, Griggs S, Howarth D (eds) (2013) Sustainable aviation futures, Transport and sustainability series. Emerald Group Publishing Limited, Bingley
Button K (2009) The impact of US-EU 'open skies' agreement on airline market structures and airline networks. J Air Transp Manag 15(2):59–71. https://doi.org/10.1016/j.jairtraman.2008.09.010
Button K, Neiva R (2013) Single European sky and the functional airspace blocks: will they improve economic efficiency? J Air Transp Manag 33:73–80. https://doi.org/10.1016/j.jairtraman.2013.07.003
Calleja CD, Fenoulhet T (2011) The single European sky (SES): building on technical progress. Transp Policy 18(6):887–893. https://doi.org/10.1016/j.tranpol.2011.05.003
Cheng T, Wen P, Li Y (2016) Research status of artificial neural network and its application assumption in aviation. In: 2016 12th international conference on computational intelligence and security (CIS). IEEE, Wuxi, pp 407–410. https://doi.org/10.1109/CIS.2016.0094
Colangelo M, Zeno-Zencovich V (2007) Introduction to European transport law, 3rd edn. Roma TrE-Press, Rome
Comenale Pinto MM (2004) "Organizzazione e responsabilità nei servizi di traffico aereo", Diritto dei trasporti:41–70
Comenale Pinto MM (2007) "Dei servizi della navigazione aerea". In: Franchi B, Vernizzi S (eds) Il diritto aeronautico fra ricodificazione e disciplina comunitaria. Giuffrè, Milan, pp 95–145
Dempsey PS (1992) Europ Laissez-faire mythology. Quorum Books, Westport
Doganis R (2001) The airline business in the 21st century. Routledge, London
Doganis R (2006) The airline business, 2nd edn. Routledge, London
Doganis R (2010) Flying off course: the economics of international airlines, 4th edn. Routledge, London
Ebke WF, Wenglorz GW (1991) Liberalizing scheduled air transport within the European Community: from the first phase to the second and beyond. Denv J Int Law Policy 19(3):494–528
EUROCONTROL (2022) One size fit all – a common unit rate for Europe? Think Paper No. 18. EUROCONTROL, Brussels
EUROCONTROL (2023) The challenge of long-haul flight decarbonisation: when can cutting-edge energies and technologies make a difference? Think Paper No. 21. EUROCONTROL, Brussels
European Court of Auditors (2017) Special report no 18/2017: single European Sky: a changed culture but not a single sky. Publications Office of the European Union, Luxembourg. https://www.eca.europa.eu/Lists/ECADocuments/SR17_18/SR_SES_EN.pdf
European Court of Auditors (2019) Special Report No 11/2019: The EU's Regulation for the Modernisation of Air Traffic Management Has Added Value – but the Funding Was Largely Unnecessary. Publications Office of the European Union, Luxembourg. https://www.eca.europa.eu/Lists/ECADocuments/SR19_11/SR_SESAR_DEPLOYMENT_EN.pdf
Havel BF (2009) Beyond open skies: a new regime for international aviation. Kluwer Law International, Alphen aan den Rijn
ICB (2019) Vision for a single European sky, 2nd edn. Industry Consultation Body, Brussels

Joint Stakeholder Declaration on Future of the Single European Sky (2019) Brussels: European Commission. https://ec.europa.eu/transport/sites/transport/files/2019-09-high-level-conference-future-of-ses-declaration.pdf
Kahn AE (1970-1971) The economics of regulation: principles and institutions, 2 vols. Wiley, New York
Kahn AE (1978a) Deregulation of air transportation – getting from here to there. In: Regulating business: the search for an optimum. Institute for Contemporary Studies, San Francisco, pp 37–52
Kahn AE (1978b) The changing environment of international air commerce. Air Law 3(3):161–174
Kahn AE (1978c) Statement before the Aviation Subcommittee of Regulatory Reform: hearings before the Subcommittee on Aviation of the House Committee on Public Works and Transportation. In: 95th Congress, 2nd Session
Kahn AE (1988) Surprises of airline deregulation. In: AEA papers and proceedings of the one-hundredth annual meeting of the American Economic Association, vol 78(2), pp 316–322
Kahn AE (2008) Airline deregulation. In: Henderson DR (ed) The concise encyclopedia of economics. Liberty Fund, Indianapolis. http://www.econlib.org/library/Enc/AirlineDeregulation.html
Kornilakis A, Nouskalis G, Tzimas T, Pergantis V (2023) Artificial intelligence and normative challenges: international and comparative legal perspectives. Springer, Cham
Kotaite A (1995) Legal aspects of the international regulation of civil aviation. Ann Air Space Law 20:9–23
Kumar M (2022) Optimized application of artificial intelligence (AI) in aviation market. Int J Recent Res Aspects 9(4):9–12
Lawless E (2014) SESAR and the single European sky. Journaal LuchtRecht 6(73):79–85
Masutti A (2011) Single European sky - a possible regulatory framework for system wide information management (SWIM). Air Space Law 36(4/5):275–292
Masutti A (2021) Il futuro del cielo unico europeo. Verso un accentramento delle competenze sul controllo del traffico aereo nell'agenzia europea per la sicurezza aerea (EASA). Diritto dei trasporti 34(2):621–640
Pilon RV (2024) Artificial intelligence in commercial aviation: use cases and emerging strategies. Routledge, London
Rizzo MP (2006) Il pacchetto di regolamenti comunitari per la realizzazione del Cielo Unico Europeo. In: La Torre U, Moschella G, Pellegrino F, Rizzo MP, Vermiglio G (eds) Studi in memoria di Elio Fanara, vol 1. Giuffrè, Milan, pp 57–88
Rizzo MP (2008) "L'accesso alla fornitura dei servizi della navigazione aerea nel diritto comunitario". In: Studi in onore di Umberto Leanza, vol 3. Editoriale Scientifica, Naples, pp 1767–1792
Rizzo MP (ed) (2009) La gestione del traffico aereo: Profili di diritto internazionale, comunitario e interno. Atti del Convegno di studio di Messina, 5–6 ottobre 2007. G. Giappichelli Editore, Turin
Rizzo MP (2022) I servizi della navigazione aerea dal SES I al SES II+: qualificazione ed accesso alla fornitura. In: Ingratoci C, Marino A (eds) Il controllo del traffico nella navigazione: Stato dell'arte ed evoluzione. Editoriale Scientifica, Naples, pp 85–110
Rosafio EG (2020) "Osservazioni in tema di trasporto aereo e ambiente". Rivista del diritto della navigazione 86(2):1011–1035
Salerno F (2017) Le recenti misure per contrastare l'impatto ambientale del trasporto aereo. Il Diritto Marittimo 119(1):68–95
Schubert F (2017) The single European sky: the way ahead. Air Space Law 42(3):257–274
SESAR Joint Undertaking (2019) A proposal for the future architecture of the European airspace. SESAR Joint Undertaking, Brussels. https://www.sesarju.eu/node/3253
Tellarini G (2018) "Trasporto aereo e ambiente: inquinamento aereo acustico e gassoso". Rivista del diritto della navigazione 84(2):585–613
Vagaggini C (2021) Sostenibilità dei voli e degli scali aeroportuali. Rivista del diritto della navigazione 87(1):217–245

Aviation and Sustainability

Francesca Salerno

Contents

Abstract This chapter examines the issue of the environmental impact of air transport. It specifically examines the measures adopted at the international level by the International Civil Aviation Organization (ICAO), together with other European Union regulations, especially those relating to the so-called Single European Sky, which aim to contribute to achieving climate neutrality in the aviation sector.

1 Introduction

The issue of air pollution and global warming attracts significant attention from international and EU legislators. Of particular interest is the regulation of greenhouse gas emissions, which cause climate change.

Air transport, like other commercial activities, raises 'environmental sustainability' issues, particularly in areas where airports are situated. Aircraft operations, both at altitude and on the ground, primarily rely on fossil fuels, which generate secondary combustion products that affect regional and global air quality and contribute to climate change. Aircraft emissions also lead to the formation of contrails and increased cloudiness.

F. Salerno (✉)
Department of Law, Parthenope University of Naples, Napoli, Italy
e-mail: francesca.salerno@uniparthenope.it

M. P. Rizzo, F. Franchina (eds.), *Drones in the Digital European Sky*,
International Aviation Law Library 1,
https://doi.org/10.1007/978-3-032-16691-3_17

Recent EU data indicate that air transport accounts for 2 to 3% of global CO_2 emissions and, after road transport, is the second largest source of climate impact generated by transport (Directive (EU) 2023/958, recital 3[1]).

Air transport also affects the climate through emissions other than CO_2, such as nitrogen oxides (NO_x), carbonaceous particulate matter, oxidised sulphur species, and the effects of water vapour, as well as through atmospheric processes triggered by these emissions, such as the formation of ozone and cirrus clouds produced by condensation trails. It is perhaps worth noting that although air transport still contributes only modestly to global warming, the rapid growth of emissions from this sector risks undermining the progress made in other sectors.

The upturn in air traffic highlights the importance of addressing the environmental challenges facing the sector at an early stage. The 2022 EASA *European Aviation Environmental Report*[2] shows an increase in traffic in 2020, returning to 2019 levels and reiterating the problems already experienced in relation to congestion and delays.

Eurocontrol data report a total of 10.2 million flights in 2023, which is 10% more than in 2022 and 92% more than in 2019. In future projections, global demand for air transport is expected to increase by an average of 4.3% per year over the next 20 years. In Europe, the number of flights is expected to grow by 44% from 11 million in 2019 (pre-pandemic) to 16 million by 2050.[3] The International Civil Aviation Organization (ICAO) also estimates European growth of up to 3.1% per year for passenger traffic and up to 2.4% per year for cargo traffic by 2050 (ICAO 2022).

In a business-as-usual scenario, air traffic is expected to continue growing considerably. Since the growth in demand for air transport services exceeds the improvements in sectoral efficiency, CO_2 emissions will continue to rise both in absolute terms and as a percentage of global emissions (ICAO 2008). This underlines the need to accelerate and intensify the decarbonisation of air transport through the adoption of measures involving all aviation operators, adopting a global approach to the issue.

2 ICAO Policy

The issue of the environmental impact of air transport has been at the heart of ICAO policies for many years.[4] In fact, the ICAO formulates policies, develops and updates the Standard and Recommended Practices (SARP) on aircraft emissions, and carries out awareness-raising initiatives.

These activities are performed by the Secretariat and the Committee on Aviation Environmental Protection (CAEP), also working with other UN bodies and

[1] Directive (EU) 2023/958 amending Directive 2003/87/EC as regards aviation's contribution to the Union's economy-wide and the appropriate implementation of a global market-based measure.

[2] See EASA European Aviation Environmental Report 2022.

[3] EUROCONTROL, Aviation Outlook 2050, Main Report, April 2022, 1.

[4] Salerno (2017), p. 69; Rosafio (2020), p. 1013; Vagaggini (2021), p. 224.

international organisations. In this regard, the Intergovernmental Panel on Climate Change (IPCC),[5] established in 1988 at the initiative of the World Meteorological Organization (WMO) and the United Nations Environmental Programme (UNEP), published the Special Report on Aviation and the Global Atmosphere in 1999 at the request of the ICAO. This was the international body's first publication concerning a single industrial sector. The report showed that the environmental benefits of technological advances, operational improvements, and sustainable alternative fuels are insufficient to achieve the ICAO's global goal of maintaining global net CO_2 emissions at the same level (carbon-neutral growth) from 2020.

More effective results can be achieved by adopting a global approach to the issue, combining the application of new technologies in the aviation sector with political and economic analysis. This approach, in line with the proposal formulated in 2003 by the Association of European Airlines (AEA), envisages the use of the balanced approach criterion enshrined in Resolution A33-7 adopted in 2001 by the 33rd ICAO Assembly to address airport noise.

This methodology involves assessing all possible solutions to mitigate noise emissions, namely the reduction of aircraft noise at source, land-use planning and management, noise abatement procedures and operating restrictions. The aim is to achieve maximum environmental benefit in the most cost-effective manner. The application of this technique, which is based on the so-called four pillars, to the issue of emissions could be achieved by working on the following elements: (1) technology; (2) operational improvements; (3) infrastructure; and (4) economic measures. From the technological perspective, it should be noted that, over the years, ICAO has developed Standards and Recommended Practices to ensure that the latest technologies are incorporated into newly built aircraft. These aircraft are now significantly more fuel-efficient per passenger kilometre than those built in 1960.

The primary reference is Annex 16 (Environmental Protection) of the Convention on International Civil Aviation, which currently comprises four volumes: Volume I—*Aircraft Noise*, containing SARPs for aircraft noise certification and international specifications for aircraft noise measurement and assessment methods; Volume II—*Aircraft Engine Emissions,* which includes SARPs for certifying aircraft engine emissions; Volume III—*Aircraft* CO_2 *Emissions*; and Volume IV—*Carbon Offsetting and Reduction Scheme for International Aviation* (CORSIA).

It must be specified that operational improvements include various practices that can reduce noise, CO_2 emissions, and fuel consumption while also improving local air quality. In the aviation context, the term 'operations' can refer to a wide range of activities, including Air Traffic Management (ATM), aircraft operator activities, airport activities, ground operator activities, flight planning, airspace design, and network management, among other things.

Operational measures identified by the ICAO include the implementation of new, innovative concepts, more efficient flight paths, aircraft weight management,

[5] IPCC (Intergovernmental Panel on Climate Change) (1999) *Aviation and the Global Atmosphere: A Special Report of IPCC Working Groups I and III.*

improved ground procedures, and the long-term integration of cleaner technological and energy solutions. It is estimated that, in the most aggressive scenario, these measures could help reduce CO_2 emissions by up to 11% in 2050.

Infrastructure improvements also represent a considerable opportunity to reduce fuel consumption and CO_2 emissions in the short term. The IPCC estimated that air transport infrastructure operated to 12% inefficiency in 1999. Much progress has been made since then, and it is estimated that greater efficiency in airport and ATM infrastructure could provide a further 70% reduction in emissions. That being said, it is also essential to implement the fourth pillar—economic measures—to achieve the goal of carbon-neutral growth.

The European Commission laid down flexible economic measures based on the 'polluter pays' principle as early as 1999.[6] Specifically, it recognised the possibility of achieving positive results on the climate impact of air transport through the emissions trading mechanism, promoted by the ICAO since 2001.

The ICAO noted this approach at the 37th Session of the Assembly, held in Montreal (28 September to 8 October 2010), and reaffirmed it at the 38th Assembly (24 September to 4 October 2013). During this session, ICAO member States proposed a global system of Market Based Measures (MBMs) to be implemented by 2020.[7]

Building on the commitments made by states in the Paris Agreement under the aegis of the United Nations Framework Convention on Climate Change (UNFCCC), Resolution A39-3, adopted at the 39th Assembly,[8] reaffirmed the importance of defining a global MBM regime for international aviation, whose implementation would make a concrete contribution to achieving the goals set out in the Paris Agreement.

Further evolution of the ICAO strategy has led to the definitive establishment of a methodology for developing and implementing a set of mitigation measures to lower CO_2 emissions. It encompasses technology, sustainable alternative aviation fuels, and other cleaner energy sources, as well as operational measures such as traffic and airspace optimisation, and market-based measures, including CORSIA, a global mechanism to offset CO_2 emissions from international air transport involving EU Member States. This methodology gives states the flexibility to combine different elements within the collection according to their specific needs.[9]

In 2019, during its 40th session, the Assembly adopted Resolution A40-18,[10] reaffirming two ambitious global targets for the international aviation sector: a 2%

[6] European Commission (1999) Communication to the Council, the European Parliament, the Economic and Social Committee and the Committee of the Regions "Air Transport and the Environment".

[7] Abeyratne (2014), p. 55.

[8] ICAO A39-3, Consolidated statement of continuing ICAO policies and practices related to environmental protection—Global Market-based Measure (MBM) scheme.

[9] Erling (2017), p. 7.

[10] ICAO A40-18 *Consolidated statement of continuing ICAO policies and practices related to environmental protection – Climate change.*

improvement in annual fuel efficiency by 2050 and carbon-neutral growth from 2020 onwards, as outlined during the 37th Assembly (2010).

On that occasion, the Assembly reached a common global standard for calculating CO_2 emissions from aircraft worldwide, as recommended by the ICAO Programme of Action on International Aviation and Climate Change (ICAO 2009). The agreement, deemed 'historic', was adopted despite conflicts among ICAO Member States due to tensions between environmental goals, concerns about market distortions, and needs and ambitions regarding development.[11]

With Resolution A41-21, adopted at its 41st Assembly (27 September to 7 October 2022), the Organisation reaffirmed its commitment to the long-term global aspirational goal for international aviation (LTAG) of achieving zero net carbon emissions by 2050, in support of the targets set out in the Paris Agreement.

3 Initiatives Within the EU

One of the latest reports published by the IPCC on 4 April 2022, titled *Climate Change 2022: Mitigation of Climate Change*, notes that international air transport is regarded as a sector where sectoral agreements have set climate change mitigation targets that are by no means sufficient to meet the long-term temperature goals of the Paris Agreement. The report therefore emphasises the urgency for the EU to address this issue by increasing its efforts and establishing itself as a global leader in the fight against climate change.

In harmony with the goals of the UN 2030 Agenda for Sustainable Development, the European Green Deal[12] aims to make Europe the first climate-neutral continent by 2050. With the Fit for 55% Package, introduced by the European Commission on 14 July 2021, Europe seeks to cut at least 55% of net greenhouse gas emissions by 2030 compared with the 1990 levels.[13] The package comprises a series of interconnected proposals designed to facilitate a fair, competitive, and green transition by 2030 and beyond. To do so, European legislation has focused on both amending existing laws and introducing new proposals. Among the measures approved by the Council in April 2023, Directive (EU) 2023/958 on the air transport sector modifies the ETS (Emission Trading Scheme) to enhance air transport's role in reducing greenhouse gas emissions in line with the new climate targets for 2030 and to enforce the international CORSIA framework for non-EU aviation.

The ETS operates on the principle of carbon cap and trade. A cap is set on the total amount of emissions of certain greenhouse gases that can be emitted by installations included in the system. The cap is reduced over time, allowing for a gradual

[11] Adam (2011), p. 25.

[12] https://commission.europa.eu/strategy-and-policy/priorities-2019-2024/european-green-deal/delivering-european-green-deal_it.

[13] https://commission.europa.eu/strategy-and-policy/priorities-2019-2024/european-green-deal/delivering-european-green-deal/fit-55-delivering-proposals_en.

reduction in total emissions. Within this limit, companies buy or receive 'emission allowances', auctioned by Member States. These credits, which correspond to one tonne of CO_2 each, can be traded for other installations if they are not used. Companies can also purchase limited quantities of international credits from emission reduction projects around the world.[14]

Specifically, Directive 2023/958 mandates phasing out free emission allowances and full auctioning from 2026. Twenty million allowances will be set aside to incentivise aircraft operators to transition away from fossil fuels by 31 December 2030. The EU ETS will apply to flights within the EU (including flights to the UK and Switzerland), and the CORSIA scheme will cover extra-European flights to and from participating third countries from 2022 to 2027 (the 'clean cut principle'). As part of the same package, Regulation (EU) 2023/2405 (ReFuelEU Aviation)[15] mandates the use of gradually increasing percentages of Sustainable Aviation Fuels (SAF) as of 2025 and a minimum quota of synthetic fuels (5%) from 2030, gradually rising to 63% in 2050 at EU airports.[16]

However, SAF production remains limited and costly. The sector, therefore, requires stronger policies and structural incentives to increase production capacity, reduce costs, and make these fuels competitive with conventional fuels. It also requires aircraft operators to ensure that the annual amount of aviation fuel loaded at a given EU airport corresponds to at least 90% of the annual fuel requirements in order to avoid 'tankering', which could result in additional emissions associated with weight gain.

'Tankering' refers to carrying extra fuel to avoid higher refuelling costs at the destination airport. This practice is associated with variations in aviation fuel prices between EU airports or between EU and non-EU airports, which may cause aircraft operators to adjust their refuelling strategies for economic reasons. This practice increases aircraft fuel consumption and generates unnecessary greenhouse gas emissions, going against the EU's efforts to protect the environment.

European policy does not fail to take into account the impact that, in the short and medium term, the introduction of new ATM technologies and procedures may have on contributing to the goal of making aviation climate-neutral through a more rational use of airspace and the elimination of inefficiencies in the various phases of flight. "Significant CO_2 emissions reductions, for example, can be achieved through traffic and airspace optimisation. In Europe, the Single European Sky project aims for the better management of air traffic that could lead to a 10% CO_2 reduction for intra-European traffic" (ICAO 2022).

From this perspective, the SESAR (Single European Sky Advanced Research) Joint Undertaking, established in 2007 to develop and implement the new European ATM system, participates in the Digital European Sky initiative, which aims to

[14] Abeyratne (2014); Simone (2014), p. 846.

[15] Regulation (EU) 2023/2405 of the European Parliament and of the Council of 18 October 2023 on ensuring a level playing field for sustainable air transport (ReFuelEU Aviation).

[16] Wittmer and Müller (2021), p. 110.

accelerate the creation of an inclusive, resilient, and sustainable Digital European Sky through research and innovation. To date, the SESAR research and innovation programme has developed 127 digital solutions that could bring significant direct and indirect environmental benefits to ATM operations. It is estimated that their implementation could already result in a 4% direct reduction in CO_2 emissions per flight. These include making taxiing and runway operations more predictable and efficient, reducing holding patterns and optimising trajectories with i4D, among other technologies, which will lead to fuel savings. Some of these solutions also support local environmental performance goals by mitigating noise and improving air quality (SESAR, EASA, EUROCONTROL 2023). The European ATM Master Plan currently aims to reduce average CO_2 emissions per flight by 5 to 10% (equivalent to 0.8 to 1.6 tonnes) by 2035, relative to 2012 levels. It is worth mentioning that improved ATM can also bring other environmental benefits, such as noise mitigation and better local air quality. In this respect, recent studies have shown that, overall, non-CO_2 emissions contribute to climate change to a similar extent to that of CO_2 emissions.

4 The SES II+ Project. Regulation (EU) 2024/2803

In the complex civil aviation system, air traffic control plays a vital role and should ensure a safe, quick, and cost-effective flow of air traffic, thereby minimising fuel consumption and, ultimately, reducing carbon emissions and flight times. The improvement of climate and environmental performance has been a key component of the reform undertaken by the Single European Sky (SES) programme since its inception.

As is well known, the project was implemented through major legislative packages: SES I and SES II. The first, approved in 2004, aimed to achieve comprehensive reform of the Air Navigation Services (ANS) sector, improving safety, capacity, economic efficiency, and environmental sustainability.[17]

The initiative seeks to address the inefficiency of the ATM system, primarily due to the fragmentation of international airspace into numerous air traffic control centres. The objective is to create a more integrated system that can decrease the average flight time in European airspace by approximately 10 min, resulting in lower fuel consumption and reduced CO_2 emissions. An additional key aspect of the system is the introduction of 'Functional Airspace Blocks' (FABs), which enable the reconfiguration of airspace based on operational needs, irrespective of national borders.[18]

The complete implementation of the SES is expected to occur between 2030 and 2035. Compared to 2004, it could potentially triple airspace capacity, reduce air

[17] Rizzo (2006), p. 407; Van Houtte (2004), p. 1561.

[18] Button and Neiva (2013), p. 74.

traffic management costs by half, significantly improve safety levels, and decrease the environmental impact of aviation by 10% (European Parliament, 2024).

Adoption of the second package in 2009 further strengthened the European project by introducing performance-based mechanisms, which include performance targets set by the Commission (supported by an expert committee) for four priority areas, defined as key performance areas, relating to safety, the environment, capacity, and cost-effectiveness. The reference period for the performance scheme spans at least three years and may extend to five.

The national supervisory authorities (NSA) are responsible for drafting performance improvement plans at the national or functional airspace block level, predicated on key performance indicators related, as previously noted, to safety, the environment, capacity, and cost efficiency. To prepare these plans, a consultation mechanism is established between the NSA, air navigation service providers, representatives of airspace users, and, where appropriate, airport operators and coordinators. The Commission is responsible for assessing whether the proposed performance targets contained in the draft performance improvement plans prepared by the Member States are consistent with the Union-wide performance targets.

The initial reference period for the performance scheme ran from 2012 to 2014. Starting in 2015, each reference period lasted five calendar years. The Commission also appointed, in compliance with Article 11 of Regulation (EC) No 549/2004,[19] the Performance Review Body (PRB), which is tasked with contributing to the formulation of the aforementioned targets and supervising the implementation of the performance scheme.

The long-term goal is to increase the efficiency of air navigation services by optimising the use of airspace via a gate-to-gate approach that covers both *en-route* and terminal air navigation services, while simultaneously contributing to the reduction of greenhouse gas emissions. The project aims to establish a common, harmonised airspace structure in terms of routes and sectors, while also achieving economies of scale and improved cost efficiency through increased cooperation between air navigation service providers.

However, despite the 'holistic innovation approach' centred on the SES, which involves all users of European airspace—including airlines, airports, air navigation service providers, and manufacturers, as well as engagement with key representatives of European aviation such as Eurocontrol and EASA—there has been no significant improvement in the European ATM system over time.[20] Against this backdrop, the European Commission therefore proposed revising the SES legal framework without deviating from its original principles and objectives by consolidating the four SES regulations into one, with the Proposal for a regulation of the European Parliament and the Council on the implementation of the Single European Sky (recast) 2013/186 (COM (2013) 410 final), known as SES II. From the operational perspective, the Proposal aims to introduce market principles into the

[19] Regulation (EC) No 549/2004 of the European Parliament and of the Council of 10 March 2004 laying down the framework for the creation of the single European sky (the framework Regulation).

[20] Motyka and Njoya (2020), p. 2.

provision of air navigation services, strengthen the role of national supervisory authorities, establish targets, and implement the performance system (also increasing the responsibilities of the Performance Review Body/Unit). It also plans to strategically reorient Functional Airspace Blocks and reinforce the governance and operational scope of the Network Manager.[21]

It should be noted that since the adoption of the Proposal and in the decade that followed, ATM underwent considerable technological evolution, which had inevitable repercussions on safety and cost efficiency (primarily understood as efficiency). At the same time, there was a marked increase in demand for air transport up until the early 2020s, resulting in traffic congestion, especially in areas of particular importance for business.

The objectives set when the SES was established were not fully met by the deadline, resulting in increased costs, delays, and higher CO_2 emissions. Furthermore, a study applying the Delphi method revealed that the environment, a key performance area (KPA), benefits from improvements in other areas. However, the survey revealed that environmentally friendly attitudes and practices are not shared by all the countries observed and that some air navigation service providers (ANSPs) have adopted additional measures to protect the environment, while others have prioritised different indicators. To promote consistency among ANSPs and address the global issue of climate change, the study suggests that a shift in mindset is necessary. This implies that airspace design should take into account the relationships between the environmental performance indicator and other KPAs, incorporating environmental externalities and social costs. Furthermore, regulators need to reconsider key indicators and include noise and local air quality pollution in performance regulation.[22]

It should also be noted that in 2017, the European Court of Auditors[23] identified shortcomings relating to some key performance indicators. Regarding those concerning environmental conditions, it recommended changes in order to assess the ability of ATM to adapt to the desired trajectories of airspace users in both their horizontal and vertical dimensions.

In September 2020, it was therefore necessary to update the 2013 document with two legislative proposals: an amended proposal to recast the SES 2+ (No 2020/579), which comprehensively defines the Single European Sky system, and a proposal (No 2020/577) to amend the EASA 2018 Basic Regulation.[24] The revision of the regulation aims "not only to remove current inefficiencies in ATM that are detrimental to the environment, but also to strengthen other useful aspects regarding ATM, such as more agile data service provision and incentives, which can actively bring improvements and contribute to further reducing the environmental footprint of aviation" (Explanatory Memorandum to Proposal 2020/579).

---

[21] Masutti (2021), p. 623.

[22] Efthymiou and Papatheodorou (2018), p. 564.

[23] European Court of Auditors (2017).

[24] Rizzo (2022), p. 85.

European legislators also took into account the EASA's indications, which, in its *Environmental Report* published in 2022, noted that the environmental performance targets for the reference period from 2015 to 2019 (RP2) had not been reached, showing a decline in performance during the second part of the period. Specifically, the report showed that the SES Key Performance Indicator (KPI), which reflects the relationship between flight paths and environmental impact, was inadequate and required reassessment, taking into account environmental indicators based on actual CO_2 emissions.

EASA therefore remarked on the necessity for EU Member States to reinforce the SES framework and develop more suitable indicators for the fourth reporting period (RP4) (2025–2029), including the introduction of local environmental incentive schemes. The amended texts emphasise the urgent need to modernise airspace management and air navigation services, aiming to increase the system's capacity to adapt to traffic changes, enhance capacity, and improve cost efficiency and environmental sustainability through the use of greener routes.

The legislative package emphasises the contribution that the new SES rules can make towards fulfilling the commitments regarding decarbonisation set out in the European Green Deal and in Regulation (EU) 2021/1119,[25] which calls for achieving climate neutrality by 2050 at the latest. This goal can be achieved by reducing greenhouse gas emissions in all sectors of the economy, including transport, with at least a 55% decrease from 1990 levels throughout the EU by 2030.

The proposal was converted into Regulation (EU) 2024/2803,[26] following a lengthy approval process, which concluded on 23 October 2024.[27] The new regulatory text formalises the principle of making more efficient use of airspace, enabling more options for optimal flight paths, which leads to increased fuel efficiency and reduced emissions. "Various climate and environmental elements should also be taken into account when optimising flight trajectories and flight profiles, in order to reduce emissions and air pollutants. A methodology on how to take into account those various elements and their interdependencies should be developed, in particular when designing performance indicators" (recital 10 Reg. (EU) 2024/2803). The new rules reaffirm the extension of binding targets and, where applicable, incentive schemes for *en-route* air navigation services, focusing on capacity, cost efficiency, and environmental concerns, which the co-legislators have renamed as a joint 'climate and environment' area.

Regarding terminal air navigation services, Art. 21(3) letter iii of Regulation (EU) 2024/2803 establishes the obligation to set binding performance targets for terminal air navigation services in the key performance area of climate and environment, and where applicable, incentive schemes. "The Commission is empowered to set key performance indicators for terminal air navigation services in the key

[25] Regulation (EU) 2021/1119 of the European parliament and of the Council establishing the framework for achieving climate neutrality and amending Regulations (EC) No 401/2009 and (EU) 2018/1999 ("European Climate Law').

[26] Regulation (EU) 2024/2803 of The European Parliament and of The Council of 23 October 2024 on the implementation of the Single European Sky, (recast).

[27] Salerno (2025), p. 93.

performance area of climate and environment once it is possible to establish indicators which are valid, reliable and measurable. Those indicators shall as a minimum be capable of demonstrating and measuring the impacts in that area which can be directly influenced by the air navigation service providers" [art. 28 g) Reg. (EU) 2024/2803].

The setting of binding performance targets for terminal air navigation services included in the performance plan should take into account local circumstances, in particular local environmental policy requirements.

The performance scheme mechanism envisaged in the new regulation requires the NSA and the Commission to jointly assess the performance of air navigation services in accordance with the principles of subsidiarity and proportionality. Of particular importance is the provision that, in order to increase the efficiency of economic regulation, the designated air traffic service providers themselves must draw up their own performance improvement plans and submit them for approval to the competent authority.

Specifically, the NSA gathers input on the performance improvement plans adopted by individual providers, reviews them, approves them, or makes the necessary changes where appropriate. Subsequently, based on this information, the same authority, possibly in cooperation with other national authorities, prepares a unified draft national performance plan to be adopted by the Member State.

The Commission evaluates the draft performance plans adopted through this process, including the consistency of the performance targets for *en-route* air navigation services with those at EU level. Under Article 23 No. 7 of Regulation (EU) 2024/2803, several Member States may develop a joint performance plan for *en-route* air navigation services and, as appropriate, for terminal air navigation services. This plan will cover at least one reference period, include at least one joint performance target and involve cross-border cooperation. Furthermore, the Commission may authorise a deviation from the Union-wide performance targets for *en-route* air navigation services concerning a key performance area if it considers such a deviation necessary and proportionate to achieve the performance targets in another key performance area.

Article 13 of the regulation stipulates the establishment of a Performance Review Board, which will replace and succeed the previously mentioned PRB—an independent and impartial entity that assists the Commission in executing tasks related to the detailed operation of performance and charging systems. The negotiators agreed to establish a stable and permanent body funded by the EU budget; however, their opinions and recommendations are non-binding, as the body will have a solely advisory role.

One way to contribute to the decarbonisation objective underpinning the EU provisions is the possible introduction of mandatory modulation of route charges to promote improved climate and environmental performance by airspace users. This assumes the use of the most fuel-efficient routes available and greater adoption of alternative clean propulsion technologies, including sustainable alternative fuels, provided that a cost-benefit analysis conducted by the Commission has determined that the modulation is feasible and adds value.

5 Conclusions

The SES system is founded on five pillars: performance, safety, technological progress, the human factor, and the optimisation of airport infrastructure. The reform, finalised by the approval of Regulation 2024/2803, as previously noted, prioritises environmental protection and is consistent with the guidelines established by ICAO at the international level, as well as with other Union regulations. It is worth recalling that in the Commission's communication on the European Green Deal, improving the standards of the SES was recognised as a measure capable of helping reduce CO_2 emissions in the aviation sector.

Within the complex framework established by the SES II+ project, consolidating the performance scheme may play a decisive role in advancing the path towards climate neutrality in air transport.

The new regulation aims for greater involvement of traffic service providers in drawing up performance plans, taking into account local politics while also reinforcing the role of national authorities in their verification and approval. The importance of cooperation among the various actors involved, a key element of the entire complex civil aviation system, thus becomes evident.

Lastly, it must be noted that the decision taken during the negotiations to broaden the key performance area of the environment so as to include the field of climate reflects European legislators' awareness of the need to address environmental issues in all their complexity, without overlooking the prominence that climate change has acquired in recent decades.

In this regard, the air transport industry is experiencing unprecedented growth, which stands in stark contrast to the objective of combating climate change. Effective air traffic management, in conjunction with other initiatives identified in the ICAO strategy and EU policy, can therefore make a vital contribution to the aviation sector's climate neutrality ambitions.[28]

References

Abeyratne R. (2014) Aviation and climate change. In: Search of a global market based measure, London

Adam M (2011) ICAO assembly's resolution on climate change: a "Historic Agreement?". Air Space Law 36(1):23–29. https://doi.org/10.54648/aila2011003

Button K, Neiva R (2013) Single European Sky and the functional airspace blocks: will they improve economic efficiency? J Air Transport Manage 33:73–80. https://doi.org/10.1016/j.jairtraman.2013.06.012

EASA (2022) European Aviation Environmental Report

Efthymiou M, Papatheodorou A (2018) Environmental considerations in the single European Sky: A Delphi approach. Transp Res Part A Policy Pract 118:556–566. https://doi.org/10.1016/j.tra.2018.09.024

[28] Müller et al. (2022), p. 16.

Erling UM (2017) European Parliament international aviation emissions under international civil aviation organization's global market based measure: ready for offsetting. Air Space Law 42(1):1–12. https://doi.org/10.54648/aila2017001
EUROCONTROL (2022) Aviation Outlook 2050, Main Report.
European Court of Auditors (2017) Special report No 18/2017: Single European Sky: a Changed Culture but not a Single Sky
ICAO (2008) Meeting, environment trend in aviation to 2050. Lima, Mexico
ICAO (2009) Programme of action on international aviation and climate change
ICAO (2022) Innovation for a Green Transition, Environmental Report
IPCC (Intergovernmental Panel on Climate Change) (1999) Aviation and the global atmosphere: a special report of IPCC Working Groups I and III. In: Penner JE, Lister DH, Griggs DJ, Dokken DJ, McFarland M (eds). Cambridge University Press, Cambridge
Masutti A (2021) Il futuro del cielo unico europeo. Verso un accentramento delle competenze sul controllo del traffico aereo nell'Agenzia Europea per la Sicurezza Aerea, in Dir. trasp.: 621–640
Motyka A., Njoya E.T. (2020), Single European Sky: the progress so far. J Aerosp Tecnol Manag 12:e3920. https://doi.org/10.5028/jatm.v12.1175.
Müller A, Walls J, Wittmer A (2022) Sustainable aviation: an introduction, in sustainable aviation. A management perspective. In: Walls JL, Wittmer A (eds)
Rizzo MP (2006) Il pacchetto di regolamenti comunitari per la realizzazione del «cielo unico europeo». In: La Torre U, Moschella G, Pellegrino F, Rizzo MP, Vermiglio G (a cura di), Studi in memoria di Elio Fanara, Milano, pp 407–442
Rizzo MP (2022) I servizi della navigazione aerea dal SES I al SES II +: qualificazione ed accesso alla fornitura, in Il controllo del traffico nella navigazione: stato dell'arte ed evoluzione, a cura di C. Ingratoci e A. Marino, 85–118
Rosafio EG (2020) Osservazioni in tema di trasporto aereo e ambiente. Riv dir nav 1011–1034. https://doi.org/10.4399/978882554082612
Salerno F (2017) Le recenti misure per contrastare l'impatto ambientale del trasporto aereo. Dir mar I:68–92
Salerno F (2025) Prospettive di riforma del cielo unico europeo e miglioramenti delle prestazioni climatiche e ambientali. Riv. di Diritto dell'Economia, dei Trasporti e dell'Ambiente, Supplemento XXIII:73–103
SESAR, EASA, EUROCONTROL (2023) Making Europe the most efficient and environmentally friendly sky to fly in the world. A Joint Discussion Paper
Simone P (2014) La compravendita di quote di emissione di gas a effetto serra nel trasporto aereo internazionale: il Protocollo di Kioto e l'ICAO. Riv. dir. nav.: 841–870. https://doi.org/10.4399/97888548834681O.
Vagaggini C (2021) Sostenibilità dei voli e degli scali aeroportuali. Riv dir. nav.: 217–239. https://doi.org/10.53136/97912599461716
Van Houtte B (2004) The single European Sky: EU reform of air traffic management. CML Rev 41:1595–1612
Wittmer A, Müller A (2021) The environment of aviation. In: Aviation systems. Management of the integrated aviation value chain, 2nd edn. Springer, pp 79–113

MIX
Papier aus verantwortungsvollen Quellen
Paper from responsible sources
FSC® C105338

If you have any concerns about our products,
you can contact us on
ProductSafety@springernature.com

In case Publisher is established outside the EU,
the EU authorized representative is:
Springer Nature Customer Service Center GmbH
Europaplatz 3, 69115 Heidelberg, Germany

Printed by Libri Plureos GmbH
in Hamburg, Germany